ELIZABETHAN PSYCHOLOGY
AND
SHAKESPEARE'S PLAYS

ELIZABETHAN PSYCHOLOGY
AND
SHAKESPEARE'S PLAYS

by

RUTH LEILA ANDERSON

HASKELL HOUSE
Publishers of Scholarly Books
NEW YORK
1964

published by

HASKELL HOUSE
Publishers of Scholarly Books
30 East 10th Street • New York, N. Y. 10003

Library of Congress Catalog Card Number: 65-15887

PRINTED IN UNITED STATES OF AMERICA

PREFACE

With the English Renaissance there came a revival of interest in psychology and ethics and an extended application of the principles of these subjects not only to individual life but also to affairs of society and of the state. As early as 1540 Ludovicus Vives' *Introduction to Wisedome* was translated into English, that it might reach many readers. Sir Thomas Elyot had already written his "disputacion Platonike," *Of the Knowledg which Maketh a Wise Man,* and his *Castel of Helth. Batman vppon Bartholome, his Booke De Proprietatibus Rerum* was printed in 1582. The abstract psychological principles of these and similar works were soon turned to practical purposes, and at the same time the principles were made specific. In 1586 there appeared two editions of Timothy Bright's *Treatise of Melancholy,* in which the author presents a "scientific" theory of the relation between body and soul, together with an elaborate application of this theory to the disease of melancholy. Thomas Wright undertook the worthy purposes of developing a complete doctrine of the passions and of showing his countrymen how, through being able to control passions in themselves and to discover them in others, they might counteract the innate tendency to imprudence. The first edition of his *Passions of the Minde in Generall* is dated 1601. Together with works of English writers, there existed translations of important foreign treatises. Among them was Huarte's *Examen de Ingenios,* a book which treats at length of humors and tempers and of their influence upon our lives. *Examen de Ingenios* is altogether modern in its purpose: "To be able then to distinguish and discerne these naturall differences of mans wit, and to applie to each by art, that science wherein he may profit, is the intention of this my worke." There were also available in English La Primaudaye's exhaustive *French Academie* and Charron's *De la Sagesse,* beginning with an exhortation to the study and knowledge of oneself as at once the foundation of all wisdom, the direct and high road to all happiness, and the first step to a knowledge of God.

The system of psychology which these and similar treatises preserve is a complex doctrine inherited from Plato and Aristotle, Hippocrates and Galen. It cannot be separated at all points from astrology, medicine, ethics, philosophy, and even theology. Back of it lies the notion that our bodies and all other matter are composed of the four elements, earth, air, fire, and water, and that the elements of one substance may act upon those of another. Eliza-

3

bethan psychology is therefore a science which involves a knowledge of the relation of man to the macrocosm. It differs from modern psychology not in its conception of human behavior, but in its way of accounting for this behavior.

Shakespeare was in all respects a man of his time. He did not seek consciously to embody psychological principles anywhere in his work, for he was pre-eminently an artist. One must not forget, however, that he was also a man living among men and thinking with them about serious problems. The world he created, like that of every other great writer, could be built only upon contemporary thought. His characters must therefore be Elizabethan. They are Elizabethan in such fullness and variety of detail that without a correct point of view we cannot account on a rational basis for all their actions. We must learn to think with Shakespeare in order to appreciate his work truly.

My research has been an attempt to determine and explain the principles of Elizabethan psychology and to consider their bearings upon Shakespeare's plays. I have made no effort to trace the origin of this science and its development in ancient and medieval times. My investigation has been confined to psychological treatises contemporary or nearly contemporary with Shakespeare and, for the most part, available to him in English. From these I have worked out an explanation of the system of psycho-physiological and psycho-ethical thought which was current among cultivated Elizabethans. Much of this theory I have related to Shakespeare's thinking; that is, to his conception of phenomena of human behavior, to character and action as they are expressed in his plays. The results, I hope, will to some degree bring us nearer the correct interpretation of his art.

This thesis owes its existence to Professor Hardin Craig, who first suggested to me the importance of Elizabethan psychology as a background for Shakespeare's plays. I therefore desire to make grateful acknowledgment of my indebtedness to him not only for invaluable criticism and encouragement, given generously throughout the progress of my work, but also for points of view derived from his lectures in the classroom before the present study was begun. I desire further to extend sincere thanks to other members of the Department of English in the University of Iowa who have assisted me with advice or interest.

R. L. A.

June 1, 1927.

CONTENTS

CHAPTER I

BODY, SOUL, AND SPIRIT

Elizabethan psychology is a classificatory science, representing man as composed of three parts: body, soul, and "spirit" or "spirits." The soul it explains in terms of operations as the internal cause of life and motion, of sense and understanding. According to Batman's translation of Bartholomaeus Anglicus' *De Proprietatibus Rerum*, the soul is a kind of spiritual and reasonable substance, which God makes of nothing to give life and perfection to man.[1] Charron considers it a very subtle substance and attempts to distinguish between corporeality such as the soul possesses and materiality,[2] but to this opinion the translator takes exception: a body, no matter how thin and subtle it may be, possesses a materiality which the soul does not possess.[3] The difference is largely in terminology, for the soul was usually thought to be incorporeal in the ordinary sense of the word. If it were a body, John Davies of Hereford argues, it could not contain many impressions or at the same time receive two such contrary forms as black and white, fire and frost.[4] By a strange process of sublimation, as we assimilate food, it turns bodies into spirits and from particular things abstracts universal qualities,

> Which bodilesse and immateriall are,
> And can be lodg'd but onely in our minds.[5]

After examining theories of pre-existence, transmigration, and traducianism, writers usually agree that the soul owes its origin in the body to divine infusion.

Elizabethan treatises explain figuratively the manner in which

---

[1] *Batman vppon Bartholome, his Booke De Proprietatibus Rerum*, London, 1582, Bk. III, ch. 4.

[2] *Of Wisdom*, 3 bks., translated by George Stanhope, D.D., London, 1697, Bk. I, pp. 48-51. The original, *De la Sagesse*, was printed at Bordeaux in 1601; there is an undated contemporary translation by Samson Lennard.

[3] *Ibid.*, pp. 72-74.

[4] "Microcosmos" (1603), *Complete Works*, ed. Grosart, 2 vols., Edinburgh, 1878, Vol. I, p. 86. The argument here is conventional.

[5] Sir John Davies, "Nosce Teipsum" (1599), *Works in Verse and Prose*, 3 vols., ed. Grosart, 1869, Vol. I, pp. 76-77.

the soul inhabits the body.   It exists there as form in matter;[6] it
is joined to the body as a mover to the thing moved or as a ship-
man to his vessel.[7]   According to Sir John Davies the soul moves
the body without touching any part of it.   It dwells within, neither
as if it were in a tent nor as a pilot in his ship, but after the fashion
of morning light in the atmosphere.   It is wholly in all parts of
the body.[8]   Nemesius, from whom Davies may have derived the
figure, gives the following description of the way in which the soul
is united to the body:

"For, as the *Sun*, so soon as it appeareth, changes the *ayre* into
light; so making it lightsome, and so diffusing it selfe with the
ayre, that is united with the same, and yet not confounded therewith: Even so, the *soul* being united with the *Body,* remaines without confusion therewith; differing in this onely, that the *Sunne*
being a *Body* . . . . is not himselfe in every place where his light is,
but . . . . is confined to a certaine *place.*

"It is not so with the *soul*. For, being void of all *Body,* and not
contained within the limits of any place, it passeth *all* and *whole,*
through it owne whole *light,* and through the whole *Body,* wherein
it is; neither is any part of it illuminated thereby, wherein it is
not fully and wholly present. Neither is it in the *body* as in some
bottle or other vessel, nor compassed in by the same; but the *Body*
is rather in the *soule,* and is thereby held in and fastened together."[9]

There was still current during the Renaissance the Aristotelian
doctrine[10] of three kinds of souls, each subsisting in a different form
of life. The vegetable soul, only, exists in plants, enabling them
to live, grow, and multiply. The sensible (or sensitive) soul con-
trols the life of beasts; besides the vegetal virtues, it imparts "feel-

[6] Charron, *op. cit.,* Bk. I, p. 60.

[7] Batman, *op. cit.,* Bk. III, ch. 3.

[8] *Loc. cit.,* pp. 99-100. The belief that the soul, although associated particularly with certain organs—the liver, the heart, and the brain—is present as
a unity in all parts of the body seems to have found wide acceptance. Senault
(*De l'Usage des Passions, derniere edition,* 1668, pp. 12-13), for example, states
that the soul is just as noble in the hand as in the heart; it extends through
all parts of the body and performs a variety of services only because it has at
its disposal a variety of instruments. Cf. Charron, *op. cit.,* Bk. I, pp. 60-61,
and *The French Academie; Fully Discoursed and Finished in Foure Bookes,*
London, 1618, p. 561. There were earlier editions of the first three books of
The French Academie. Unless otherwise indicated, my references are to the
edition printed in 1618.

[9] *The Nature of Man,* George Wither, tr., London, 1636, pp. 197-198.

[10] See *Aristotle's Psychology,* W. A. Hammond, tr., Macmillan Co., 1902,
pp. 54-56.

ing,"[11] movement of the body, and an inclination to possess the good and to withdraw from evil. The rational soul is found only in man. In addition to the powers of the two inferior kinds, it possesses an intellectual faculty which includes reason and will. Batman states the doctrine clearly:

"In diuerse bodyes the soule is sayde to be three folde, that is to saye, *Vegetabilis* that giueth lyfe, and no feeling, and that is in plants and rootes, *Sensibilis*, that giueth life & feeling, and not reason, that is in unskilfull beasts, *Racionalis* that giueth lyfe, feeling and reason, and this is in men. The Philosopher lykeneth the soule that is called *Vegetabilis*, to a Triangle. For as a Triangle hath three corners, this manner soule hath three vertues, of begetting, of nourishing, and of growing. And this soul *Vegetabilis* is lyke to a Triangle in Geometrie. And hee lykeneth the soule *Sensibilis*, to a quadrangle square, and foure cornered.[12] For in a Quadrangle is a line drawne from one corner to another, before it maketh two Triangles, and *the* soule sensible maketh two triangles of vertues. For where euer the soule sensible is, there is also the soule Vegetabilis, but not backwards. And hee lykeneth the soule *Racionalis* to a circle, because of his perfection and conteining."[13]

Sir Toby in *Twelfth Night* asks, "Shall we rouse the night-owl in a catch that will draw three souls out of one weaver?"[14] He probably has in mind the three kinds of souls which we have just described. Elizabethan treatises, also, refer at times to groups of faculties as if each constituted a separate soul in man. Almost invariably, however, the soul is said to be a unity—"one *Essence* entire and undivided"[15]—operating through different instruments and thereby producing many kinds of activity. The body contains three principal organs—the liver, the heart, and the brain—and each of these enables the soul to perform a special kind of work.

---

[11] The term is here applied to those processes of knowing common to man and beast: "The vertue of feeling that cometh of the soule sensible, is a vertue by which the soule knoweth & iudgeth of coulours, of sauours, and of other obiects that be knowne by the vtter wits."—Batman, *op. cit.*, Bk. III, ch. 11.

[12] Cf. *King Lear*, I, i, 76: "the most precious square of sense," and Edmund Spenser, *The Faerie Queene (Complete Works*, 10 vols., ed. Grosart, 1882, vols. 5-8), Bk. II, canto ix, ll. 195 ff.

[13] *Op. cit.*, Bk. III, ch. 7. Almost the identical passage appears in *Wits Theater of the Little World*, printed by "I. R." for "N. L.," 1599, pp. 37-38.

[14] Act II, sc. iii, ll. 59-61. Cf. *Much Ado*, II, iii, 61-62. Unless otherwise indicated, all quotations from Shakespeare are made from the text as edited by William Allan Neilson in the Tudor Edition.

[15] Charron, *op. cit.*, Bk. I, p. 54. Often psychologists present extended arguments to prove that the soul is a unity.

The liver serves a vegetal, the heart a vital, and the brain an animal faculty. With the first two organs are associated the maintenance of life and the emotions; with the last, ideation and will. Or, following Aristotle's doctrine of three kinds of souls, we may arrange the powers of the human soul to form three other groups: the vegetal, the sensible, and the rational. The soul of man is a single entity, possessing in addition to the powers of the two inferior kinds of soul, a rational faculty which renders man superior to beasts and enables him to contemplate spiritual truths; it is a single entity capable of a multiplicity of operations.

In order to make possible these operations, God provided man with "spirits" (or "spirit"), the Elizabethan equivalent of the nervous system and therefore the chief instrument of the soul. These "spirits," fumes or subtle vapors that arise in the blood, are maintained within the body by means of nourishment. The Elizabethan regarded all matter, inanimate as well as animate, as being permeated by a spiritous substance.[16] Food consists not only of a corporal matter but also of a "spiritual matter," which unites with and sustains our "spiritual matter," the spirits; "so nothing of other nature can haue corporall coniunction with vs except their Spirits with ours first grow into acquaintance: which is more speedily done a great deale then the increase of the firme substance."[17]

As the operations of the soul are generally said to be threefold in kind, each centralized in one of the chief organs of the body, so are the spirits. To speak more precisely, the spiritous substance, arising in the liver, undergoes successive processes of sublimation in the heart and in the brain. In each of its three stages of purity, this spirit, designated according to its degree of purity and according to the function it performs as natural, vital, or animal spirit

---

[16] "If you demaund whereof this Spirit is made, I take it to bee an effectuall, and pregnant substance, bred in all thinges, and at what time the Spirit of the Lord did as it were hatch, and breed out all liuing thinges, out of the Chaos mentioned in Genesis. Which Chaos, as it was matter of Corporall, and Palpable Substance to all things, so did it also minister this liuely Spirit vnto them, diuerse and seuerall, according to the diuersitie of those seedes, which God indued it withall: to some more pure, to othersome more grosse, according to the excellencie of the creature, and dignitie of the vses whereto it is to be employed. From this power of God, sprang the Spirit of man . . . ."— T. Bright, *A Treatise of Melancholy*, newly corrected and amended, London, 1613, pp. 54-55. Two editions were printed in 1586.

[17] Bright, *op. cit.*, pp. 43-44.

(or spirits),[18] serves a group of powers of the soul.   The natural, instruments of the vegetal faculty, arise in the liver from the boiling and seething of the blood.   With the humors[19] they pass through the veins[20] to all parts of the body.   Some of them enter the left cavity of the heart and here, "by mouing & smiting togethers of the parts of *the* hart," they become vital spirits, a substance less gross than that which arises in the liver.   The vital spirits are carried to members of the body by the arteries.[21]   They make possible the functioning of the vital virtue, the virtue which gives man life.   Their office is "to carry naturall heate to the other members, and to giue them vertue & strength to put in practise those actions and offices, which exercise by the same heate."[22]   In the brain[23] vital spirits are "concocted, refin'd, wrought off, and subtiliz'd, by means of an infinite number of small and exceeding fine Arteries, which, like so many little Threads plaited and interwoven with each other, make a sort of Labyrinth, or double Net . . . .

---

[18] Batman, *op. cit.*, Bk. III, ch. 22: "Then one and the same spirit corporall, subtill, and airely, through diuerse offices in diuerse lims, is named by diuerse names.   For by working in *the* liuer it is called *Spiritus Naturalis*, in the heart *Vitalis*, & in the head *Spiritus animalis.*"   Cf. Bright, *op. cit.*, pp. 56-57, 80; Charron, *op. cit.*, Bk. I, p. 26.   La Primaudaye (*op. cit.*, p. 564) states that all spirits are bred in the heart.   The spirits then change their nature according to the place in which they work.

[19] The humors will be considered below, pp. 33-35.

[20] "Veins are hollow and round like pipes, arising from the liver, carrying blood and natural spirits; they feed all the parts."—Burton, *Anatomy of Melancholy*, 3 vols., George Bell and Sons, London, 1896, Vol. I, p. 171.

[21] "As for the *Arteries* or pulses they are pipes that proceede from the heart.   For in that is the great artery planted, which is the stocke of all the rest, which serue to carry the vitall spirits throughout the body: they are couered with little skins that are strong and thicke to keepe the spirits from breathing out, and for the same cause they haue their passages more streight.   So that they haue two skinnes or couerings, whereof that which is vnderneath is fiue times thicker then the skin of a veine.   To conclude, the arteries and veines are ioyned together, to the end that the vital spirits might draw and receiue from the veines conuenient matter for their nourishment, as also that by their heat they might warme the blood that is within them."—La Primaudaye, *op. cit.*, p. 350.

[22] La Primaudaye, *op. cit.*, p. 564.

[23] Frequently the brain is said to be divided into four compartments—a right and a left ventricle (sometimes spoken of as a single ventricle) in the forepart of the brain, a middle ventricle, and a hindmost ventricle "common to the *cerebel* or little brain, and marrow of the backbone."—Burton, *op. cit.*, Vol. I, p. 176.   According to Batman (*op. cit.*, Bk. III, ch. 22), Burton (*op. cit.*, Vol. I, p. 176), and John Davies of Hereford ("Mirum in Modum," 1602, *loc. cit.*, Vol. I, p. 7) spirits are concocted in the right and left ventricles; according to Charron (*op. cit.*, Bk. I, p. 110) and John Huarte (*Examen de Ingenios*, translated into English by "R. C." from an Italian translation of the original, London, 1596, p. 54) they are formed in the hindmost ventricle.

in which the Vital Spirit being kept, by perpetual Motion back-
ward and forward, is exalted and refin'd, till it becomes *Animal*,
that is, sublimated and spiritous to the last and highest Degree.''[24]
The resultant animal spirits flow from the brain through the nerves,
frequently called sinews,[25] to other parts of the body; they render the soul capable of sense and of motion. If the vital spirits
are impure, the animal spirits derived from them are likely to be
correspondingly impure. The soul can function properly only
when the spirits are perfectly wrought, for by them its faculties
exercise all their powers. These faculties we must now consider
separately.

The vegetal faculty of the soul promotes nutrition, growth, and
reproduction. Its nutritive power works by means of a number
of subordinate virtues or powers—appetite for food and drink,
retention, digestion, distribution, assimilation, and expulsion. In
the liver, the chief organ of nourishment and growth, arise the
four humors, which carry sustenance to the body in their progress
through the veins; here, also, are made the natural spirits, which
enable the vegetal powers to perform their tasks. A natural appetite, guided by the light of nature, instructs these various powers.
Since the vegetal faculty cannot function in a state of separation
from the body, it is mortal. According to Batman, it withers with
age and when the body dies consumes itself;[26] according to Charron,
neither the vegetal nor the sensitive faculty dies, but rather each
ceases functioning when its instruments, the parts of the body, fail.
If a soul could be returned to a sound body, all its faculties would
continue operation.[27]

In the middle region of the body resides a vital faculty or virtue.
Its chief organ, the heart, is divided into two parts. The right

---

[24] Charron, *op. cit.*, Bk. I, p. 28.

[25] Often the words nerve and sinew are used interchangeably for what is
now called nerve: ''*Nerves*, or sinews, are membranes without, and full of
marrow within; they proceed from the brain, & carry the animal spirits for
sense and motion.''—Burton, *op. cit.*, Vol. I, p. 171. Sometimes, however,
they are synonymous with tendon or muscle. (Cf. Edward Dowden, ''Elizabethan Psychology,'' *Essays Modern and Elizabethan*, New York, 1910, pp.
318-319.) Sinews that are hard are fittest for motion; they come from the
hindmost portion of the brain or from the marrow of the back bone. Those
that are soft and delicate, coming from the foremost cells, are fittest for sense.
In fact the most tender and delicate sinews are used only for sense; they
carry very subtle and highly attenuated spirits.—Nemesius, *op. cit.*, pp. 317,
426; La Primaudaye, *op. cit.*, p. 349; Burton, *op. cit.*, Vol. I, p. 171.

[26] *Op. cit.*, Bk. III, ch. 14.

[27] *Op. cit.*, Bk. I, p. 55.

receives blood from the liver and sends the thicker portion to nourish the lungs. The left is the seat of life. From the right compartment it draws the thinner portion of blood, "as a torch doth oil," and begets of it the vital spirits, sometimes called the spirits of life. By means of the aortic system it disperses to all parts of the body blood more "frothy" and "yellowish" than that coming from the liver; in this the vital spirits are contained. When the heart expands, it cools and refreshes itself by means of air drawn from the lungs; when it contracts, it expels smoky excrements also by way of the lungs. These motions are natural to the organ: "For the heart hath his filaments or small threeds, apt and conuenient for that purpose."[28] In one of his sonnets John Davies of Hereford, who may be counted among the psychologists of his day, writes:

> Worke on my Hart, sterne *Griefe,* and do thy worst:
> Draw it togeather till his Strings do crack.[29]

The notion expressed here, that death may result from the breaking of heart-strings, seems to underlie the following from Shakespeare:

> The tackle of my heart is crack'd and burn'd,
> And all the shrouds wherewith my life should sail
> Are turned to one thread, one little hair.
> My heart hath one poor string to stay it by,
> Which holds but till thy news be uttered.[30]

The heart is the seat of life, of heat, of pulse, of the vital spirits, and of the perturbations of the soul. It is the organ which lives first and dies last.[31]

The animal faculty of the soul resides in the brain. According to La Primaudaye[32] and John Davies of Hereford,[33] whose "Mirum in Modum" and the "Microcosmos" present a complete system of psychology derived from *The French Academie,*[34] this faculty contains motive, sensitive, and principal virtues. The first enables the body and its members to move. The sensitive virtue includes the functioning of the external senses; the principal consists of common

---

[28] La Primaudaye, *op. cit.,* p. 451.

[29] "Wittes Pilgrimage," *loc. cit.,* Vol. II, No. 68, p. 15.

[30] *King John,* V, vii, 52-56. Cf. *King Lear,* V, iii, 216-217.

[31] Burton, *op. cit.,* Vol. I, p. 175.

[32] *Op. cit.,* p. 401.

[33] "Mirum in Modum," *loc. cit.,* p. 6.

[34] See my article, "A French Source for John Davies of Hereford's System of Psychology," *Phil. Quar.,* VI (1927), 57-66.

sense, fantasy, and imagination—capacities sometimes considered
as belonging to a single power designated by any one of the three
terms—reason or a judging faculty, and memory. In other words
it includes the powers that are sometimes called the five wits.[35]

Upon the basis of Aristotelian theory, the soul may be said to
possess a vegetal, a sensitive, and a rational faculty. The first we
have already considered: it is that faculty which promotes nourishment, growth, and reproduction. The sensitive and rational faculties dwell principally in the brain. The former may be defined
broadly as an act of an organical body by which it lives, has sense,
appetite, judgment, breath, and motion; for, in addition to certain
functions dependent upon the animal virtue or spirit formed in
the brain, it includes the powers exercised by the natural and vital
virtues.[36] Usually, however, the term sensitive faculty is restricted
to designate only a power of apprehension and a power of "motion," both inferior to the understanding and the will.[37]

In the process of sensitive apprehension the outer and the inner
senses, "particular or outer wit" and "common or inner wit," as
Batman calls them, co-operate. Of the former group hearing, sight,
and smell are senses of commodity or convenience; touch and taste
are necessary to the preservation of life. The external senses are
the doors through which knowledge comes to man. Each is capable
of a rudimentary perception of things that are actually present to
sense, a perception based of course upon a single kind of impression; each is capable also of pleasure and pain.

Writers disagree regarding the classification and number of the

----

[35] Batman (*op. cit.*, Bk. III, ch. 16) has a similar classification from which
La Primaudaye may have borrowed. He divides the animal virtue into three
powers, the ordinative, the sensitive, and the motive, which correspond to those
described above. Of the first he says: "That part that is named *Ordinatiua,*
fulfilleth the brayne by it selfe alone. For in the first part in the foremost
chamber it ordeineth the fantasie or imagination: in the middle chamber it
ordeineth the vertue estimatiue and reason. And againe in the uttermost
chamber it maketh perfect the memorie, and the memorial acte . . . ."

Reference to the five wits is made frequently of course in literature. See
Shakespeare, *Much Ado,* I, i, 66; *Romeo and Juliet,* I, iv, 47; II, iv, 75; *King
Lear,* III, vi, 60; etc. Stephen Hawes (*The Pastime of Pleasure,* 1509, *Publ.
of Percy Society,* XVIII, 108-111) calls them common wit, imagination, fantasy, estimation, and memory.

[36] Burton, *op. cit.,* Vol. I, p. 179.

[37] Occasionally the sensitive faculty is described as a power which makes
possible the operation of the external senses. The functioning of the internal
senses is then said to proceed from a cogitative virtue. See La Primaudaye,
op. cit., p. 590.

internal processes of perception. Batman, in considering the relation of the soul to the body, names five virtues:

"The first whereof . . . . is feeling, and by that vertue the Soule is moued, and taketh heede to the bodylye wittes, and desireth those things, that belong to the bodye. . . . . The second power is wit: that is the vertue of the soule, whereby shee knoweth things sensible and corporall, when they bee present. The third is imagination, whereby the Soule beholdeth the lykenesse of bodylye thinges when they bee absent. The fourth is *Racio,* Reason, that deemeth and iudgeth betweene good and euill, truth and falsenesse. The fifte is *Intellectus,* understanding and inwit. The which comprehendeth thinges not material but intelligible, as God, Angel, and other such."[38]

The first three virtues cannot function apart from the body; they are common to man and beast. Reason and understanding may be separated from the body; hence they are immortal. Farther on,[39] Batman names as inner senses imagination, sensible reason or a virtue estimative, and memory; he assigns each respectively to the foremost, the middle, and the hindmost ventricle of the brain. Edmund Spenser gives a similar classification.[40] Coeffeteau,[41] Sir John Davies,[42] Burton,[43] and Phineas Fletcher[44] consider common sense, imagination or fantasy,[45] and memory the internal senses. Coeffeteau has nothing to say about the localization of these powers. The others agree in placing memory in the hindmost cell. Sir John Davies and Burton assign common sense to the foremost and fantasy or imagination to the middle portion of the brain. Fletcher reverses this localization.

Common sense, imagination, and fantasy, La Primaudaye says,

---

[38] *Op. cit.,* Bk. III, ch. 6. Almost the identical passage appears in *Wits Theater of the Little World,* p. 37.

[39] Bk. III, ch. 10.

[40] *Faerie Queene, loc. cit.,* Bk. II, canto ix, ll. 420 ff. He calls the power dwelling in the forepart of the brain fantasy. The second power, which he does not name, is clearly a form of reasoning.

[41] F. N. Coeffeteau, *A Table of Humane Passions,* Edward Grimeston, tr., London, 1621, Preface.

[42] *Loc. cit.,* pp. 110-113.

[43] *Op. cit.,* Vol. I, p. 182.

[44] "The Purple Island" (1633), in Giles and Phineas Fletcher, *Poetical Works,* F. S. Boas, ed., 2 vols., Cambridge Press, 1909, Vol. II, pp. 78-79.

[45] Sir John Davies makes the term imagination synonymous with common sense; the second power of the internal senses he calls fantasy. Some writers call fantasy or imagination, the estimative or the cogitative virtue. See Burton, *op. cit.,* Vol. I, p. 182.

were sometimes differentiated and sometimes described as a single
power, ordained to collect images from the external senses and to
prepare them for the consideration of reason. He accepts the term
common sense as the name of a virtue which receives impressions
from the outer world and reduces them to a unit of apperception.
No distinction need be made between imagination and fantasy, he
says, as names of a power which continues the formation of ideas.[46]
Batman apparently follows those who do not differentiate the terms.
La Primaudaye[47] and John Davies of Hereford,[48] although they
distinguish between the functioning of common sense and the imagination, place both powers in the forepart of the brain and assign
reason, a faculty usually said to be a part of the rational "soul,"
to the middle cell. Their classification agrees essentially with that
which Batman gives; one cannot be certain, however, that their
"reason" corresponds exactly to his "sensible reason." The reason
which they describe is clearly a part of the immortal "soul."

From these and other divergent opinions it appears that there
existed during the Renaissance several theories as to the faculties
of the mind. Certain writers, we have seen, consider common sense,
imagination, and memory as three separate powers arising from
the sensible "soul"; with some variation in opinion they assign
each to a separate cell of the brain. Batman, also insisting upon
localization, divides the "inner wit" into imagination, sensible
reason, and memory. Spenser, La Primaudaye, and John Davies
of Hereford probably continue his theory. Some writers do not
divide the faculties of mind into the sensible and the rational.
They call imagination, reason, and memory powers of the rational
"soul."[49] A few writers, including Charron[50] and Huarte,[51] oppose
theories which confine the operations of a faculty to a single portion
of the brain. Shakespeare, upon the evidence of his works, believed
in localization. Once, in *Love's Labour's Lost*,[52] he refers to the

---

[46] *Op. cit.*, pp. 401, 410, 414.

[47] *Op. cit.*, pp. 414, 416-417.

[48] "Mirum in Modum," *loc. cit.*, p. 7.

[49] See, for example, Huarte, *op. cit.*, pp. 40-41, 50 ff. Bacon (translation of
De Augmentis, Bk. II, ch. 1, in *The Works of Francis Bacon*, edited by Spedding, Ellis, and Heath, new ed., Vol. IV) derives his classification of human
learning from the three faculties of the "rational soul": memory, imagination,
and reason.

[50] *Op. cit.*, Bk. I, p. 111.

[51] *Op. cit.*, pp. 51 ff.

[52] Act IV, sc. ii, l. 71.

ventricle of memory, and once, in *Macbeth*,[53] to the "receipt of reason." Apparently he agreed with those contemporaries who associate reason with the middle cell of the brain.

Fortunately this confusion of terms and disagreement regarding the relation of the mind to its organ does not alter in any essential either the explanation of the process of apprehension or the description of the powers by which that process is performed. The outer wits, since each receives a different kind of impression, must submit their images by means of the animal spirits to a higher power. This faculty we may call the common sense, for it provides a storehouse for all forms of images from the outer world. Its function is usually said to be threefold: to receive, to act as first judge or arbiter of all reports from the senses, and to transmit results to a "more inward" faculty.[54] By reducing contrary images to a unity of apperception it destroys many false ideas which might arise from several impressions of an object taken by different senses.[55] "Common sense" therefore signifies rudimentary perception.

Images that have been collected and sorted by the common sense are ready for the imagination or fantasy. The chief function of this faculty is to continue the thought process, to recommend to the consideration of reason forms that are of importance, and to store ideas in the ventricle of memory. It retains impressions longer than does common sense and tries them in a balance,

> Where some things good, and some things ill doe seem,
> And neutrall some, in her fantasticke eye.[56]

The imagination is always busy. During sleep it does not receive reports from the outer world; hence it may create dreams. In beasts it has no superior; in man it should be subject to reason but usually it dominates thought.

Except by those who oppose localization, memory, "the Register and Storehouse of all the Idea's and Images first perceiv'd by the Senses, and then collected and seal'd up by the Imagination,"[57] is said to reside in the hindmost portion of the brain. As a writer records on paper that which he would not forget and later returns

---

[53] Act I, sc. vii, l. 66.

[54] Coeffeteau, *op. cit.*, Preface; Charron, *op. cit.*, Bk. I, p. 80; John Davies of Hereford, "Mirum in Modum," *loc. cit.*, p. 7; Burton, *op. cit.*, Vol. I, p. 182; etc.

[55] Cf. *All's Well*, II, i, 180-181.

[56] Sir John Davies, *loc. cit.*, p. 112.

[57] Charron, *op. cit.*, Bk. I, p. 110.

to read, so the imagination writes in the memory "figures" of things known by the five senses and by the understanding, as well as certain "figures" of its own framing. Later it may return to behold and contemplate these forms.[58] Since the memory receives actual impressions—as one records on paper or as wax takes the print of a seal—it is described as a "tendernesse" of the brain disposed with a "certaine kinde of moisture" to admit and pre-serve whatever the imagination apprehends. The functioning of memory thus depends largely upon the composition of its cell. A brain that is too moist cannot retain distinct impressions; one that is too hard is likely to be unreceptive:

> Therefore, hir parte and portion of the braine,
> Is much lesse humid, and more firmly fixt,
> Because it so the better may retaine,
> Th' impressions by the *Sences* there infixt,
> And for its *Fount* of marrow in the raine,
> Whereof the strongest sinewes are commixt,
>   For both which reasons *Nature* had respect,
>   To binde the *Braine* behind to that effect.
>
> And yet too hard the *Braine* may there be bound,
> For so twill hardly open to conceiue,
> And beeing ouer-moyst, it will confound
> All the impressions which the *Sences* giue.
> Well temp'red therefore needs must be the ground,
> That truly yeelds the seede it doth receiue;
>   Yet the moyst braine conceiues more readily,
>   But the drie braine retaines more steadily.[59]

A normal child learns more readily than an old man because the temper of his brain is better adapted to the needs of memory and because the organ is not yet so filled with forms that it is hardly capable of holding more. Sir John Davies writes of an intellectual memory united to the understanding and will.[60] Those who describe only one form of memory make imagination the custodian that lays up reports from the understanding as well as from its own court. The storing of ideas completes the operations of the sensitive powers of apprehension—common sense, imagination or fantasy, and memory; or imagination, sensible reason, and memory.

The sensitive "soul" consists not only of these processes of know-ing but also of a motive virtue (or power) which renders man cap-able of action. The motive virtue includes the appetites—inclina-tions by which the soul likes or dislikes whatever comes to it—and

---

[58] Huarte, *op. cit.*, pp. 78-79.
[59] John Davies of Hereford, "Mirum in Modum," *loc. cit.*, p. 9.
[60] *Loc. cit.*, p. 121.

a power enabling man to move parts of his body and to move from place to place. The appetites La Primaudaye and John Davies of Hereford divide into two kinds, as they arise with or without touching. Of the first La Primaudaye writes:

"Pleasure and griefe belong properly to the first kinde, and the instruments and seates thereof are in the sinewes, or els in that small sinewy skinne, which giueth the sense. For those things delight the sinewes which agree with their nature, and looke what is contrary vnto them, the same affecteth them with griefe . . . ."[61]

These appetites do not proceed from the imagination. Obviously they are inclinations arising from the sense of touch—from any of the external senses, in fact, for all of them are capable of pleasure and pain. They are the inclinations or motions to which Shakespeare refers in *Measure for Measure* when he describes Lord Angelo as

> one who never feels
> The wanton stings and motions of the sense.[62]

The second form of appetite, that which arises without touch, follows imagination or thought. It possesses a desiring or concupiscent and an angry or irascible inclination from which spring the affections of the heart. These affections, especially in their initial stages, are also called motions. They are impulses which incite the soul to reach out for the good and to withdraw from the evil.

The second power of motion belonging to the sensible "soul" is one that enables man to move parts of his body and to move from place to place. It is dispersed throughout the sinews, which it holds as one does the reins of a bridle,

> And makes the Body to aduance, retire,
> To turne or stop, as she them slacks, or straines.[63]

The "efficient cause" of bodily motion is reason, or its subordinate, the fantasy, which, when it apprehends a good or bad object, arouses the sensitive appetite. The appetite, in turn, commands the virtue which makes movement possible. The spirits, through contracting and relaxing, then draw the nerves, the muscles, and the joints to the place intended, and thus man moves a member of his body or

---

[61] *Op. cit.*, p. 439. Cf. John Davies of Hereford, "Microcosmos," *loc. cit.*, p. 24.
[62] Act I, sc. iv, ll. 59-60 . Cf. *Cymbeline*, I, vi, 103.
[63] Sir John Davies, *loc. cit.*, p. 115.

carries himself from one place to another.   Only by the functioning
of this last power can he effect what is begun in thought.[64]

Superior to the vegetal and sensitive activities of the soul is a
rational power capable of functioning without using bodily instruments and consequently immortal.   Fletcher describes this faculty
as a Prince whose countenance is sun-like, whose body, matter without matter, is never filled, although it may hold within its compass
all heaven and earth.   When his kingdom sleeps, he keeps watch;
his virtue is present in every part of the body.   As a Viceroy of
the divine Judge, he dwells within a tower, the little world of man,
constantly assaulted by a thousand enemies:

> Hence while unsetled here he fighting reignes,
> Shut in a Tower where thousand enemies
> Assault the fort, with wary care and pains
> He guards all entrance, and by divers spies
> Searches into his foes and friends designes:
> For most he fears his subjects wavering mindes.
> This Tower then only falls, when treason undermines.[65]

If he does not yield to inferior powers, he is capable of inclining
man to God and of obtaining for himself eternal joy.

This rational nature, as does the sensitive faculty, includes a
power of apprehension and a power of motion—the understanding
and the will—under which may be described all its operations.   The
two powers taken together are frequently named intellect.   The
former, to which alone the term intellect is sometimes applied, is
also called reason or wit.   As the final thought process, it receives
and illuminates ideas that have come from imagination.   There is
associated with it a reflective power, by which it examines its own
actions, and certain innate criteria, which provide a knowledge of
the law of God and of Nature.   By virtue of these innate notions
the soul not only comprehends particular and material forms, but
also, as a result of several processes, distinguishes between good and
evil and arrives ultimately at universal and divine truths:

"From this [innate knowledge] do spring three seuerall actions,
whereby the whole course of reason is made perfect.   First, that
which the *Greeks* call *Sinteresis*, the ground whereupon the practise
of reason consisteth, answering the proposition in a sillogisme: the
conscience, applying the assumption: and of them both, the third,
a certaine trueth concluded."[66]

---

[64] Burton, *op. cit.*, Vol. I, pp. 184-185.

[65] *Loc. cit.*, p. 77.

[66] Bright, *op. cit.*, p. 89.   Burton (*op. cit.*, Vol. I, pp. 189-190) describes

These functions the soul performs without using instruments of the body, "and neuer faileth therein, so farre as the naturall principles leade, or outward obiects be sincerely taken, and truly reported to the minds consideration."

The understanding, as it functions differently, receives different names. Considering successive powers that continue work begun by the imagination, Charron, for example, enumerates reason, discourse or ratiocination, penetration or sagacity, judgment, understanding, and will or volition, a consequence of the knowing process by which the mind reaches out for a good.[67] Similarly Sir John Davies makes a distinction between reason, rating from ground to ground, and understanding, the recognition of truth, and between opinion, assenting lightly, and judgment, the definition of truth by principles.[68] Reason seems generally to have been regarded as the process by which the intellect considers material things, and understanding as the process by which it comprehends universal and spiritual truths. The following from La Primaudaye presents this distinction clearly; it suggests also the manner in which rational apprehension functions:

"For it [reason] goeth from things knowne, to them that are vnknowne, and descendeth from generals to specials, and from them to particulars, and mounteth aloft againe by the same steps from one to another, and compareth one with another. For after that *imagination* hath receiued the images and impressions of things offered vnto it by the outward senses, the consideration of *Reason* followeth, which enquireth of all that may be in the mind, of the plenty or want that is there, and causeth it to returne to it selfe: as if it did behold and consider it selfe, to take knowledge what it hath, or what it hath not, how much it hath, & of what qualitie and nature it is. After this, reason draweth out and concludeth invisible of visible, of corporall things it concludeth things without bodies, and secret things of plaine and euident matters, and generals of particulars: then it referreth all this to the vnderstanding which is the chiefe vertue and power of the soule, and that which comprehendeth all the faculties thereof . . . . yea that which

---

three innate "species" of the understanding: "*Synteresis,* or the purer part of the conscience, is an innate habit, and doth signify *a conuersation of the knowledge of the law of God and Nature, to know good or evil* . . . . The *dictamen rationis* is that which doth admonish us to do good or evil . . . . The *conscience* is that which approves good or evil, justifying or condemning our actions . . . ." Fletcher (*loc. cit.,* p. 82) makes conscience a counselor of will rather than of the understanding.

[67] *Op. cit.,* Bk. I, pp. 129-130.
[68] *Loc. cit.,* p. 117.

finally resteth in the contemplation of the spirit, which is the end
of all enquiry of truth, and as it were a setled and assured view
of all those things that haue been culled out by reason and approued
by iudgement.''[69]

Rational apprehension is described in still another way according to the end toward which it strives. When it seeks truth by
means of contemplation, it is called speculative or contemplative
reason—*intellectus speculativus*; when it seeks the good and, having found it, goes forward to the will in order that the soul may
follow after the good or flee from evil, it is called practical or active
reason—*intellectus practicus*. The first Nemesius calls mind or
wisdom and the second reason or prudence.[70] From each of the
forms a habit of life may develop: from the functioning of understanding, the life contemplative and from the functioning of reason,
inasmuch as the power does not stop with the discovery of good
but goes forward to the will, the life active.[71]

Joined with rational apprehension is a virtue which covets the
good and hates the evil. This faculty, will, is the intellect in action,
a virtue which carries out what the understanding advises. Like
the sensitive appetite, will is blind, ordained to follow the light of
reason, and consequently by some termed the intellective appetite.
Will differs, however, from the affections. ''The object of Appetite,'' writes Hooker, ''is whatsoever sensible good may be wished
for; the object of Will is that good which Reason doth lead us to
seek.'' Appetite may desire anything that seems good, ''be it never
so impossible,'' but will does not incline to possess or to do whatever
reason pronounces good unless reason also teaches a way to obtain
or to do the good. The affections are not wholly within our power,
for they ''can neither rise at the conceit of a thing indifferent, nor
yet choose but rise at the sight of some things''; acts arising from
the disposition of will are in the power of will to be performed or
stayed. ''Finally,'' Hooker concludes, ''Appetite is the Will's
solicitor, and the Will is Appetite's controller; what we covet by
the one by the other we often reject; neither is any other desire

[69] *Op. cit.*, p. 418. Cf. Batman (*op. cit.*, Bk. III, ch. 6): ''For it [the
soul] beholdeth the higher things and so it is called *Intellectus*: and beholdeth
the neather things, and so it is called *Racio*.''

[70] *Op. cit.*, pp. 565-566.

[71] Batman, *op. cit.*, Bk. III, ch, 13. Cf. La Primaudaye, *op. cit.*, p. 423;
John Davies of Hereford, ''Mirum in Modum,'' *loc. cit.*, p. 9; Fletcher, *loc.
cit.*, pp. 80-81.

termed properly Will, but that where Reason and Understanding, or the show of Reason, prescribeth the thing desired."[72]

There is ingrafted in will a desire for good so strong that it cannot love anything that does not possess the appearance of good:

> If *ill* for *good* shee choose, hence it doth gro
> Because *ill* seeming *good*, shee takes it so.

> Shee nought can loue but hath some show of *good*;
> Nor ought can loath but hath like show of *ill*;
> Desire of *good* by her may be with-stoode,
> But *it* shee cannot loath, or leave it still:
> So may shee choose to execute her will,
> When ill is tendred her *in deede*, or *sho*,
> But cannot leaue it, or her wil fulfill,
> Because to *ill* she is a mortall foe,
> And lothes it as sole worker of her woe.[73]

That He might have voluntary service, God gave the will freedom. Will depends for its guidance upon reason, yet it is not so subject thereunto that it must follow all the conclusions that are propounded to it or even accept any of them, "but that always she hath her libertie to make choice of which reason shee pleases, out of all those that are set before her."[74] Nothing can restrain the freedom of will. As understanding is the highest form of apprehension, will is the highest power of desire. The sensitive appetites should remain obedient to it; thus will is finally responsible for action.

Let us note now the entire process of thought and the manner in which action results therefrom. When an object presents itself to the outward senses, animal spirits enable each organ affected to receive a particular kind of impression to which it has been adapted. These impressions are crude and often contradictory. The animal spirits, therefore, hasten to the foremost cell of the brain, the ventricle of common sense, where their reports are reduced to a unity and preserved in the absence of the object for the consideration of the imagination. This power, having elaborated ideas by means of the animal spirits, may assign them to the memory or it may recommend them to reason and the understanding before storing them for future use. If action is required, the imagination communicates with the heart, informing the affections whether the object is pleasing or displeasing. At the same instant, the

---

[72] *Of the Laws of Ecclesiastical Polity*, 2 vols., Everyman's Library, Vol. I (I, vii, 3-5), pp. 170-171.

[73] John Davies of Hereford, "Microcosmos," *loc. cit.*, p. 25.

[74] La Primaudaye, *op. cit.*, p. 442.

"form" or idea, purged from "sensible" and "singular conditions," may be perceived by the understanding and represented to
the will as a good or as an evil. The will, being queen of the powers
of the soul, ordains what shall be embraced and what avoided, "as
it pleseth her," and sensitive appetite, yielding obedience, "quick-
neth all the powers and *passions* ouer which shee commands, and
sets to worke those which are necessary to that action, and by their
meanes commands the mouing *power*, dispersed ouer all the members, to follow or fly, to approach or recoyle, or to do any other
motion which it requireth." In this fashion arises all action when
man "will obserue the order which he ought." Often, because of
bad education, wrong habits, unsound organs, or a perverse will,
he does not permit reason to hold the supremacy which it deserves.
At such times sensitive appetite does not stay to have ideas judged
by the understanding and chosen by the will, but of itself, in response to the imagination, commands the moving power. In either
case, with the functioning of the motive virtue, thought eventuates
in action.[75]

The powers of apprehension co-operate in such a way that each
of the inferior powers provides an image or stimulus adequate to
the needs of its immediate superior. Impressions received by the
external senses become increasingly purified until they culminate
in the wisdom of which the intellect is capable. The soul thus gives
to man several kinds or degrees of knowledge, varying from crude
sensation to the perception of spiritual truths. Finally it understands many things which the senses do not really declare unto it:

  ". . . . as the qualities of externall things are the matter subiect
  of the internall senses, so their images conceiued by the internall
  senses, and purged from all bodily matter, are the matter subiect
  of the vndèrstanding and spirit. And the spirit labouring about
  them draweth out certain motions, and knoweth many things from
  them, which cannot mooue the senses and which the senses cannot
  know. And yet the spirit is first mooued by these images, as the
  senses are by externall things."[76]

In the following passage La Primaudaye considers the relative
clarity of knowledge in each of its successive stages:

  ". . . . wee are now to obserue and note this, that the knowledge
  of things which we haue by the outward senses, is as if wee beheld

---

[75] Coeffeteau, *op. cit.*, Preface.
[76] La Primaudaye, *op. cit.*, p. 611.

the shadowes of them: and that knowledge which we haue by the common sence, by Imagination and Fantasie, is as if we did looke vpon the images, which represent vnto vs those things whereof they are images more liuely and cleerely then their shadowes can doe. And the knowledge we haue by vnderstanding . . . . is as if we viewed not only the shadowes or images of things, but also their very bodies, which is more. And that knowledge which we haue by reason is as if, besides all this, we saw their effects and vertues: Therefore there is as much difference betweene the knowledge that a man may haue by euery one of these faculties and powers, as there is betwixt the shadowe, and image, and body, and effects or vertues of one and the same thing, to the end that the nature thereof may be throughly knowne.''[77]

From analyses of the thought process it is obvious that Shakespeare and his contemporaries regarded the faculties of apprehension as powers which evolve ideas in varying stages of completion. They distinguish several kinds or degrees of knowledge and several correspondent inclinations of desire. The first kind belongs to the external senses, for the animal spirits present in the organs are capable of giving an elemental knowledge of an object from which a stimulus comes. "And the Senses are not purely *Passive*," writes Charron; "for, notwithstanding that they receive an Impression, and in that respect are acted upon, yet do they likewise act in some Degree themselves, so far as they perceive the Image and apprehend the Object propounded to them.''[78] Perception that arises in the external organs is limited of course in many respects. When an object is too large, for example, to be "apprehended at one aspect," sight needs the help of internal faculties.[79] By itself alone the eye is sensible of number as far as two or three;[80] nor can feeling distinguish a higher number than two or three.[81] None of the senses, without the assistance of the imagination and of the memory, can build up sensation from successive stimuli: "For, that thing onely which moves the *sense* by *one only attempt,* is wrought by the *sense* alone (without the helpe of *memory* and *cogitation* :) but, such things as are felt at divers times are not wrought by the *sense* onely, but by the aide of *memory* and *cogitation* . . . .''[82] Superior

[77] *Op. cit.,* p. 418. Cf. John Davies of Hereford, ''Mirum in Modum,'' *loc. cit.,* p. 9.

[78] Charron, *op. cit.,* Bk. I, p. 79.

[79] Nemesius, *op .cit.,* p. 292.

[80] *Ibid.,* p. 293.

[81] *Ibid.,* p. 313.

[82] *Ibid.,* p. 295.

to the functioning of the outer wits is perception of things that are absent by the internal senses and of things not bodily by the understanding. Each of these powers may give rise to appetite, for man "may take pleasure by all those partes whereby he may knowe, as well by the internall as the externall senses, and by all the powers of the minde and soule."[83] With the outer wits are associated a love of that which gives pleasure and a hatred of that which gives pain, inclinations readily observable in connection with touch and taste.[84] From the imagination proceed the affections of the heart, and from the understanding proceeds will. There is a knowledge of sense and a pleasure of sense, a knowledge of the imagination and a pleasure of the imagination, a knowledge of the intellect and a pleasure of the intellect.

The doctrine that there are three degrees of knowledge and three correspondent inclinations of desire was so essential a part of Elizabethan psychology that it frequently became a basis for estimating character. Judgment and action, it was thought, may be determined by any one of the three. One need not be surprised, then, to find that Shakespeare describes clearly the nature of judgment and action arising from each of the forms. Iachimo, misrepresenting Posthumus to Imogen, thinks in terms of the pleasures of sense:

> Had I this cheek
> To bathe my lips upon; this hand, whose touch,
> Whose every touch, would force the feeler's soul
> To the oath of loyalty; this object, which
> Takes prisoner the wild motion of mine eye,
> Fixing it only here; . . . .[85]

In *The Merchant of Venice* we are told that the "fool multitude" choose by show,

> Not learning more than the fond eye doth teach;
> Which pries not to the interior, but, like the martlet,
> Builds in the weather on the outward wall,
> Even in the force and road of casualty.[86]

Aragon knows that judgment based upon the dictates of sense is

---

[83] La Primaudaye, *op. cit.*, p. 475.

[84] See Charron, *op. cit.*, Bk. I, p. 85; Nemesius, *op. cit.*, p. 271.

[85] *Cymbeline*, I, vi, 99 ff.

[86] Act II, sc. ix, ll. 27-30. Cf. the King's reference to the multitude (*Hamlet*, IV, iii, 5),
"Who like not in their judgement, but their eyes."

unsound. In *Measure for Measure* Angelo says of his passion for Isabella,

> I have begun,
> And now I give my sensual race the rein.[87]

The man who heretofore has never known the wanton stings and motions of sense, through yielding to this grossest form of apprehension and of appetite, all but loses himself.   The way of sense is dangerous.

> Minds sway'd by eyes are full of turpitude.[88]

Let us consider for a moment the nobler powers of knowledge and desire.   In a familiar lyric Shakespeare tells us that fancy is engendered in the eyes,

> With gazing fed; and fancy dies
> In the cradle where it lies.[89]

The imagination, that faculty by which fancy is begot, is more likely, we shall discover, to follow sense than reason; with satiation of sense fancy therefore dies, and the imagination becomes free to busy itself with other "forms."   The imagination is never idle. From impressions received from common sense or from the memory it may create new images, sometimes monstrous or startling.   In *Romeo and Juliet* fantasy (or imagination) is said to be as thin of substance as the air and more inconstant than the wind.[90]   Often it leads man to confusion.

> How many actions most ridiculous
> Hast thou been drawn to by thy fantasy?

asks Sylvius of Corin in *As You Like It*.[91]   Disregarding the voice of reason, the imagination may prompt unadvised action such as that of Hotspur at Shrewesbury, who, according to comment in *2 Henry IV*,

> Lin'd himself with hope,
> Eating the air, and promise of supply,
> Flatt'ring himself in project of a power
> Much smaller than the smallest of his thoughts;
> And so, with great imagination
> Proper to madmen, led his powers to death,
> And winking leap'd into destruction.[92]

---

[87] Act II, sc. iv, ll. 159-160.

[88] *Troilus and Cressida*, V, ii, 112.

[89] *Merchant of Venice*, III, ii, 68-69.

[90] Act I, sc. iv, ll. 99-100.

[91] Act II, sc. iv, ll. 30-31.

[92] Act I, sc. iii, ll. 27 ff.   Cf. references to Hotspur's imagination, *1 Henry IV*, I, iii, 199-200 and 209-210.

To the messenger from Rome, whom he has urged to rail with "full license," Mark Antony says:

> O, then we bring forth weeds
> When our quick minds lie still.[93]

His self-accusation comes during a moment of regret as the pronouncement of reason upon the folly of a course directed by inferior faculties. The conception of imagination suggested by these and other passages in Shakespeare is but the expression in literature of a notion one finds everywhere in psychological treatises: the imagination is exceedingly variable; it is the source of "all our Evils, our Confusions and Disorders, our Passions and Troubles."[94] Right conduct springs from reason; reason must not be allowed to "fust" in us unused.[95]

---

[93] *Antony and Cleopatra*, I, ii, 113-114.

[94] See Charron, *op. cit.*, Bk. I, pp. 158-162.

[95] For a discussion of the powers of knowledge and desire in relation to the psychology of love, see below, pp. 121-124.

CHAPTER II

ELEMENTS, HUMORS, AND TEMPER: SOME CHARACTERISTICS OF THE SOUL

Whether the faculties of the soul perform their tasks skilfully depends upon the fitness of the instruments they have at their disposal. The fitness of these instruments, varying not only for different individuals but also for the same individual under changing circumstances, the Elizabethan explained in terms of a theory of elements, humors, and temper. The four elements, earth, water, air, and fire, are the simplest particles of all that is material; they are the simplest particles of our bodies. Huarte tells us that the elements, "according to the waight and measure by which they enter into the composition must alwaies so indure in the mixture."[1] To each of them are joined two[2] of the four first[3] qualities. Earth is dry and cold, water cold and moist, air hot and moist, and fire hot and dry. Earth is contrary to air and water to fire. Union is possible, however, for water serves as a mean between earth and air, and air as a mean between water and fire. The elements possess an inclination not only to ascend and descend but also to move in a circular[4] direction. Each element is joined by one of its qualities to that which is below and by the other to that which is above it: water to earth beneath by coldness and to air above by moisture; air to water beneath by moisture and to fire above by heat; fire to air beneath by heat and to earth toward which it declines, "as it were in a circular motion," by dryness; earth to water above by coldness and to fire, which declines toward it, by dryness.[5] The elements are continually engendered one of another and perpetually

---

[1] *Examen de Ingenios*, p. 301.

[2] Bright (*A Treatise of Melancholy*, pp. 69-70) argues that each element possesses only one quality.

[3] So called because they "slide first from the Elements into the things that be made of Elements" and because from them come all the "secundarie effects."—*Batman vppon Bartholome*, Bk. IV, ch. 1. They are the only qualities which may effect a whole change in a substance.—Nemesius, *The Nature of Man*, pp. 231-232.

[4] David Person (*Varieties: or, a Surveigh of Rare and Excellent matters ....*, London, 1635, p. 7) states that circular motion in no way pertains to elements of material bodies.

[5] Nemesius, *op. cit.*, pp. 232-234.

preserved from being wasted.[6]   The elements are never idle but always doing and suffering.   Accordingly, two of their qualities are called active and two passive:

"Two of these qualytyes be called Actiue, able to worke hot, and coldnesse.   The other two bee drye and wetnesse, and be called Passiue, able to suffer.   And so as these qualyties preuaile and haue maisterie, the Elements be called Actiue and Passiue able to do & suffer.   The first two be principally called Actiue, not because they worke alone, for there is none idle qualitye in the bodie: But therefore they be called Actiue, for by working of them the other be brought in & kept saued.   For heate sometime bringeth in and keepeth moistnesse, and sometime drines . . . ."[7]

Within the body, bones represent earth, flesh air, vital spirits fire, and· all the humors water; choler represents fire, blood air, phlegm water, and melancholy earth.   There is a correspondence between understanding and fire, reason and air, imagination and water, all the external senses and earth; between sight and fire, hearing and air, taste and smell and water, feeling and earth.[8]   La Primaudaye assures us that all the elements exist in every part of the body, but that in each part one predominates:

"This is to bee seene in the blood, which is the first & chiefest of those 4 humours in the body, and is properly of the nature of aire.   For the muddy dregs, which commonly thicken and settle in the bottom of it, are of the nature of the earth, & are called *Melancholy,* and the pure blood that swimmeth in the midst doth represent vnto vs the aire: that humor that swimmeth in a round circle is watry fleame, and the skum that appeareth aboue, is the choler, which is of the nature of the fire."[9]

The Elements, inseparably linked together within the body by their tendencies to ascend and descend and to incline in a circular motion, give to man an elemental temperament or complexion:[10]

---

[6] *Ibid.,* pp. 234 ff.

[7] Batman, *op. cit.,* Bk. IV, ch. 1.

[8] *Ibid.,* Bk. XI, ch. 7.   Cf. La Primaudaye, *The French Academie,* p. 341.

[9] *Op. cit.,* p. 341.

[10] In exact usage the term complexion refers to the mixture of qualities resulting from the combination of elements in man.   The following passages suggest this usage:

"Complexion is a combynation of two dyuers qualities of the foure elementes in one bodye, as hotte and drye of the Fyre, hotte and moyst of the Ayre."— Quoted in *N.E.D.* from Thomas Elyot's *Castel of Helth,* London, 1541.

"Againe, it fareth oft-times that this or that humour aboundeth by disordered diet, yet the complexion all one, neither purgations of humour alter complexion a fixed thing, ingenerate by nature, and not ouerthrowne but by

> The Elements of *Nature's* famelies
> Produce the *Elemental's* temprament,
> Which is a mixture of the *Qualities*
> Or composition of each *Element*:
> (As *these* doe bend, so are their *bodies* bent)
> Which we *Complexion* cal; whereof are two,
> Well, and ill tempred; And the *Aliment*
> That feeds the *Body*, herein much can doe,
> For that can make & marre *Complexion* too.[11]

Parts of the body, as well as man himself, are well tempered if there is an equal counterpoise of the four qualities, and ill tempered if one of them predominates.[12] An equal counterpoise, if it prevails generally throughout the body, produces a man like Brutus, whose

---

some venimous quality directly opposit against it, or long custome of other disorder, whereby nature is supplanted in time, & growing in acquaintance with which it first misliked, and is ouermatched with a counterfet nature, gotten by vse of that otherwise is vnnaturall."—Bright, *op. cit.*, p. 104.

"A bodie of sanguine complexion (as commonly we call it, although complexion be another thing then condition of humors) .... breedeth an indifferencie to all passions."—*Ibid.*, p. 118.

Frequently "complexion" and "temper" or "temperament" are made synonymous as being the combination of qualities which results from the condition of the humors within the body. This sense of the word complexion, if not its exact usage, seems to underlie the words of Isabella to Angelo (*Measure for Measure*, II, iv, 128-130):

> "Nay, call us ten times frail;
> For we are soft as our complexions are,
> And credulous to false prints."

Cf. *Hamlet*, I, iv, 27. In *Love's Labour's Lost* (I, ii, 82 ff.) Armado asks Moth of what complexion Samson's love was. The page replies, "Of all the four, or the three, or the two, or the one of the four." Since one or another of the elements and of the humors always predominate in a body there can be only four complexions.

"Complexion" (*N.E.D.*) has certain meanings derived from the above usages. Among those which Shakespeare employs are the following: (1) Bodily habit or constitution (determined of course by the combination of qualities): "Methinks it is very sultry and hot for my complexion."—*Hamlet*, V, ii, 102. (2) Constitution or habit of mind, disposition (determined by combination of qualities): *Salanio* of *Jessica's* flight: "And then it is the complexion of them all to leave the dam."—*Merchant of Venice*, I, i, 32. Cf. *Much Ado*, II, i, 305; *Measure for Measure*, III, i, 187. (3) Natural color, texture, and appearance of the skin (as showing bodily constitution, and thus disposition): *Morocco*: "Mislike me not for my complexion."—*Merchant of Venice*, II, i, 1. Cf. *Love's Labour's Lost*, IV, iii, 234; *Henry V*, II, ii, 73; *Comedy of Errors*, III, ii, 103. (4) Countenance or face: "Turn thy complexion there."—*Othello*, IV, ii, 62. (5) Transferred, to indicate color, visible aspect, or appearance of things or qualities: "Complexion of the sky."—*Richard II*, III, ii, 194. Cf. *Much Ado*, I, i, 315 (love's complexion); *2 Henry IV*, II, ii, 6 (complexion of greatness); *Henry V*, III, iii, 17 (complexion of war); etc.

[11] John Davies of Hereford, "Microcosmos," *loc. cit.*, p. 30. The statement from Huarte (above, p. 29) and the quotations from Bright (above, n. 10) imply that complexion, according to the exact usage of the term, is hardly subject to the influence of nourishment.

[12] *Ibid.*, pp. 30-31.

> life was gentle, and the elements
> So mix'd in him that Nature might stand up
> And say to all the world, ''This was a man!''[13]

Men in whom one quality predominates unduly over others possess a "vicious mole of nature"; their bodies are not well suited to the needs of the soul. The proportion in which the elements are united within the body has an influence, of course, upon action. Slow and heavy moving signifies a predominance of earth, fearfulness and sluggishness of water, cheerfulness of air, and sharp, angry violence of fire.[14]

In a number of passages Shakespeare analyzes action or state of mind in terms of this relation between the elements and conduct. Cleopatra, aroused by her resolve to follow Antony in death, feels herself made only of the swift and light particles, air and fire. Earth and water, which make man sluggish, she gives to baser life.[15] Of his horse, which is the color of nutmeg, the Dauphin in *Henry V* says, "He is pure air and fire; and the dull elements of earth and water never appear in him, but only in patient stillness while his rider mounts him."[16] La Primaudaye tells us that choler (fire) engenders the bay horse, blood (air) the russet, phlegm (water) the gray, and melancholy (earth) the black. The bay horse is hardy in war; the russet is quick and prompt but of less force than the bay; the gray is heavy and fearful, and the black unsound.[17] Here again Shakespeare makes a distinction between the light and dull elements in their relation to behavior. A more extended analogy appears in *Sonnets* Nos. 44 and 45. The poet, wrought so much of earth and water, cannot speed with thought across the distance that separates him from his friend; he must attend time's leisure, receiving nothing but tears from the gross elements predominant in his being. His portion of air and fire are with his friend, for the first is thought and the other desire. Left with only two elements, he becomes oppressed with melancholy and sinks down to death until the swift messengers, air and fire, return and re-establish life's composition. Assured of his friend's health he becomes for

---

[13] *Julius Caesar*, V, v, 73-75.

[14] Batman, *op. cit.*, Bk. XI, ch. 7.

[15] *Antony and Cleopatra*, V, ii, 292-293.

[16] Act III, sc. vii, ll. 22-25.

[17] *Op. cit.*, p. 826.

a moment happy; then his messengers are off again and he grows sad.[18]

The body, according to Elizabethan psychology, is sustained and nourished by four humors—melancholy, phlegm, blood, and choler —corresponding respectively to earth, water, air, and fire, and subject to variation in quantity and in degree of purity. These, also, we must consider in order to understand human behavior.

The humors arise in the liver or develop one from another.[19] In their progress through the body, choler, phlegm, and melancholy unite with blood, the most temperate and essential of all the humors and the one after which the entire mass is named. When blood is let from the body—

". . . . vppermost we see as it were a little skim like to the floure or working of new wine, or of another wine when it is powred forth [choler]. Next we may see as it were small streames of water mingled with the blood [phlegm]. And in the bottome is seene a blacker and thicker humor, like to the lees of wine in a vessell [melancholy]."[20]

Although the four humors unite in the veins, each maintains its

---

[18] Dowden ("Elizabethan Psychology," *loc. cit.*, pp. 328-329) directs attention to the sonnets and to the two preceding passages from Shakespeare.

The word element sometimes signifies that one of the four elements which is the natural abode of any particular class of living beings. In a transferred and figurative sense it may thus mean a person's ordinary range of activity, the surroundings in which one feels at home, or the appropriate sphere of operation of any agency.—"Element," 12, *N.E.D.* This usage of the term underlies several passages in Shakespeare: *Clown to Viola* (*Twelfth Night*, III, i, 64-65): "Who you are and what you would are out of my welkin—I might say 'element,' but the word is overworn." Cf. (*ibid.*, III, iv, 137) "I am not of your element"; (*Merry Wives*, IV, ii, 186) "Such daubery as this is beyond our element"; (*King Lear*, II, iv, 57-58) "Down, thou climbing sorrow, Thy element's below!"

[19] "The breeding of them is made & beginneth in the lyuer, but it endeth not ther at ful. First working heate turneth what is cold & moyst into the kind of fleme, & then what is hot & moyst into the kinde of bloud: and then what is hot and drye into the kinde of *Cholera*: and then what is colde and drye into the kinde of *Melancholia*. Then the processe is such First, fleame is bread, as an humour halfe sod: second bloud, that is perfectly sodde: the thirde *Cholera*, that is ouer sodde: the last is *Melancholia*, that is more earthly, and the dregges of the other. . . . . The breeding of the Elements be straight, and returning into the same. For of aire fire is bread, and of fire aire, and euery Element of other. The breeding of the humors is straight, and not by contrary. By seething bloud is bred of fleame, and not that it retourneth. Likewise bloude is made cholar, by great heate drieing and making subtill the humour, but not that it returneth. And by burning of cholar in lyke manner *Melancholia* is made, and not that it retourneth."—Batman, *op. cit.*, Bk. IV, ch. 6.

[20] La Primaudaye, *op. cit.*, pp. 523-524.

own characteristics. Blood, which in an equal temper exceeds the others in quantity,[21] is hot and moist, sweet and red. It imparts strength and color to the body and serves for the engendering of spirits. Phlegm, next to blood in quantity, is watery, cold, moist, and white. It moderates the strength, heat, and thickness of blood, nourishes the brain, and moistens and nourishes such parts of the body as are concerned in motion. If blood fails, heat dissolves phlegm into blood. Melancholy, sometimes called black choler, is earthy and gross, thick, black, and sour. A part of it passes to the spleen and a part remains with the blood. Melancholy feeds the bones, the spleen, and other parts of the body which are gross or "melancholy" in nature; it tempers the two hot humors, and serves to stay and retain the floating spirits that arise from blood, "least if they should be made more pure and subtill then is expedient for the bodie, they vanish and passe away altogether." Melancholy thickens the blood and thus prevents it from flowing too freely through the veins and arteries.[22] Choler, least in quantity, is hot, dry, yellow or red, and bitter. A part of it passes from the liver to the gall, and a part, flowing thence with other humors, moderates moisture and makes the blood subtle so that it may pass easily through "straight wayes." Choler prevents the body from becoming heavy, sleepy, and dull; it penetrates and opens passages and feeds members of the body in which the fiery element predominates.

From the natural predominance of a humor in man, spring definite characteristics of physique and conduct. The phlegmatic are generally slothful, given to bodily pleasures, sleepy, idle, dull of wit, heavy, and slow. They love delicate food and drink. Their stature is short and fat; their hair soft, yellow, and straight. The melancholic are hard to please, obstinate, suspicious, sorrowful, and given to fearful thoughts. The sanguine are cheerful, courageous, kind, and ingenious. Their blood, if subtle, makes the wit keen. As fatness increases, blood diminishes. The choleric are easily provoked, given to treachery, and vehement in action; fierce in assailing but inconstant in sustaining the assault; inclined to envy, pride, prodigality, and wrath. They are tall, lean, and brown. Their hair is black, crisp, and hard. If choler is corrupt, they are subject to evil passions and dreadful dreams. Huarte tells us (upon

---

21 The statement of proportions follows Bright, *op. cit.*, pp. 6-7.
22 La Primaudaye, *op. cit.*, p. 530. Cf. Batman, *op. cit.*, Bk. IV, ch. 11.

the basis of Galenic doctrine) that moist humors make man blockish and foolish. Wisdom springs from choler; firmness and constancy from melancholy.[23]

Although there may be in man a more or less habitual predominance of one humor over others, the composition of what we call blood is by no means unchanging. The humors are exceedingly variable in quantity and in quality. During the day they reign by turns—blood from 3 A.M. to 9 A.M., choler from 9 A.M. to 3 P.M.,[24] phlegm from 3 P.M. to 9 P.M., and melancholy from 9 P.M. to 3 A.M.[25] In the spring blood begins to flow more freely and to increase. The heat of summer dissolves superfluities, wastes the humors, and opens the pores. Spirits escape from the body with exhalations, moisture, and vapors. Choler is in ascendancy. Autumn breeds phlegm. Winter thickens the humors, constrains the sinews, and sends natural heat inward. Melancholy increases, and makes men sluggards.[26]

A humor may be corrupt in substance or it may become disproportionately mixed with other humors. In either case it affects the state of man's well-being:

"Neither doe diseases proceede but onely of the distemperature that is in mens bodies, and in the humours of which they are compounded. For as long as they are in a good, moderate, and proportionable temper, and are distributed to all parts of the body according as neede requireth, so that none of them exceedeth, then is there an equality in all the body, which doth not onely preserue it in life, but in health and good disposition."[27]

From the elements and humors of the body arises temperament, a "Mixture and Proportion of the *Four* Prime *Qualities, Hot* and *Cold, Moist* and *Dry*; or rather a *Fifth Quality*, which is, as it were, a Harmony resulting from a due Conjunction of all these together, like that Concord in Sounds, which arises from a Complication of

---

[23] *Op. cit.*, p. 60. See also *ibid.*, p. 95; Batman, *op. cit.*, Bk. IV, chs. 9-10; La Primaudaye, *op. cit.*, p. 535; John Davies of Hereford, "Microcosmos," *loc. cit.*, p. 31.

[24] The notion that strength increases until noon thus has a physiological basis.

[25] Bright, *op. cit.*, pp. 139-140; John Davies of Hereford, "Microcosmos," *loc. cit.*, p. 31.

[26] Batman, *op. cit.*, Bk. IX, chs. 5-8; John Davies of Hereford, "Microcosmos," *loc. cit.*, p. 31.

[27] La Primaudaye, *op. cit.*, p. 528.

different Notes.''[28]   This temperament, according to Elizabethan theory, determines largely the way in which the soul functions. Huarte goes so far as to make nature and temperament synonymous. He argues, for example, that the ventricles of the brain are uniform in composition; no variation in activity can arise therefrom. Differences among men, as well as differences in individual behavior under changing circumstances, must issue from differences in temperament.[29]   La Primaudaye states that the temperature of liquors, humors, and qualities (under which he comprehends the spirits) is the fittest instrument of the soul.[30]   Other writers hold essentially the same opinion. They present an intricate series of relationships between each of the four first qualities and the functioning of the soul.

During the progress of man's life, moisture, heat, dryness, and cold reign respectively by turns. The vegetal faculty functions readily in childhood because the body contains much heat and moisture. The understanding lies dormant. Man, while these qualities are predominant, is subject to passions that are hot. Dryness and cold facilitate rational activity. Since they are not conducive to growth, they finally prevent the vegetal faculty from keeping the body in repair. Old age gives rise to sorrow and to other passions agreeable to a cold and dry temperament. In every age man has ''a diuers temperature, and a contrary disposition, by means whereof, the soule doth other workes in childhood, other in youth, and other in old age.''[31]

Shakespeare thus at times describes behavior in terms of physiological accompaniments. After a moment of triumph at Alexandria, Mark Antony says to Cleopatra:

> Though grey
> Do something mingle with our younger brown, yet ha' we
> A brain that nourishes our nerves, and can
> Get goal for goal of youth.[32]

The brain supplies the nerves with animal spirits, which render man capable of thought and action. Extreme dryness, such as that which comes with age, destroys the spirits. Cold, in the real sense of the word, benumbs all the faculties of the soul. Antony means

---

[28] Charron, *Of Wisdom*, Bk. I, p. 114.

[29] *Op. cit.*, p. 56.

[30] *Op. cit.*, p. 566.

[31] Huarte, *op. cit.*, p. 21.

[32] *Antony and Cleopatra*, IV, viii, 19-22.

that although he is old his brain still feeds the nerves an abundance of spirits; he has not lost the virility of youth. Falstaff makes a difference in physiological conditions the basis of his argument that age cannot understand youth: "You that are old consider not the capacities of us that are young; you do measure the heat of our livers with the bitterness of your galls."[33] Old age is normally cold and dry. It is probable that to account for this envy and peevishness in old age, the Elizabethan thought of choler, the humor which collects in the gall, as having lost much of its heat, a quality which renders man active, and therefore as being unduly dry and bitter. Of the Senators in Athens, Timon remarks:

These old fellows
Have their ingratitude in them hereditary.
Their blood is cak'd, 'tis cold, it seldom flows;
'Tis lack of kindly warmth they are not kind;
And nature, as it grows toward earth,
Is fashion'd for the journey, dull and heavy.[34]

Here the dramatist characterizes in terms of the inevitable physiological changes that come with age. The difference between youth and age results from a difference in temperament. Life itself, according to La Primaudaye, consists in the preservation of the instruments the soul uses in the body, and the chief of these are heat and moisture.[35]

---

[33] *2 Henry IV*, I, ii, 196-198. According to Professor R. P. Cowl in the Arden edition of the play (London, Methuen and Co.) Shakespeare was indebted for this contrast between youth and age to Lyly, *Euphues, Anatomy of Wit* (Bond, i, 192-193): "Doe you measure the hotte assaultes of youth, by the cold skirmishes of age? whose years are subject to more infirmities than our youth, we merry, you melancholy . . . ."

[34] *Timon of Athens*, II, ii, 223-228. Cf. *Cleopatra* to *Charmian* (*Antony and Cleopatra*, I, v, 73-75):

"My salad days,
When I was green in judgement; cold in blood,
To say as I said then!"

Youth is hot and moist; therefore judgment is immature—green. There is a difference in opinion as to the interpretation of the rest of the passage. If we agree with Warburton that "cold in blood" is said in reproach of Charmian, the words derive significance from the fact that cold benumbs the soul. If, on the other hand, we accept as does Professor R. H. Case (Arden Edition) the pointing of Ff, the lines have no exact psychological meaning. Rash love springs from hot blood. Youth is not cold. The folly of its judgment results from moisture and the excess of its imagination from heat.

[35] *Op. cit.*, p. 554. The chief natural cause of long life is a constitution combining heat and moisture in due proportion; a second cause is a long continuance of this temperature: "So that death is a defect of those instruments of the soule, whereby life is prolonged. For the soule leaueth the bodie by reason of the defect of instruments, and not for any disagreement that is between the body and it . . . ."—*Ibid.*, pp. 554-555.

There is a correspondence, also, between the temperature of the
brain and the functioning of the powers which dwell there. "Only
This is Man's great Unhappiness, that the *Three Faculties, Understanding, Memory*, and *Imagination*, do each of them require different, nay, contrary Temperaments, for their Exercise and Perfection."[36] Cold, when it is merely a moderate degree of heat, promotes understanding; it also induces stability of character and
makes man firm in opinion, for it enables the brain to retain
"figures" easily without allowing them to rise.[37] Whenever the
quality becomes extreme, however, it benumbs the powers of the
soul. Cold, in the real sense of the word, is therefore detrimental
to man:

". . . . *Hot*, and *Moist*, and *Dry* only, can contribute to Mens In-
genuity. The Other is a sluggish, unactive Principle, and, instead
of quickening, does only benumb and stupifie the Soul, and put a
Stop to all its Motions. Therefore, when in reading some Authors,
we find them recommending *Cold*, as of use to the *Understanding*,
and saying, that Men of a Cold Brain . . . . are Prudent, Wise, Ingenious and the like, we must not there understand the Word *Cold*
in its Natural and most received Sense, but interpret it of a large
Abatement and more moderate Degree of *Heat* only."[38]

Unlike cold, which agrees well with virtuous action, heat may
incline one to vice and to passions that are hot. By refining the
spirits and lifting up "images" in the brain it stimulates the imagination. This faculty is more vigorous, therefore, in youth and
early manhood, the years during which poets reach their height.
Dryness facilitates the understanding, for it makes the spirits subtle,
pure, and swift. Melancholy, grief, and fasting thus dispose one
to think. Dryness wastes the humors and makes the body lean. It
may preserve life by drying up humors that stop the motion of
spirits but when it becomes excessive it kills the body. Moisture
promotes growth; it dulls the understanding. In order to receive
impressions easily, the brain must be soft and pliable; hence moisture is necessary to memory. That faculty is most active in youth
and in the morning, after the brain has been moistened by sleep.
Since cold, except in so far as it is a moderate heat, hinders the
soul, there are, then, three principal temperaments of the brain—

---

36 Charron, *op. cit.*, Bk. I, p. 114.

37 Huarte, *op. cit.*, pp. 57-58.

38 Charron, *op. cit.*, Bk. I, p. 117.

hot, dry, and moist—facilitating respectively imagination, understanding, and memory.

There is only one temper that makes a man "so surpassing wise,
as by nature he can be"—the perfect temperament—

"wherein the first qualities are in such waight and measure, that
the heat exceedeth not the cold, nor the moist the drie; but are
found in such equalitie and conformitie, as if really they were not
contraries, nor had any naturall opposition. Whence resulteth an
instrument so appliable to the operations of the reasonable soul,
that man cometh to possesse a perfect memory of things passed, and
a great imagination to see what is to come, and a great vnderstanding to distinguish, inferre, argue, iudge, and make choice."[39]

Upon this temper rests the office of a king. The more nearly man's
temperament approaches perfection, the more quiet, comely, moderate, and gracious will he be naturally. No one, however, is without
some predominance of one of the four qualities. As a humor rules
more or less in everyone, so is man called sanguine, phlegmatic,
choleric, or melancholic; and so, we have seen, is he likely to possess
definite physical and mental characteristics.[40]

Physical features, inasmuch as they depend upon the combination
of the first qualities within the body, may serve as an index of
temperament and thus of an individual's habitual mode of behavior.
Since moisture promotes growth but dulls the understanding, men
of large stature are ordinarily less wise than those of small stature.
"Nothing offends the reasonable soule so much as to make his abode
in a body surcharged with bones, fat, and flesh."[41] A little head,
according to Galenic doctrine, is faulty in any man: it lacks brain.
Huarte adds that a head which is large because of an abundance
of matter and because of ill-tempered substance also lacks brain.
In small men the head should incline toward greatness; in large
men it should be small.[42] Choler and melancholy harden the body;
hence one may judge wit by the quality of the flesh:

"And so in men who haue an equall temperature throughout
their whole bodie, it is an easie matter to gather the qualitie of
their wit by the tenderness or hardness of their flesh: For if it be
hard & rough, it giueth token either of a good vnderstanding or a
good imagination; and if smooth and supple, of the contrary, name-

[39] Huarte, *op. cit.*, pp. 239-240.
[40] La Primaudaye, *op. cit.*, p. 535.
[41] Huarte, *op. cit.*, p. 26.
[42] *Ibid.*, pp. 25-26. Cf. Batman, *op. cit.*, Bk. I, ch. 1.

ly of good memory, and small vnderstanding, and lesse imagination . . . .''[43]

The quality of the flesh is not always a trustworthy basis upon which to estimate the nature of wit, however, for the temperature of the brain may differ from that of the body. It is necessary, also, to consider the hair. Hair grows from fumosities or excrements of the brain.[44] The color and amount of it depend upon the color and amount of the fumosity. Auburn or yellow hair proceeds from blood; it indicates a gentle nature.[45] White or flaxen hair springs from a predominance of phlegm; red from gross humors and ill blood; black from choleric humors mixed with melancholy; and gray from corrupt phlegm and a defection of natural heat.[46] Hair which is ''big, blacke, rough, and thicke'' is a sign of a good imagination, or of a good understanding; hair which is soft and smooth is a sign of ''much memorie and nothing else.''[47] Excessive heat burns the scalp and closes the pores through which the hair must pass. It actually burns the excrements which engender hair. Baldness, therefore, indicates a degree of imagination; a degree which, when found in a warrior, presages success.[48] These and other physical characteristics the Elizabethan psychologist enumerates as a means of discovering temperament and wit; rather than consider all of them, let us turn for a moment to Shakespeare.

To Antony, Julius Caesar remarks:

> Let me have men about me that are fat,
> Sleek-headed men and such as sleep o' nights.
> Yond Cassius has a lean and hungry look,[49]
> He thinks too much, such men are dangerous. . . . .
> Would he were fatter! but I fear him not.
> Yet if my name were liable to fear,
> I do not know the man I should avoid

---

[43] *Ibid.*, pp. 80-81.

[44] Batman, *op. cit.*, Bk. V, ch. 65. Men and women living in hot and dry countries have hard, crisp hair, because the earthy and dry part of the fumosity, coming out of the skin, moves downward, and the hot and light part upward. Thus the hair is ''bowed and bent.''

[45] According to Huarte, auburn hair results from an equal proportion within the brain of choler (hot and dry) and phlegm (cold and moist); it suggests temperance. See his discussion of signs indicative of temperance, *op. cit.*, pp. 243-263.

[46] Batman, *op. cit.*, Bk. V, ch. 66.

[47] Huarte, *op. cit.*, p. 81.

[48] *Ibid.*, p. 213. There is another type of baldness, one in which the hair which remains is hard and earthy, that indicates a lack of understanding and imagination.

[49] Cf. *Antony and Cleopatra*, III, xi, 37: ''The lean and wrinkled Cassius.''

So soon as that spare Cassius. He reads much;
He is a great observer, and he looks
Quite through the deeds of men. He loves no plays
As thou dost, Antony; he hears no music,
Seldom he smiles, and smiles in such a sort
As if he mock'd himself and scorn'd his spirit
That could be mov'd to smile at anything.
Such men as he are never at heart's ease
Whiles they behold a greater than themselves,
And therefore are they very dangerous.[50]

According to Elizabethan science, the qualities which make the
body lean dispose one to think. The choleric, we have found, are
tall and lean, men who are easily provoked, given to treachery,
vehement in action, envious, proud and wrathful. Envy and pride
lead Cassius to form a conspiracy against Caesar.[51] In Act IV he
becomes angry with Brutus, and undergoes a real struggle to maintain a degree of patience:

Urge me no more, I shall forget myself;
Have mind upon your health, tempt me no farther.[52]

Brutus questions:

Must I give way and room to your rash choler?

Later he adds:

Fret till your proud heart break;
Go show your slaves how choleric you are.
And make your bondmen tremble.

is right in fearing the spare Cassius.

later play Cleopatra sends Alexas after a messenger whom
chided hence, to bid him give an account of the features
racteristics of Octavia—her age, her inclination, her height,
color of her hair.[53] The messenger, having returned to the
describes Octavia as a widow thirty years of age, low of
not so tall as Cleopatra, and without majesty of bearing.
er to find Octavia an unworthy rival, Cleopatra interprets the
rt of voice and stature as "dull of tongue" and "dwarfish."
questioning continues:

Cleo.   Bears't thou her face in mind? Is't long or round?
Mess.   Round even to faultiness.
Cleo.   For the most part, too, they are foolish that are so.
        Her hair, what colour?

---

[50] *Julius Caesar*, I, ii, 192 ff.
[51] Note, for example, Act I, sc. ii, ll. 94-131.
[52] Sc. iii, ll. 35-36. Cf. ll. 28-29 and 63-64.
[53] *Antony and Cleopatra*, II, v, 111 ff.

Mess. Brown, madam; and her forehead
As low as she would wish it.[54]

Upon the basis of what she has heard, Cleopatra decides that Octavia is "no such thing"—that she is one who is too ordinary actually to gain Antony's affection. Steevens quotes from Thomas Hill's *A Pleasant History: declaring the whole Art of Physiognomy* .... (1613), to show that a round face is indicative of foolishness. In contemporary literature a low forehead is several times considered among features that discredit beauty.[55] There can be no doubt that Cleopatra's conclusion depends in part upon her desire to believe Octavia a poor creature; nevertheless the principle upon which she proceeds is sound. The passage gives evidence of Shakespeare's familiarity with the notion that temperament reveals itself in physical features. An attempt to estimate the exactness of his knowledge in this respect, here and in several other instances,[56] would carry us into the literature of physiognomy.

The soul depends for its operation upon the body and spirit. These instruments have no impulsion in themselves; that can come only from the soul. Nothing is comparable in swiftness of motion, however, to spirit once set to work. In its several forms, it is capable of responding to all the varied operations of the soul, whereas the body, made up of many parts each adapted to a special duty, is of more restricted use. Having received impulsion, spirit directs and guides the soul "vnto more particular instruments, for more speciall and priuate vses, as to the Eye, to see with, to the Eare to heare, to the Nose to smell, to the Bowels, Stomacke, and Liuer to nourish, to the heart, to maintaine life: and to other parts, to the end of propagation . . . ."[57]

Spirit is the "verie hand" of the soul; the body and its members are to the soul as flails, saws, and axes are to the one who uses them. By means of spirit the soul exercises all its powers:

". . . . and it [spirit] being light, subtle, and yeelding, yet forceth it the heauiest and grossest, and hardest parts of our bodies, chewing with the teeth, and striking with the fist, & beating downe with the thrust of shoulder, the resistance of that which standeth

---

[54] Act III, sc. iii, ll. 32 ff.

[55] See Professor R. H. Case, Arden Edition of the play, Act III, sc. iii, l. 33, n.

[56] Note especially *Midsummer Night's Dream*, III, ii, 290 ff. and 325 ff.

[57] Bright, *op. cit.*, p. 54.

firme: and containing alone the force of all the members, seeth with the eye, heareth with the eares, vnderstandeth organically with the braine, distributeth life with the heart, and nourishment with the liuer, and whatsoeuer other bodily action is practised. This hand is applied to the grosse instrument, and the effect brought to passe, yet not absolutely of it selfe, but by impulsion of the mind . . . .''[58]

From Elizabethan reasoning as to elements, humors, and temper arise several considerations which explain further the nature of the soul and of its functioning. Generally the soul is said to be of equal excellency in all men. ''For all reasonable soules and their vnderstandings (sundered from the body) are of equall perfection and knowledge,'' says Huarte in discussing the question of a difference in men's wits.[59] The mind can judge only according to the impression it receives; hence the idiot possesses faculties capable of the same existence as are those of the prudent. The difference consists in the nature and present disposition of the instruments the soul has at its command: as a prince who depends for information upon spies,

> If they returne no newes doth nothing know;
> But if they make aduertisement of lies,
> The Prince's counsel all awry doe goe.

> Euen so the soule to such a body knit,
> Whose inward senses vndisposed be,
> And to receiue the formes of things vnfit;
> Where nothing is brought in, can nothing see.

> This makes the idiot, which hath yet a mind,
> Able to know the truth, and chuse the good,
> If she such figures in the braine did find,
> As might be found, if it in temper stood.[60]

Batman assures us that the soul is of such a nature that it ''may grow and waxe, neither more neyther lesse one time then at an other. And therefore in the greater bodye it is no greater, nor in the lesser bodie lesser . . . .''[61]

The theory of the body as composed of elements, humors and qualities accounts, then, for the differences in mental capacity among men and for differences in the clarity of one's own powers under changing circumstances. ''Now the Brain is properly the

---

[58] *Ibid.*, pp. 79-80.
[59] *Op. cit.*, p. 75.
[60] Sir John Davies, ''Nosce Teipsum,'' *loc. cit.*, pp. 144-145.
[61] *Op. cit.*, Bk. III, ch. 4.

Instrument of the Reasonable Soul," writes Charron, "and therefore upon the due Temperament of This, a great deal must needs,
indeed the Whole in a manner, will depend."[62] Huarte argues
that the temperature of the four first qualities may be called nature
and that from this issue "al the habilities of man, all his vertues
and vices, and this great varietie of wits which we behold."[63] In
the following passage La Primaudaye presents the same opinion
and a conventional argument of proof:

> "Some others . . . . haue rendred this reason of the quicknes or
> slownes of mans wit, saying, that it commeth of the good or im-
> moderate mixture & temperature of the elements, of which our
> bodies are compounded and framed, and of the symmetrie and
> proportion of the organicall or instrumentall parts ioyned togither
> in him. And surely these seeme to giue the true reason therof. For
> we see many, who in their beginning and first age shew that they
> haue a prompt and sharp wit, but when they come to old age are
> changed, & become slow and dul to conceiue. Which is a great
> token and argument that a good or bad complexion and constitu-
> tion of the body, is the cause of such a disposition, either in quick-
> ness or slowness of spirit, as the difference of yeeres doth affoord
> them."[64]

Some lines in *Troilus and Cressida* suggest that Shakespeare agreed
with these writers in making temperament the basis of variation
among men:

> Here's Nestor;
> Instructed by the antiquary times,
> He must, he is, he cannot but be wise:
> But pardon, father Nestor, were your days
> As green as Ajax' and your brain so temper'd,
> You should not have the eminence of him,
> But be as Ajax.[65]

The soul thus definitely instrumentalized remains unmarred by
physiological changes within the body. It is like an excellent work-
man who "continueth alwayes in the same estate, and hath no lesse
knowledge and arte in him without his instruments, then when he
hath them."[66] The operation of a faculty may be interfered with

---

[62] *Op. cit.*, Bk. I, p. 114.

[63] *Op. cit.*, pp. 20-21.

[64] *Op. cit.*, 1586, p. 90.

[65] Act II, sc. iii, ll. 261-267. Cf. the use of the word temper in the following (*2 Henry IV*, V, ii, 15-16):
> "O that the living Harry had the temper
> Of him, the worst of these three gentlemen!"

[66] La Primaudaye, *op. cit.*, p. 405.

by anything which disturbs its instruments, but the disturbance in no way alters the nature of the faculty, for the body may give to the soul only such discontentment as a false-stringed lute may give the musician or a rough and ill-fashioned pen the cunning writer.[67] Even under stress of emotion the soul continues unchanged:

". . . . in the mean time of these stormes and tempests of passion, these delusions, feares, false terrours, and poeticall fictions of the braine, [the soul] sitteth quiet and still, nothing altered in facultie, or any part of that diuine and impatible disposition, which it ob- taineth by the excellencie of creation: no more than the Sunne is moued in the heauens, or receaueth in it selfe an obscurity, when stormes arise . . . ."[68]

Accordingly, the soul does not grow old; rather it continues in its original state during one's entire life. If the proportion of qualities necessary to wisdom could be established in a moment, man would suddenly possess greater skill in discoursing than he can gain from long continued study. As love or anger heats and dries the brain, the prosaic may become poetic. Because of a sudden change of temperament the wise may become foolish and the foolish wise.[69] The weakness of the aged is due not to a decay of faculties but to "excrementitious humiditie and Rhumaticke Superfluities, which drowne the instrument, and an internall drynesse, whereby all wayes to that small remnant of Spirit is stopped."[70] Faculties seem either to develop or wither under varying circumstances only because their instruments change. When the body and its organs become "sore bruised, and distorted very grievously," life ends: "The Lodging is no longer fit to entertain her [the soul], and she must be gone."[71] Reason and understanding, inasmuch as they are capable of functioning apart from the body, continue existence.

---

[67] Bright, *op. cit.*, p. 46.

[68] *Ibid.*, p. 140. For a similar comparison see Nemesius, *op. cit.*, pp. 197 ff. and Sir John Davies, *loc. cit.*, pp. 99-100.

[69] Huarte, *op. cit.*, pp. 40 ff.

[70] Bright, *op. cit.*, p. 147. Cf. *Aristotle's Psychology* (ed. Hammond), p. 29.

[71] Charron, *op. cit.*, Bk. I, p. 113.

CHAPTER III

THE RELATION OF DIET, CLIMATE, AND THE STARS TO THE FUNCTIONING OF THE SOUL

The soul, we have found, is definitely instrumentalized except in its contemplation of spiritual truths. Significant to an understanding of the way in which this conception of the soul was made to account for human behavior, is a theory that every part of the universe is composed of elements.[1] The elements of all matter (celestial as well as earthly) possess qualities, and the qualities of one substance are capable of acting upon those of another. Man thus lives in close relationship with the world about him. Diet, climate, and the stars may alter his temperament and his spirits; they may therefore exercise an influence upon the operations of his soul.

Nourishment in general produces heat in the body, a quality which promotes good disposition. Upon the basis of this principle, obviously, Menenius argues that Cominius did not meet Coriolanus under favorable circumstances; he decides to make his plea for Rome at an opportune moment:

> He was not taken well; he had not din'd.
> The veins unfill'd, our blood is cold, and then
> We pout upon the morning, are unapt
> To give or to forgive; but when we have stuff'd
> These pipes and these conveyances of our blood
> With wine and feeding, we have suppler souls
> Than in our priest-like fasts: therefore I'll watch him
> Till he be dieted to my request,
> And then I'll set upon him.[2]

All food, Bright tells us, contains a "spiritous substance."[3] The ease and rapidity with which this substance alters our "spiritual matter" varies according to the kind of nourishment that is being assimilated. Furthermore, nourishment may alter the humors within the body; and as these change, the spirits, rising from them, must also change. Thus the nature of our spirits (and consequent-

---

[1] For a possible distinction between the elements of earthly and of heavenly substances, see below, p. 54, n. 35.

[2] *Coriolanus*, V, i, 50-58.

[3] *A Treatise of Melancholy*, pp. 43-44.

ly the kind of action of which we are capable) at any time depends to an extent upon the nature of our food.

Beef is good meat for the English because it makes them strong:

"Beefe is good meate for an Englysshe man, so be it the beest be yonge, & that it be not koweflesshe; For olde beefe and koweflesshe doth ingender melancholye and leporouse humoures. yf it be moderatly powderyd, that the groose blode by salte may be exhaustyd, it doth make an Englysshe man stro*n*ge, the educacion of hym with it co*n*syderyd."[4]

The Constable of France in *Henry V* tells us that when the English have "great meals of beef and iron and steel," they "eat like wolves and fight like devils"; but that when they are "shrewdly out of beef," they have "only stomachs to eat and none to fight."[5]

Food that is fine and delicate the vegetal faculty converts into blood which, in the brain, breeds spirits well adapted to the work of the rational "soul."[6] Wine, in a moment, repairs our spirits; bread and flesh work more slowly, for their spirits are not so subtle "or at least they are fettred as it were in a more grosse body."[7] Wine, used moderately, is of great efficacy; it is, according to many authorities—

"the most sweet licour of all others, the principall aide, and chiefe proppe of human life, the chiefe restorer of the vitall spirits, the most excellent strengthener of all the faculties and actions of the body, reioicing and comforting the heart very much . . . . For it engendereth very pure bloud, it is very quickly conuerted into nourishment, it helpeth to make digestion in all parts of the body, it giueth courage, purgeth the braine, refresheth the vnderstanding, reioiceth the heart, quickeneth the spirits . . . . augmenteth naturall heate . . . . purifieth the troubled blood, openeth stoppings, maketh good colour . . . ."[8]

Reference to the physiological effects and to the consequent revivifying power of wine is frequent in Shakespeare. "Prove that

---

[4] Andrew Boorde, *A Compendyous Regyment or a Dyetary of Helth*, E.E.T.S. (Ex. Ser.), No. 10, p. 271.

[5] Act III, sc. vii, ll. 160-166. Cf. *1 Henry VI*, I, ii, 9-12.

[6] John Davies of Hereford, "Mirum in Modum," *loc. cit.*, p. 6. Good odors, also, stimulate rational activity, for they purify the brain, awaken fantasy, and refine the wits. Incense makes the spirits apt for divine thoughts.—Sir John Davies, "Nosce Teipsum," *loc. cit.*, p. 109.

[7] Bright, *op. cit.*, pp. 43-44.

[8] La Primaudaye, *The French Academie*, p. 810. Cf. Bright, *op. cit.*, p. 43; John Davies of Hereford, "Microcosmos," *loc. cit.*, p. 33; Boorde, *loc. cit.*, p. 254.

ever I lose more blood with love than I will get again with drinking,"[9] says Benedick, insisting upon his callousness to love. Because wine heats the blood and comforts the heart, captains frequently carouse before combat: on the eve of battle, when he feels
his alacrity of spirit and cheer of mind waning, Richard III calls
for a bowl of wine.[10] A passage in *Henry V* suggests the relative
efficacy of ale and wine to heat the blood for fighting. The Constable of France is amazed because the English, whose cold blood
has been tempered only by "sodden water," "their barley broth
[ale],"[11] make the quick blood of the French, "spirited with wine,"
seem "frosty."[12] Falstaff, in *2 Henry IV*, indirectly points a contrast between the sober-blooded John of Lancaster, who drinks no
wine, and Prince Harry, who has tempered his naturally cold blood
by drinking a goodly store of sherris.[13] In the same passage he
gives an elaborate and exact analysis of the power of wine:

"A good sherris-sack hath a two-fold operation in it. It ascends
me into the brain; dries me there all the foolish and dull and crudy
vapours which environ it; makes it apprehensive, quick, forgetive,
full of nimble, fiery, and delectable shapes; which, deliver'd o'er
to the voice, the tongue, which is the birth, becomes excellent wit.

---

[9] *Much Ado*, I, i, 252-254. Professor M. P. Tilley ("Good Drink Makes
Good Blood," *Mod. Lang. Notes*, XXXIX, 1924, pp. 153-155) shows that the
belief that wine begets blood (and water phlegm) had become proverbial. He
directs attention to the idea several times expressed in Shakespeare that every
sigh costs the heart a drop of blood. (See *2 Henry VI*, III, ii, 60-62; *3 Henry
VI*, IV, iv, 21-22; *Midsummer Night's Dream*, III, ii, 97.) This last notion
I have not found in psychological treatises. Professor H. C. Hart (*3 Henry
VI*, Arden Edition, IV, iv, 22, n.) states that the idea is extant in folklore,
particularly in certain parts of Scotland. It may be a poetical and popular
development from the general belief that extreme passion consumes blood.
The purpose of sighing is, normally, to ease the heart by cooling and refresh-
ing it: "Sighing hath no other cause of mouing then to coole and refresh
the heart, with fresh breath, and pure ayre . . . . besides the cooling which the
heart it selfe receiueth thereby."—Bright, *op. cit.*, p. 193. Cf. La Primaudaye, *op. cit.*, p. 468: "For howsoeuer griefe shutteth vp the heart . . . . yet
by groning, sighing, and weeping, the heart doth in some sort open it selfe,
as if it would come foorth to breathe, least being wholly shut vp with sorrow
it should be stifled." To this use Shakespeare refers twice, in passages which
suggest further the pain we habitually associate with sighing: *Hamlet* IV, vii,
123-124; *Merchant of Venice*, I, ii, 81-82.

[10] *Richard III*, V, iii, 72-74.

[11] *N.E.D.* defines barley broth as strong ale. Note the following: "Ale
for an Englysshe man is a naturall drynke. . . . . Barly malte maketh better
ale then oten malte or any other corne doth: it doth ingendre grose humoures;
but yette it maketh a man stronge."—Boorde, *loc. cit.*, p. 256.

[12] Act III, sc. v, ll. 18-22.

[13] Act IV, sc. iii, ll. 94-96 and 127-133. Professor Tilley (*loc. cit.*, p. 155)
cites this passage.

The second property of your excellent sherris is, the warming of the blood; which, before cold and settled, left the liver white and pale, which is the badge of pusillanimity and cowardice; but the sherris warms it and makes it course from the inwards to the parts extremes. It illumineth the face, which as a beacon gives warning to all the rest of this little kingdom, man, to arm; and then the vital commoners and inland petty spirits muster me all to their captain, the heart, who, great and puff'd up with this retinue, doth any deed of courage; and this valor comes of sherris.'"[14]

Fumes, rising from the stomach or from the humors, may ascend to the brain and dull the operations of the soul. They may enter the sinews and retard the progress of the spirits. It is by means of such fumes, coming in this case from excessive drinking, that Mark Antony wishes to steep sense in "soft and delicate Lethe,"[15] and Lady Macbeth to benumb the powers of Duncan's guardsmen:

> His two chamberlains
> Will I with wine and wassail so convince
> That memory, the warder of the brain,
> Shall be a fume, and the receipt of reason
> A limbeck only.[16]

In this connection one should note, also, some further effects of fumes or vapors upon the functioning of the soul. Such diseases as apoplexy and palsy are caused by the dulling and binding of the spirits in the brain and in the sinews. Thus Don John, although he wilfully mis-states the reason for Hero's swooning, makes use of sound physiology when he says:

> These things, come thus to light,
> Smother her spirits up.[17]

Elizabethan treatises define sleep as a rest of the outward senses and of the common sense. It is a state induced whenever vapors so completely fill the sinews that the spirits cannot pass to the external senses. The imagination, cut off from reports of subordinate powers, is left free to create dreams. Waking comes with the liberation of the spirits: waking is "nought els but free shedding of spirits into the lyms of feeling and of mouing, & doing the worke of the animate vertue in the body.'"[18]

---

[14] Act IV, sc. iii, ll. 103 ff.
[15] *Antony and Cleopatra*, II, vii, 113-114.
[16] *Macbeth*, I, vii, 63-67.
[17] *Much Ado*, IV, i, 112-113.
[18] *Batman vppon Bartholome*, Bk. VI, chs. 25-26.

Several passages in Shakespeare are related to this explanation of sleep. The Player King in *Hamlet* says:

> My spirits grow dull, and fain I would beguile
> The tedious day with sleep.[19]

According to Elizabethan theory, the smoke or vapor that produces sleep, as it fills the sinews, thickens and dulls the spirits. To Ferdinand, who has just fallen in love with Miranda, Prospero says:

> Thy nerves are in their infancy again
> And have no vigour in them.[20]

He probably means that Ferdinand's spirits do not flow freely in his nerves to give the body erection and strength necessary for movement.[21] Ferdinand replies:

> My spirits, as in a dream, are all bound up.

As sleep binds the spirits so that they cannot deliver to the imagination reports from the outer world and thus forestall the framing of strange dreams, Ferdinand's love for Miranda engages his spirits to such an extent that they cannot perform the normal operations of the soul. Ferdinand is forgetful of all else save his love. For a moment, he cannot follow Prospero. In the same play, Antonio and Sebastian declare that they are not disposed to sleep.[22] Antonio's spirits are "nimble"—they can proceed readily to the external organs of sense. Batman assures us that when the spirit "moueth alway outwarde" there can be no rest.[23]

A second influence upon the soul is one which comes from climatic conditions and from the nature of the region in which man lives. This influence is so important that Charron ascribes to it the "First, most remarkable, and universal Distinction between Some Men and Others"—a distinction which involves both the mind and the body. From their countries, he says, men receive "different Complexions, and Statures, and Countenances; nay, different Manners and Dispositions; and different Faculties of the Soul too." Men owe their

---

[19] Act III, sc. ii, ll. 236-237.

[20] *Tempest*, I, ii, 484-485.

[21] In considering this passage, Dowden ("Elizabethan Psychology," *loc. cit.*, p. 319) makes "nerves" synonymous with what we call tendons. Spirits provide erection of body and vigor. During infancy, they are kept sluggish by the predominance of moisture over other qualities. "Nerves" here may therefore mean the vessels which carry animal spirits.

[22] Act II, sc. i, ll. 201-202.

[23] *Op. cit.*, Bk. VI, ch. 26.

temper to their country; consequently, according to the locality in which they are born, they bring into the world with them ''Dispositions Greater or Less, to War, Courage, Justice, Temperance, Docility, Religion, Chastity, Wit, Goodness, Obedience, Beauty, Health, and Strength.''[24]

Upon the basis of this doctrine, psychologists sometimes divide the world into three regions, each the home of a different type of people. Charron, who treats the subject at length, tabulates for each type characteristics of body, mind, religion, and manners. Men of the North are tall and big, phlegmatic or sanguine, white or light tawny. Their voices are strong; their skin is soft and hairy. These men are great eaters and drinkers, strong and robust. Of mind they are heavy, dull, stupid, foolish, credulous, easy to be imposed upon, inconstant in their humors and opinions. They are not much addicted to religion. In manner they are warlike, hardy, laborious, chaste, not likely to be jealous, but cruel, and inhuman. Men of the South are small and short of stature, cold and dry of constitution,[25] black and tawny. They love solitude. Their voices are small and weak; their skin is hard; their hair frizzled and shaggy. In the South men are weak and abstemious. Of mind they are ingenious, apt, wise, prudent, subtle, positive in opinion, and obstinate. They are studious and contemplative, but given to superstition. In manner they are averse to war, cowardly, lascivious, jealous, cruel, and inhuman. Men of the middle region are likely to incline in characteristics toward those resulting from the region nearest them.[26] Inhabitants of the North excel in memory, those of the South in understanding, and those of the middle region in imagination.[27]

Since climatic conditions modify temperament, much depends upon the air man breathes daily. Subtle air moves the simple

---

[24] *Of Wisdom*, Bk. I, pp. 383-384.

[25] As a cave or well is warmest during winter, men who live in the North contain much natural heat. In the South the warmth of the sun draws heat outward; men are cold of constitution.—Charron, *op. cit.*, Bk. I, p. 391. John Davies of Hereford (''Microcosmos,'' *loc. cit.*, p. 31) states that men of the South are hot and men of the North cold; he lists, however, characteristics essentially the same as those given above.

[26] *Op. cit.*, Bk. I, p. 386.

[27] *Ibid.*, pp. 115-116. Variation from the general rule results from intermarriages, the nature of the winds and water, differences in altitude within the same region, etc.—*Ibid.*, p. 387.

David Person (*Varieties*, p. 90) states that men of the South possess imagination, those of the middle district reason, and those of the North understanding. He agrees with John Davies of Hereford in considering the Southerner hot and dry and the Northerner cold and moist.

mind; air infected by lakes, vales, moors, carrion, or filth dulls the
understanding. The winds, finding a way to the brain and the
heart, modify the spirits. A change of climate may indeed alter
one's mode of behavior:

> The *Aire* we breath doth beare an Ore herein,
> And being subtil moves the simple *Minde;*
> For, never yet was *foole* a *Florentine,*
> (As by the wise hath well observed byn)
> So subtill is the *Aire* hee draweth in:
> The *influences* of malignant *Starres,*
> *Vales, Caves, Stanckes, Moores,* and *Lakes* that never ryn,
> *Carion,* and *filth,* all such the *Aier* marres,
> Which killes the *Corpes,* and *Witt's* Carreer barres. . . . .

> The *winds,* though *Aire,* yet *Aire* do turne & wind;
> Which passions of the *Aire,* our *sp'rits* affect;
> These by the *Nose* and *Mouth* a waie doe find
> To *Braines,* and *Hart,* and there their *kindes* effect,
> And as they are, make them, in some respect:
> For, where the *Windes* be cold and violent,
> (As where rough *Boreas* doth his *Throne* erect)
> There are the *People* stronge, and turbulent,
> Rending the *Sterne* of *civill government.*[28]

Elizabethan theory as to the way in which climate affects the
operations of the soul was familiar to Shakespeare, for it underlies
several passages in his plays. Astonished at the valor of the English, the Constable of France in *Henry V* says:

> *Dieu de batailles!* where have they this mettle?
> Is not their climate foggy, raw, and dull,
> On whom, as in despite, the sun looks pale,
> Killing their fruit with frowns?[29]

In the same play Henry V attributes his boastfulness to the effect
of the air of France upon him:

> Yet, forgive me, God,
> That I do brag thus! This your air of France
> Hath blown that vice in me.[30]

Confessing his guilt, Iachimo says to Cymbeline:

> Well may you, sir,
> Remember me at court, where I was taught
> Of your chaste daughter the wide difference
> 'Twixt amorous and villanous. Being thus quench'd
> Of hope, not longing, mine Italian brain
> Gan in your duller Britain operate
> Most vilely.[31]

---

28 John Davies of Hereford, "Microcosmos," *loc. cit.,* p. 32.
29 Act III, sc. v, ll. 15-18.
30 Act III, sc. vi, ll. 159-161. Cf. *Cymbeline,* V, ii, 2-4.
31 *Cymbeline,* V, v, 192-198.

Here Shakespeare's conception of character turns upon his knowledge of the extent to which climate may affect the soul. At the British court Iachimo learns of Imogen the nobility of true love; he realizes that he cannot accomplish his purpose by fair means. His Italian brain, under the influence of foreign air, operates vilely, however, and he devises a plan whereby he procures a report sufficiently startling to convince the trustful Posthumus. When Iachimo left Italy, he intended either to seduce Imogen or to lose his wager. At heart he is not a villain.[32]

In thinking thus of Iachimo we are merely accepting with the dramatist a theory well known among his contemporaries. The Elizabethan still adhered to the Galenic doctrine that the nature of thought and action depends upon the temperature of the body. He believed that temperature is exceedingly changeful and that this variability accounts for differences in human behavior:

". . . . by reason of the heat, the coldnesse, the moisture, and the drouth, of the territorie where men inhabit, of the meats which they feed on, of the waters which they drinke, and of the aire which they breath: some are blockish, and some wise: some of woorth, and some base: some cruel, and some merciful: many straight brested, and many large: part liers, and part true speakers: sundrie traitors, and sundrie faithfull: somewhere vnquiet, and somewhere staied: there double, here single: one pinching, another liberall: this man shamefast, that shameless: such hard, and such light of beleefe."[33]

Even a wise and virtuous man may suddenly change his manners, "and the reason is, because he hath gotten a new temperature, moist and full of vapours, whence it follows that the figures are cancelled which tofore he had in his brain, and his vnderstanding dulled."[34]

There is another influence upon the life of man, very potent in

---

[32] The eagerness with which Iachimo makes confession (Act V, sc. v, ll. 141 ff.) and his references to the pricking of conscience (Act V, sc. ii, l. 1; Act V, sc. v, ll. 141-142; etc.) suggest that villainy is not ingrained in his nature. Note also the lines (Act V, sc. v, ll. 147-149):

"That paragon, thy daughter,—
For whom my heart drops blood, and my false spirits
Quail to remember,—"

By "false spirits" the dramatist may mean spirits which, because they have undergone alteration, differ in temper and in substance from the spirits of an individual under ordinary circumstances; in other words, spirits which lead the faculties of the soul to function in ways contrary to their normal mode of operation.

[33] Huarte, *Examen de Ingenios*, pp. 21-22.

[34] *Ibid.*, p. 60.

determining individual differences at birth and in shaping the
courses of our lives—the influence of the stars. Hence the study
of mind did not for the Elizabethan exclude a study of astrology.
The stars, although probably not composed of elements exactly such
as one finds in earthly substances,[35] possess elemental qualities
through which they produce an effect upon the elements of the
body and thus, by altering temper, serve to urge man either to
virtue or to vice. These qualities, particularly those of the planets
and of the signs of the zodiac, the astrologer had carefully worked
out; sometimes one finds them catalogued in discussions of mind
and ethics. Saturn, for example, is cold, dry, and pale. The child
born under it is full of evil qualities, slow and seldom glad; melancholy, the cold and dry humor, predominates in his complexion.
Mars is hot and dry. It disposes the soul to unsteadfast wit, to
wrath, boldness, and other choleric passions. As the moon wanes,
the brain, the humors, and the marrow of the bones decrease in
quantity; as it waxes, they increase. The moon makes a man un-
stable; it makes him disordered in the eyes.[36] In a similar way
each sign of the zodiac exercises an influence upon a particular
portion of the body—Taurus upon the neck and throat rather than
upon either the sides and the heart or the thighs and the legs, as
Sir Andrew Aguecheek and Sir Toby Belch, in *Twelfth Night*,[37]
think.

Among the elaborate correspondences of the microcosm to the
macrocosm there was found, of course, a place for the stars. Each
age of man was said to be under the governance of a particular
planet, at which time the qualities of the body were thought to
conform to the qualities of the planet. John Davies of Hereford
presents the theory concisely:

> And as these *humors* haue their turnes in time,
> So rule the *Planets* in like consequence:
> For, by the *Moone* is governed our *Prime*

---

[35] David Person (*op. cit.*, p. 7) states that the heavens and the stars are
composed of a substance to which a circular motion appertains and that the
elements of material bodies have motion only to fall and to rise. According
to ancient and medieval philosophy, heavenly bodies are composed of a quintessence, or "fifth essence," more subtle than any of the material elements.
A passage from a translation of Le Clerc's *Prim. Fathers* (1702) (quoted in
N.E.D. under "quintessence," 1) implies that the soul was sometimes thought
to be made of this quintessence. The soul would then be subject in a special
way to influences from the stars.

[36] See Batman, *op. cit.*, Bk. VIII, ch. 23 ff.; La Primaudaye, *op. cit.*, p. 703.

[37] Act I, sc. iii, ll. 146-151. Batman (*op. cit.*, Bk. VIII, ch. 10 ff.) considers the relation of the various signs to the body.

That's *hot* and *moist*, but the preheminence
The *moisture* hath; So our *Adolescence*
Is swaid by *Wit*-infusing *Mercury*
Being *hot* and *moist*, yet doth more *heate* dispense,
Which tunes the *voice's Organes* erst too hy,
Making them speake with more profundity.

Then, *youth* (our third age) *Loue's Queene, Venus* swa'es
Bee'ng *hot* and *dry*, but yet more hot, then drie;
In this we *Wantons* play, in *Venus'* plaies
And offer *Incense* to a rowling *eie:*
Bright *Sol* (the gloriou'st *Planet* in the *sky*)
Doth rule our *Manhoode* which is temperate:
Hee *Author* is of *grace* and *gravity*;
Of hapless life this is the happi'st state,
Which they hold long'st that are most moderate.

And lastly *old age* being *cold*, and *dry*,
By al-wise *Iupiter* is governed,
Author of *Councell, Craft,* and *Policy:*
Which *Age* againe in two's distinguished,
The first *yonge old age* may be Christened;
The last *Decrepit* is, and so is call'd;
Which *Saturn* rules with *Scepter* of dul *lead:*
This *Age* to *Life* like *Death,* is stil enthrall'd,
Thus in our life the *Planetts* are enstall'd.[38]

Numerous passages in Shakespeare's plays indicate some specific developments from this theorizing. In addition to the general belief that stars exert an influence upon an individual at the time of his birth,[39] there is, in several cases, the idea that nobler stars govern nobler people.[40] Prospero finds that his zenith depends upon a most auspicious star and that, if he does not court its influence, his fortunes will ever after droop.[41]

Yet cease your ire, you angry stars of heaven![42]

says Pericles, having been cast from the sea upon the shore of Pentapolis. Hermione, in *The Winter's Tale,* after Leontes has commanded her imprisonment, says:

There's some ill planet reigns;
I must be patient till the heavens look
With an aspect more favourable.[43]

One may invoke the stars, or even bide one's time with them.

---

[38] "Microcosmos," *loc. cit.,* pp. 31-32. According to those who divide life into seven ages, Mars governs a period preceding "old age."

[39] *Richard III,* IV, iv, 215; *Much Ado,* II, i, 349; *All's Well,* I, i, 205-206; *Cymbeline,* V, iv, 105; *King Lear,* IV, iii, 34-37; etc.

[40] *All's Well,* I, i, 197; *Twelfth Night,* II, v, 156; *Hamlet,* II, ii, 141. Cf. *Two Gentlemen of Verona,* II, vii, 74.

[41] *Tempest,* I, ii, 180-184.

[42] *Pericles,* II, i, 1.

[43] Act II, sc. i, ll. 105-107. Cf. *Pericles,* I, iv, 108.

The stars may prove favorable to man or they may hinder him in what he undertakes to do. Hence the Elizabethan thanked his stars with good grace for a happy turn in his affairs and blamed them for misfortune. To a messenger from Caesar, Mark Antony says:

> He makes me angry;
> And at this time most easy 'tis to do 't,
> When my good stars, that were my former guides,
> Have empty left their orbs, and shot their fires
> Into the abysm of hell.[44]

Antony of course has been defeated; his words may therefore represent merely the attempt of a baffled soul to understand and account for a reversal of fortune by blaming conditions over which man has no control. The person who blames the stars is not always a tragic hero, however. After the battle of Alexandria, Caesar laments that his star and Antony's have been unreconciliable.[45] Bedford, in *1 Henry VI*, refers to the bad revolting stars that have consented to the death of Henry V;[46] he invokes the ghost of the dead king to combat with adverse planets.[47] "My stars shine darkly over me," says Sebastian in *Twelfth Night*.[48] Having consoled himself by assuming that many wives are as faithless as he thinks Hermione to be, Leontes argues:

> Physic for 't there is none.
> It is a bawdy planet, that will strike
> Where 'tis predominant; and 'tis powerful, think it,
> From east, west, north, and south.[49]

To an extent these men are right. Celestial bodies may provoke innumerable evils upon an individual—if that individual is not well fortified against them. The fortunes of a lover may indeed be "star-crossed," if that lover is unable, except in death, to "shake off the yoke of inauspicious stars."

One finds also, in Shakespeare and in Elizabethan treatises, the notion that the heavens may foretell future events and that they may be in some way associated with disaster coming upon a group

---

[44] *Antony and Cleopatra,* III, xiii, 143-147.

[45] *Ibid.,* V, i, 46-48.

[46] Act I, sc. i, ll. 4-5.

[47] Act I, sc. i, ll. 52-54.

[48] Act II, sc. i, l. 4.

[49] *Winter's Tale,* I, ii, 200-203. Cf. *1 Henry VI,* IV, v, 6; *2 Henry VI,* III, i, 206; *3 Henry VI,* IV, vi, 22; *Romeo and Juliet,* First Prologue, 6, and V, iii, 111; etc.

of people. Comets, according to Shakespeare, import changes of times and states;[50] eclipses in the sun and moon portend no good to us;[51] meteors in the air and a moon that looks bloody upon the earth are signs that forerun the death or fall of kings.[52]

> When beggars die there are no comets seen;
> The heavens themselves blaze forth the death of princes.[53]

Disturbances among the planets mean commotion upon earth:

> But when the planets
> In evil mixture to disorder wander,
> What plagues and what portents! what mutiny!
> What raging of the sea! shaking of earth!
> Commotion in the winds! Frights, changes, horrors,
> Divert and crack, rend and deracinate
> The unity and married calm of states
> Quite from their fixure![54]

Of the certainty with which comets presage evil, David Person says,

"Always leaving Philosophicall alterations, thus much by naturall experience we may resolve upon; that they never appeare but some bad event followeth thereon, either to the country over which it blazeth, or to which it aspecteth; or else to that countrey over which ruleth a starre which that comets tayle tendeth towardes or followeth; though much rather to that countrey which it hath aspect unto: not by vertue of its influence, but by reason of the superabundancie of maligne, dry, and hot exhalations regorging and dispersing themselves over it."[55]

The Elizabethan explained the disastrous effects following an alteration in the heavens upon the basis of the quality of the air at such times as the phenomenon appears. Meteors, according to Person, are made of dry and moist vapors and exhalations extracted from the earth and water and elevated to a region of the air where they are fashioned diversely, according to the degree of the region or according to the matter of which they are formed.[56] Comets are made of a similar matter.[57] From the presence in the

[50] *1 Henry VI*, I, i, 2.

[51] *King Lear*, I, ii, 112-113. Cf. *Othello*, *V*, ii, 99-101.

[52] *Richard II*, II, iv, 9-10; *Hamlet*, I, i, 117-118.

[53] *Julius Caesar*, II, ii, 30-31.

[54] *Troilus and Cressida*, I, iii, 94-101. Cf. *Love's Labour's Lost*, V, ii, 394; *Hamlet*, I, i, 162; *Timon of Athens*, IV, iii, 108-110.

[55] *Op. cit.*, p. 69.

[56] *Op. cit.*, pp. 49-50.

[57] *Ibid.*, p. 61.

air of these exhalations spring numerous evils among men. Astronomical philosophers say:

". . . . the exhalations of hot and dry vapours from the Earth, whereof these Comets are made, betoken a bilious and wrathful, sudden and irefull disposition of the in-dwellers of these Countries; for the same ayre which they attract, and emit, doth someway affect them, and this ayre is filled with these exhalations, resolved by the heat of the incumbing Sun; so no question but this same way it moueth their bodies and minds to feare fiery and sudden revolts, fightings, seditions, and uproares."[58]

In answer to the question why common people, as well as kings, may not die under the influence of comets, Person replies only that the supereminency of great persons causes their death to be noted more widely.[59] La Primaudaye, however, finds a reason for the death of kings. His explanation of comets and of the evils accompanying them differs in some detail from that of Person:

"[A comet is] a globe placed in heauen, which being enlightened by the Sunne doth plainely appeare: and when his rayes passe farther, they shew like the fashion of a beard, or of a tayle. Whereupon it appeareth that this flaming globe may be made in the midst of the spheres, if the generation thereof be in them: or else we must say (and that seemeth true) that the heauen is full of many starres, not very massie, which (the aire being dry and attenuated) doe present themselues to our sight. . . . . Then through the drines of the aire it commonly happeneth, that the seas are much turmoiled with tempests, and that great blustring windes doe follow thereupon, and that Monarches and great Princes, who are most dry through cold and watchings, or else through abundance of hot and delicate meates and of strong wine, doe thereupon die: So likewise the dry and attenuated aire causeth the waters to diminish, fishes to die, and scarcity of victuals, which oftentimes stirreth vp seditions, and the change of lawes, and finally the subuersion of states. All which things . . . . doe seeme in some sort to proceed through the great tenuity and drines of the aire: and thereof the comet then appearing may be a signe and token, but not the cause."[60]

La Primaudaye then argues that no matter what may be the cause of astral phenomena we should regard them as forerunners of the justice of God.

Although he did not doubt that the stars exercise an influence

---

58 *Ibid.*, p. 67.
59 *Ibid.*, p. 68.
60 *Op. cit.*, p. 746.

upon men and even foretell disastrous events, the Elizabethan was uncertain as to how far this influence actually extends. Usually the philosopher and moralist stopped short of the extreme position held by the astrologer. David Person admits that the nature and seat of the planets argue of necessity the nature of the people who seem to live under them.[61] He does not believe, however, that the planets have any enforcing power over the body at birth: "They may well . . . . incline and helpe our propensnes, force them they cannot . . . ." The heavens work only through the mediation of the air; hence, since the air is always in motion and varies constantly in quality, they cannot always produce "such and such like infallible dispositions proper to any one alone more then to others, in, and of that same time and place: the contrary whereof we see."[62] In the following passage La Primaudaye, also, states that the stars have power merely to incline the soul in one way or another. He suggests further that few men are able to resist this power:

"The stars influence men onely that in disposing their bodies, beeing compounded of the elements, vpon which the planets worke, they serue to aide them to abound in vertues or vices, according as their minde being moderatrix of all their actions, doth dispose her faculties, to intend good or euill. For this cause we say, that to those which want the gifts and graces of Gods spirit, all things cannot but succeed badly, and the influences of the spheres hurt them rather then otherwise, yea some more then other some: as to the contrarie, the minde of the faithfull and well instructed doth correct the nautines of the stars, and deliuereth himselfe from all peruerse inclination."[63]

Shakespeare seems to have held essentially the same position, for Helena, in *All's Well,* understands the limits of astral influence:

> Our remedies oft in ourselves do lie,
> Which we ascribe to heaven. The fated sky
> Gives us free scope, only doth backward pull
> Our slow designs when we ourselves are dull.[64]

---

[61] *Op. cit.,* pp. 85-86.

[62] *Ibid.,* p. 186.

[63] *Op. cit.,* p. 703.

[64] Act I, sc. i, ll. 231-234. Cassius' reference to the stars ("The fault . . . . is not in our stars . . . .,"—*Julius Caesar,* I, ii, 140 ff.) is, of course, colored by his philosophy. The Elizabethan moralist would agree, however, that will is ultimately responsible for the affairs of men. Edmund's "We make guilty of our disasters the sun, the moon, and stars . . . ."(*King Lear,* I, ii, 130 ff.) may be just censure of a tendency to blame the stars, but his denial of all planetary influence (ll. 143-145) is, in effect, a denial of religion. (See Professor Hardin Craig, "The Ethics of *King Lear,*" *Phil. Quar.,* IV, 1925, p.

The stars are not all-powerful but they incline man to follow one way or another, and when he is dull, they may work their malignancy. One may show wisdom,

> By spying and avoiding Fortune's malice,
> For few men rightly temper with the stars.[65]

Only the faithful and well instructed are able to correct the naughtiness of the stars and to deliver themselves from all perverse inclination.

Back of all this reasoning about the relation to life of diet, climate, and the stars, is the Elizabethan theory that all matter possesses elemental qualities. Food is compounded of elements; hence, when it is converted into humors, it may modify the proportion of qualities within the body. The air varies constantly; through its qualities it may alter temperament. The multitudinous stars also exercise upon man an influence that only the bravest can thwart. Temper is indeed variable. And temper, to a very large extent, determines the nature of the activity of the soul!

104.) Hotspur's argument against the power of the stars and of other natural phenomena to foretell events (*1 Henry IV*, III, i, 13 ff.) probably springs from his impulsiveness and from his antipathy to Glendower.

[65] *3 Henry VI*, IV, vi, 28-29.

CHAPTER IV

THE MICROCOSM

In considering the question as to why the soul is united to the body, Sir John Davies writes:

> This substance, and this spirit of God's owne making,
> Is in the body plact, and planted heere,
> That both of God, and of the world partaking,
> Of all that is, Man might the image beare.

> God first made angels bodilesse, pure minds,
> Then other things, which mindlesse bodies be;
> Last, He made Man, th' horizon 'twixt both kinds,
> In whom we doe the World's abridgement see.[1]

The Elizabethan, whose mental habits were averse to abstractions, found in the doctrine underlying these stanzas a concrete embodiment of psychological thought. He considered man an epitome of the entire universe, a little world unto himself. Inasmuch as man has a body composed of the four elements, he partakes of the nature of inanimate substances. Like plants he has a vegetal power, and like beasts such powers as those of voluntary motion, appetite, and sensation. His intellectual faculties—reason, understanding, and a will inclined to the pursuit of good—enable him to communicate with incorporeal natures.[2] To state the resemblance differently, the lowest part of the body corresponds to earth, the thorax or middle portion to air, and the head to heaven.[3] The series of relationships between man and the universe is extremely elaborate, for in him all natures are bound up together:

"Man thus Compounded, became a Model of the Universe, having a *Rational* Soul, with ability fit for the Government of the World; an *Intellectual* Soul common with Angels and *Sensitive* with Beasts; thus he became a little World in the Great, in whom all Natures were bound up together; our *Flesh* is heavy like *Earth*, our *Bones* hard as *Stones*, our *Veins* as the *Rivers*, *Breath* as the *Air*, Natural *Heat*, like the *warmth* inclosed in the *Earth*, which the Sun stirreth up in procreation; *Radical moisture*, which feeds that Natural *Heat*, is as the fatness in the Earth; our *Hairs* as *Grass*, our *Generative*

---

[1] "Nosce Teipsum," *loc. cit.*, pp. 97-98.
[2] Nemesius, *The Nature of Man*, pp. 6-8.
[3] Charron, *Of Wisdom*, Bk. I, p. 27.

Power is as *Nature* which produceth; our *Determinations* like wandering *Clouds,* our *Eyes* like the *Lights* in Heaven; our *Youth* like the *Spring,* our *setled Age* like the *Summer,* declining like *Autumn,* and *old Age* like *Winter;* our *Thoughts* are the *motions of Angels,* our pure *Understanding* like the *Intellectual* Natures always present with God; and the habitual Holiness and Righteousness of our Immortal Soul was the *Image* of God, as a shadow may be like the substance. Man's Four *Complexions* like the Four Elements, and his Seven *Ages* like the Seven *Planets.* Our *Infancy* is like the *Moon,* in which it seemeth only to grow, as Planets; in our next age we are instructed as under *Mercury,* always near the Sun: Our *Youth* is wanton, and given to pleasures, as *Venus;* our Fourth Age Strong, Vigorous, and Flourishing, is like the *Sun:* Our Fifth Age like *Mars,* striving for Honour; our Sixth like *Jupiter,* Wise and stayed; our Seventh like *Saturn,* slow and heavy when by irrecoverable loss we see that of all vain Passions and Affections the Sorrow only remains, and our Attendants are various Infirmities and Diseases . . . ."[4]

Man thus completes creation. In the words of Charron, he is *a sort of God in Miniature.* Man is "the Universe in one small Volume," and as such, "the Prodigy, and miraculous Production of Nature":

"Man is likewise not only the Creator, but the whole Creation in Little; the Universe in one small Volume: Whence it is that Man is sometimes styled a *Little World;* and by the same reason the World might be called a *Great Man.* He is, as it were, the Mediator of the different parts of Nature, that Link of this long Chain, by which Angels and Brutes, Heaven and Earth, the Spiritual and Corporeal Creation, are ty'd together; and that void Space supply'd, which wou'd make a wide and most unseemly Gap in the Universe, if not fill'd up, and the Series thus continu'd, by a Creature partaking of both Extremes. In a word, This was the last Touch, the Master-piece, the Honour, and Ornament, nay, the Prodigy, and miraculous Production of Nature."[5]

There is analogy, also, between man and a commonwealth. Flesh corresponds to the vile and stupid common people, and the irrational "soul" to persons of quality. The understanding is king of the little world. A subordinate magistrate, the imagination, examines reports from the outer senses and commands the affections to execute judgments that are made. For direction in fulfilling his

<hr>

[4] *An Abridgment of Sir Walter Raleigh's History of the World,* 5 bks., London, 1698, pp. 12-13. Cited by Professor John D. Rea, "Jacques on the Microcosm," *Phil. Quar.,* IV (1925), 347.

[5] *Op. cit.,* Bk. I, p. 16. The doctrine of the microcosm is frequently made a basis for praising the excellency of man. See Burton, *Anatomy of Melancholy,* Vol. I, p. 149. Cf. *Hamlet,* II, ii, 316-321.

office, he has the light of nature and the dictates of reason. Matters of great import he refers to the king. Or the functioning of the soul is like the governance of a military state. The outer wits are sentinels, who guard the safety of the state; they are also scouts, who reconnoiter and bring to the inner senses reports which may be passed to the understanding, "the Supreme *Commander* of the Soul." The peace and prosperity of a civil or military state depend upon the proper subordination and co-operation of various powers; the state of well-being in man depends upon the orderly subordination and co-operation of his faculties. As in the one there may be dissension or revolution, in the other there may be great perturbation.[6]

To the literary artist of the Renaissance, the doctrine of the microcosm, with its intricate series of relationships between the world of man and the universe, was peculiarly attractive. It became the basis of such poems as John Davies of Hereford's "Microcosmos" and Phineas Fletcher's "The Purple Island." Shakespeare saw in it a means of making thought concrete. In *Richard II* the King says to Aumerle:

> Our lands, our lives, and all are Bolingbroke's,
> And nothing can we call our own but death,
> And that small model of the barren earth
> Which serves as paste and cover to our bones.[7]

David Person tells us that the body of man may be compared to the earth, "the rocks and stones whereof are his bones, the brookes and rivers serpenting thorough it, the veynes and sinewes conveying moistnesse from their fountaines unto all the members; the hollow of our bowells and of the trunke of our bodies, to the vast and spacious cavernes and caves within the body of this earth . . . ."[8] "That small model," to which King Richard refers, is the body.[9] A more detailed notion of the correspondence between man and the universe may have been in the dramatist's mind when he wrote the lines, "By my troth, Nerissa, my little body is aweary of this great

---

6 Charron, *op. cit.*, Bk. I, pp. 23, 170 ff.

7 Act III, sc. ii, ll. 151-154.

8 *Varieties*, p. 27.

9 Compare the use of the word model in the following lines from *Henry V* (Prol. Act II, ll. 16-17):

> "O England! model to thy inward greatness,
> Like little body with a mighty heart."

The country, England, is a body (model); it serves as a cover to inward greatness—a mighty heart (the political state).

world.''[10]   If so, the speech becomes more pointed: Portia's microcosm does not respond sympathetically to the macrocosm.

In *Coriolanus*, Menenius refers to his face as the map of his microcosm.[11]   The conceit was familiar enough to an Elizabethan, who
believed in a natural correspondence between inner being and outer
seeming.   In the following sonnet John Davies of Hereford makes
use of it:

> Giue mee (faire-*Sweete*) the Mapp well coloured,
> Of that same little *World*, your selfe, to see
> Whether those *Zones* of hott Loue, and colde Dreade
> Bee so extreame in you, as th' are in mee.
> If on the Hart (that small World's Center greate)
> Such *Heate*, and *Cold* their vtt'most Powers imploy
> No *Thoughts* could dwell therein for *Cold*, and *Heate;*
> Which my distem'pred-dismall Thoughts annoy.
> But, if I finde the *Climes* more temperate
> In your World then in mine, Ile thether send
> My Thoughts by *Colonies,* in wretched State,
> Sith there, for'thwith, they cannot choose but mend:
> And by your temp'rance, when they betterd bee
> If you'l transplant Them, Them re-plant in mee.[12]

Shakespeare draws frequently upon the similarity between the
orderly co-operation of man's faculties and the successful governance of a commonwealth; between the perturbation of the soul and
a revolution.   Falstaff thinks in terms of the body politic when
he says in praise of sherris-sack: ''It illumineth the face, which
as a beacon gives warning to all the rest of this little kingdom, man,
to arm; and then the vital commoners and inland petty spirits
muster me all to their captain, the heart . . . .''[13]   At times the analogy serves to intensify the description of conflict within a character under stress of emotion.   It lurks in the mind of Brutus when
he reflects that between the acting of a dreadful thing and the first
inclination toward it, the state of man, ''like to a little kingdom,''
suffers the ''nature of an insurrection.''[14]   Achilles, refusing to

---

[10] *Merchant of Venice*, I, ii, 1-2.   Professor John D. Rea, (*loc. cit.*, p. 345)
cites this and the preceding passage from Shakespeare. Franz Boll, *Die Lebensalter, Neue Jahrbücher für das klassiche Altertum, Geschichte und deutsche
Literatur*, Bd. XXXI, pp. 89-145, gives an exhaustive discussion of the com-
posite character of thought embodied in Jacques' speech (*As You Like It*, II,
vii, 139 ff.) on the seven ages of man.

[11] Act III, sc. i, l. 69.   Cf. *Richard II*, V, i, 12; *2 Henry VI*, III, i, 203;
Titus Andronicus, III, ii, 12.

[12] ''Wittes Pilgrimage,'' *loc. cit.*, No. 69, p. 15.

[13] *2 Henry IV*, IV, iii, 116-120.

[14] *Julius Caesar*, II, i, 69.   Cf. *Macbeth*, I, iii, 139-142.

fight for his people, endures a struggle between reason and the powers of executing thought, the affections and the will.

> Imagin'd wrath
> Holds in his blood such swoln and hot discourse
> That 'twixt his mental and his active parts
> Kingdom'd Achilles in commotion rages
> And batters 'gainst itself.[15]

Lear upon the heath tears his white hair, which the impetuous blasts catch in their fury. His powers are so distracted that he seems striving in his little world to out-scorn

> The to-and-fro conflicting wind and rain.[16]

In a later scene, Gloucester reflects that as Lear has become a ruined piece of nature, so this great world shall wear out to nought.[17]

Shakespeare makes use of the microcosmic theory not only in describing a conflict among the faculties of the soul, but also in presenting political situations. Frequently he refers to the state as if it were a microcosm. The body of Rome is headless; it must have a better head than one which shakes with age and feebleness.[18] Brutus is the soul of Rome.[19] The body of England is foul. Rank diseases grow near the heart of it, but, with advice and medicine, like a distempered human body, it may be restored to its former strength.[20] Ophelia must not consider Hamlet's advances seriously, for the Prince will be circumscribed in his choice of a wife by the body (Denmark), whereof he is the head.[21] Because of their excellent fighting against the Romans, Cymbeline calls Belarius, Guiderius, and Arviragus the liver, heart, and brain of Britain.[22] Jacques, in *As You Like It*, is ready to cleanse of its disease the foul body of the world.[23]

In *Henry V* the theory of the microcosm underlies a passage[24] which has to do with a defense against the Scots while the King

[15] *Troilus and Cressida*, II, iii, 182-186.
[16] *King Lear*, III, i, 11.
[17] Act IV, sc. vi, ll. 137-138.
[18] *Titus Andronicus*, I, i, 185-188.
[19] *Julius Caesar*, II, i, 321. Cf. Act II, sc. i, l. 163.
[20] *2 Henry IV*, III, i, 38 ff.
[21] *Hamlet*, I, iii, 20 ff.
[22] *Cymbeline*, V, v, 14.
[23] Act II, sc. vii, ll. 58-61.
[24] Act I, sc. ii, ll. 178 ff.

invades France. Representing England as a little world, Exeter argues:

> While that the armed hand doth fight abroad,
> The advised head defends itself at home.

A government, "though high and low and lower, Put into parts," still functions in an orderly manner. Canterbury continues the reasoning suggested in Exeter's reference to the several parts of a government working to one purpose:

> Therefore doth heaven divide
> The state of man in divers functions,
> Setting endeavour in continual motion,
> To which is fixed, as an aim or butt,
> Obedience.

Heaven divides the state (in this case the body politic rather than the "little world") into various functions. The many branches of a government work harmoniously, however, because they yield obedience to authority. Canterbury next pictures co-operation as it exists among the honey bees,

> Creatures that by a rule in nature teach
> The act of order to a peopled kingdom.

From this analogy he infers

> That many things, having full reference
> To one consent, may work contrariously.

A thousand actions, once set afoot, end in a single purpose. He addresses the King:

> Therefore to France, my liege!
> Divide your happy England into four,
> Whereof take you one quarter into France,
> And you withal shall make all Gallia shake.
> If we, with thrice such powers left at home,
> Cannot defend our own doors from the dog,
> Let us be worried and our nation lose
> The name of hardiness and policy.

In terms of the world of man and of nature, Shakespeare here solves a problem confronting the state.

He uses a similar method in *Troilus and Cressida*. After a siege of seven years, the walls of Troy still remain. Ulysses analyzes the situation by reference to the microcosm and to the macrocosm. He begins:

> Agamemnon,
> Thou great commander, nerve and bone of Greece,
> Heart of our numbers, soul and only spirit,

> In whom the tempers and the minds of all
> Should be shut up . . . .[25]

Greece is the little world. Agamemnon is the nerve which carries animal spirits that enable man to feel, to move, to act; he is the bone which supports the body, the heart which commands the affections that control action, the soul and spirit of his kingdom. In him should be the tempers and the minds of all his people. Ulysses goes on to point out that the siege has failed because the Greeks have neglected "the specialty of rule"; they have formed factions. What happens when degree is vizarded?

> The unworthiest shows as fairly in the mask.[26]

He shows that the heavens themselves observe degree; that communities, rank in schools, commerce, brotherhoods, the primogenitive and the due of birth, the prerogative of age, crowns, sceptres, and laurels maintain their places but by degree. He describes the evils attendant upon a disruption of order in the cosmos and in the state.[27] Next he speaks in terms of the world of man:

> Then everything includes itself in power,
> Power into will, will into appetite;
> And appetite, an universal wolf,
> So doubly seconded with will and power,
> Must make perforce an universal prey,
> And last eat up himself.[28]

The theory of the microcosm underlies the wording of his conclusion, the application of the whole matter to the Greeks,[29] and his reference to the great Achilles, the sinew of the army.[30] It reappears in Act V: Hector is the heart, the sinews, and the bone of Troy.[31]

A familiar passage in *Coriolanus* describes a particular kind of rebellion within man, that between the members of the body and the belly. As Menenius narrates the fable, the Second Citizen, suddenly realizing the complexity of the analogy—

---

[25] Act I, sc. iii, ll. 54-58. Professor Murray W. Bundy ("Shakespeare and Elizabethan Psychology," *Jour. Engl. Germ. Phil.*, XXII, 1924, pp. 526-527) points out Shakespeare's use of the microcosmic theory here and in several other passages which analyze the situation at Troy.

[26] Act I, sc. iii, l. 84.

[27] Act I, sc. iii, ll. 85 ff.

[28] Act I, sc. iii, ll. 119-124. Note the exact psychology of the lines. When the will yields to appetite, the state of man is lost.

[29] Act I, sc. iii, ll. 127 ff.

[30] Act I, sc. iii, l. 143.

[31] Sc. viii, l. 12.

> The kingly-crowned head, the vigilant eye,
> The counsellor heart, the arm our soldier,
> Our steed the leg, the tongue our trumpeter,
> With other muniments and petty helps
> In this our fabric—[32]

begins to wonder what answer the belly could make to the powerful insurgents. Menenius gives the answer and drives to his conclusion:

> The senators of Rome are this good belly,
> And you the mutinous members.[33]

In another part of the play,[34] the Tribunes and Menenius visualize Rome as a microcosm. Sicinius says that Coriolanus is a disease that must be cut away. Menenius corrects him:

> O, he's a limb that has but a disease;
> Mortal to cut it off; to cure it, easy;

and goes on to show that a people cannot shed the blood of one who has spent himself for his country, without branding themselves to the end of the world. Sicinius calls the reasoning "clean kam." Brutus says that it is merely awry. When Coriolanus loved his country, the people honored him. Catching up the thought Brutus has suggested, Menenius turns the attack upon the Tribunes:

> The service of the foot
> Being once gangren'd, is not then respected
> For what before it was—

but his speech is broken off by the impatient Brutus. In Act I the old fable drawn from Plutarch renders a political situation concrete; the analogy it suggests is kept throughout the play. Shakespeare's use of the microcosmic theory here and in other passages we have considered points not only to his familiarity with psychological thought of his contemporaries, but also to his skill in adapting that thought to his purpose.

[32] Act I, sc. i, ll. 119-123.
[33] Act I, sc. i, ll. 152-153.
[34] Act III, sc. i, ll. 295 ff.

CHAPTER V

THE PASSIONS: THEIR PHYSIOLOGICAL BEHAVIOR

With the sensible or irrational part of the soul is joined a power of appetite common to man and beast. Its operations receive different names: motions, affections, passions, perturbations. If a response of appetite remains agreeable to nature, it is called a motion.[1] The term motion is not always so definitely restricted in usage, however; any operation of appetite, inasmuch as it stirs the soul to desire or to abhor, is motion. Those responses that disturb our physical well-being but still continue light, are affections; those that are violent are passions or perturbations.[2] In another sense the motions of appetite are called affections, because by them the soul either affects the good or, because of affecting the good, detests evil. They are called passions because, through altering the humors and the spirits, they actually produce physical distress; and perturbations because, through physiological changes, they corrupt judgment, seduce the will, and thus annoy the faculties of mind.[3] The passions are motions of the sensible appetite, caused by the apprehension of good or evil, which produce alteration in the body contrary to the laws of nature. Physiological changes inseparably accompany them.[4] In so far as they disturb the processes of thought, they may be called perturbations or maladies of the soul.

All these terms appear in Shakespeare's dramas and occasionally in lines that suggest distinctions similar to those given above. The word motion is used at times to designate an impulse of desire or

---

[1] Nemesius, *The Nature of Man*, p. 357.

[2] *Ibid.*, p. 359; La Primaudaye, *The French Academie*, p. 463; John Davies of Hereford, ''Microcosmos,'' *loc. cit.*, p. 38.

[3] Thomas Wright, *The Passions of the Minde in Generall*, London, 1630, p. 8. (Contemporary editions were printed in 1601 and 1604.) This last distinction is of course etymological.

[4] Passions do not arise in the rational part of the soul because the intellect does not depend for its operations upon bodily organs. Its motions, immaterial and spiritual, produce no physical change unless they pass into the region of sensitive faculties. Properly speaking, therefore, they are not passions.— Coeffeteau, *A Table of Humane Passions*, pp. 2-3, 253-254; Wright, *op. cit.*, p. 32.

of abhorrence, an inclination of appetite in response to a message from the brain:

> Between the acting of a dreadful thing
> And the first motion, all the interim is
> Like a phantasma or a hideous dream.[5]

As in Elizabethan treatises "motion" is applied generally to any operation of sensitive appetite, so in Shakespeare the term is not restricted in usage to the initial stage of emotion: "But we have reason to cool our raging motions, our carnal stings, our unbitted lusts . . . ."[6] Shylock asks: "Hath not a Jew hands, organs, dimensions, affections, passions . . . .?"[7] Obviously he thinks of affections and passions as being different states, or at least different aspects of the same state of the soul. Just what distinction one should make is not clear. In *1 Henry IV*, Falstaff, impersonating the King, speaks to Prince Harry "not in pleasure but in passion."[8] La Primaudaye tells us that as soon as knowledge is taken of a good propounded to man, that good is "well liked of." When this pleasure, which is at first moderate ("And this liking or delight is as it were a little pleasant winde of motion in the heart, which beginneth to arise and to follow after this good."), grows strong, it is turned to love.[9] Falstaff does not regard the light motion of pleasure as a passion; he speaks to Hal in the stronger motion—love. Of Beatrice, Hero says:

> She cannot love,
> Nor take no shape nor project of affection,
> She is so self-endeared.[10]

The lines seem to indicate that the motions of Beatrice cannot develop into the passion of love; her affections remain affections. A passage in *The Merchant of Venice* suggests more clearly a distinction between affection and passion:

> for affection,
> Master of passion, sways it to the mood
> Of what it likes or loathes.[11]

---

[5] *Julius Caesar*, II, i, 64-66. Cf. *Twelfth Night*, II, iv, 18; II, iv, 101; *Midsummer Night's Dream*, I, i, 193; *King John*, IV, ii, 255; *Cymbeline*, II, v, 20; etc.

[6] *Othello*, I, iii, 334-336. Cf. *Julius Caesar*, III, i, 70; *1 Henry IV*, II, iii, 63.

[7] *Merchant of Venice*, III, i, 62-63.

[8] Act II, sc. iv, l. 458.

[9] *Op. cit.*, p. 465.

[10] *Much Ado*, III, i, 54-56.

[11] Act IV, sc. i, ll. 50-52. Dowden ("Elizabethan Psychology," *loc. cit.*, p. 324) quotes this passage.

Here Shakespeare agrees with his contemporaries in regarding affection as an inclination of the soul toward or against an object— that is, as a response of appetite whereby the soul "either affecteth some good, or for the affection of some good, detesteth some ill"— and passion as the emotional state arising from this inclination and altering the humors and the spirits within the body. Elsewhere Shakespeare several times associates passions with physiological change—that part of an emotion which can be felt in oneself and observed in others.[12] Sometimes, indeed, the word distemper becomes synonymous with passion:

> O gentle son,
> Upon the heat and flame of thy distemper
> Sprinkle cool patience.[13]

In Shakespeare, as in Elizabethan treatises, "perturbation" suggests distress of soul rather than of body.[14]

The sensitive appetite, from which the passions spring, possesses a concupiscent and an irascible inclination. Some authorities define the first as a disposition that covets the good easily obtained and withdraws from minor evils, and the second as a disposition that desires the good and abhors the evil whenever great difficulty is involved. This distinction Wright passes over as an opinion commonly accepted but unsound. The irascible appetite does not covet. God and Nature gave to man an inclination to provide for himself that which is profitable and to shun that which is hurtful. Foreseeing that many impediments would confront man, God gave him also an inclination to overcome difficulties in the way either of good or of evil. The former is the concupiscent instinct, and the latter the irascible.[15] Coeffeteau, who agrees fully with Wright, describes the irascible as a sword and target to the concupiscible. It aims

---

[12] *Tempest*, IV, i, 153; *As You Like It*, IV, iii, 172; *Othello*, V, ii, 44; *Troilus and Cressida*, II, ii, 169; etc.

[13] *Hamlet*, III, iv, 123-125. Cf. *ibid.*, II, ii, 55; III, ii, 312; III, ii, 351; *King John*, IV, iii, 21; etc.

[14] The word is used only five times: (1) *Benedick* (of Beatrice): "So, indeed, all disquiet, horror, and perturbation follows her."—*Much Ado*, II, i, 268-269. (2) *Falstaff*: "Apoplexy hath it original from much grief, from study, and perturbation of the brain."—*2 Henry IV*, I, ii, 131-132. (3) *Prince Harry* (of the crown): "O polish'd perturbation! golden care!"— *2 Henry IV*, IV, v, 23. (4) *Doctor*: "A great perturbation in nature, to receive at once the benefit of sleep, and do the effects of watching!"—*Macbeth*, V, i, 10-12. (5) *Ghost*: "Richard, thy wife . . . . Now fills thy sleep with perturbations."—*Richard III*, V, iii, 159-161.

[15] Wright, *op. cit.*, pp. 19-22.

always at an object environed with difficulty and strives to remove anything that may interfere with the contentment of the desiring power.[16]   Charron refers to the irascible nature as the place in which the soul is active, contriving means to obtain the good and to escape the evil.[17]   The concupiscible inclination is a coveting or desiring instinct, and the irascible an invading or impugning instinct.   They are not separate faculties but different tendencies of a single power, the sensitive appetite.   From them arise all the passions.

Writers disagree as to the actual number and classification of the passions.   Coeffeteau, dividing them upon the basis of the instinct from which they spring, names eleven primary states.   Those that regard good or evil "absolutely and simply" are concupiscible in nature.   Three—love, desire, and pleasure—have for their object the good, and three—hatred, flight, and pain—have for their object the evil.   Those that regard good or evil environed with difficulty are irascible.   They are fear, courage, hope, despair, and choler.[18] Subordinate to these general passions are certain particular states which regard an object as limited to some special condition.   Desire considers the good merely as a good: it is a general passion.   If man inclines toward a specific good, a "particular" passion follows. Thus the desire for honor is ambition; for riches, covetousness.[19] Coeffeteau terms pleasure and pain, included among the primary states, the fountain whence flow all the emotions.[20]

Frequently the passions are classified according to the complexity of their composition.   Bright divides them into the "simple" and the "compound."   The former, such states as are unmixed with other emotions, he divides further into two kinds: the "primitive" and the "derivative."   Love and hate are "primitive" in so far as from them may spring certain "derivative" emotions.   The love of a good, present and possessed, is joy, and of a future good, hope; hatred of an evil, present and possessed, is sorrow or grief, and of an evil to come, fear.   The soul is subject also to passions compounded of two or more "simple" passions.   Love joined to hope, for example, produces trust, and hate to hope, anger.[21]   Sir John

16 *Op. cit.*, pp. 5-6.
17 *Of Wisdom*, Bk. I, p. 175.
18 Cf. *ibid.*, Bk. I, pp. 174-176.
19 Coeffeteau, *op. cit.*, pp. 32 ff.
20 *Op. cit.*, pp. 244-246.
21 *A Treatise of Melancholy*, pp. 99-102.

Davies[22] and Wright[23] likewise name six primary emotions. Batman,[24] La Primaudaye,[25] and John Davies of Hereford[26] name only four: joy, hope, sorrow, and fear.[27] According to Senault[28] there is only one basic passion—love. Hope, fear, joy, and sorrow are merely properties or movements of love to obtain a good or to avoid an evil. Hope is the natural course of love, fear its flight, sorrow its torment, and joy its repose.

The Elizabethan was uncertain whether all passions rise from a common center or certain kinds from organs of their own. Nemesius places the concupiscible inclination of appetite in the liver and the irascible in the heart.[29] There was also a tendency to assign joy, anger, and love respectively to the spleen, the gall, and the liver. Coeffeteau holds the notion most generally accepted that all passions reside in the heart, which, as the fountain of life and of the vital operations, must also be the retreat of the appetites which nature has given man to preserve his life and to chase away any peril that may threaten him. Men who are choleric are prone to anger not because that passion dwells in the gall, but because the predominance of a hot and dry humor renders them subject to anger. An abundance of blood inclines men to love not because the concupiscible inclination resides in the liver, where blood is made, but because hot and moist qualities are favorable to the passion. Nor does joy reside in the spleen because a distemperature of the organ produces melancholy. The heart is the seat of all emotions.[30] With this opinion Wright, Bright, Sir John Davies, John Davies of Hereford, and La Primaudaye agree. They admit, however, that the liver, the spleen, and the gall are in a special way related to the emotions. Let us consider what Shakespeare and psychologists contemporary with him have to say of these organs.

Frequently Shakespeare associates the liver with love.[31] In *The*

---

[22] "Nosce Teipsum," *loc. cit.*, p. 113.

[23] *Op. cit.*, p. 25.

[24] *Batman vppon Bartholome*, Bk. III, ch. 6.

[25] *Op. cit.*, 1586, p. 33.

[26] "Microcosmos," *loc. cit.*, p. 27. On the title page of Grimeston's translation of Coeffeteau, *op. cit.*, are four female figures: Pleasure, Pain, Hope, and Fear.

[27] La Primaudaye calls them desire, joy, fear, and grief.

[28] *De l' Usage des Passions*, pp. 28-29.

[29] *Op. cit.*, pp. 352-353. Cf. Charron, *op. cit.*, Bk. I, pp. 27-28, 54.

[30] *Op. cit.*, pp. 21 ff.

[31] *Merry Wives*, II, i, 121; *As You Like It*, III, ii, 443; *Much Ado*, IV, i, 233; *Twelfth Night*, I, i, 37; II, iv, 101; *Antony and Cleopatra*, I, ii, 23; etc.

Merchant of Venice, Bassanio describes cowards as men whose livers are white as milk.[32] In *Twelfth Night* we are told that if the cowardly Sir Andrew Aguecheek can be found to have enough blood in his liver to clog the foot of a flea, Sir Toby will eat the rest of his anatomy.[33] The liver converts chyle into blood. An abundance of blood produces the sanguine temperament and this inclines man to love. The liver is thus intimately connected with love, if not actually the seat of the passion.[34] Heat is conducive also to action. In the heart vital spirits are made from blood. These, when converted into animal spirits, enable man to act. A red liver means valor. A liver "white and pale" is a "badge of pusillanimity and cowardice."[35]

The gall extracts from the liver a choleric excrement, hot, dry, and bitter. According to Fletcher this humor is a fluid like fire,

> All flaming hot, red, furious, and fell,
> The spring of dire debate, and civile ire;
>   Which wer't not surely held with strong retention,
>   Would stirre domestick strife, and fierce contention,
> And waste the weary Isle with never ceas'd dissension.[36]

When it is not kept in its proper place, it fills the body with bitterness and gnawing. An abundance of choler renders an individual subject to passions that are hot; it makes him bold and wrathful. The condition of the gall may thus account in part for the nature of one's actions.

Contemporary thought regarding the relation of gall to life underlies numerous passages in Shakespeare. Buckingham in *Henry VIII* rightly associates with the flow of gall hasty and malicious motions of the soul.[37] A similar idea is expressed in *2 Henry IV*: the bitterness of gall prevents old age from understanding rightly hot-livered youth.[38] From the gall spring rancor and a desire for revenge.[39] The word is thus at times synonymous with that which distresses the soul,[40] and at times, as a verb, it means

---

[32] Act III, sc. ii, l. 86.

[33] Act III, sc. ii, ll. 65-67.

[34] See below, pp. 126-127.

[35] *2 Henry IV,* IV, iii, 113. Cf. *ibid.,* V, v, 33; *Twelfth Night,* III, ii, 21; *Troilus and Cressida,* II, ii, 50.

[36] "The Purple Island," *loc. cit.,* p. 40.

[37] Act I, sc. i, l. 152.

[38] Act I, sc. ii, ll. 197-198.

[39] *Henry V,* II, ii, 30; *King Lear,* I, iv, 292; *Othello,* IV, iii, 93-94.

[40] *Twelfth Night,* III, ii, 52; *Troilus and Cressida,* IV, v, 30; V, i, 40; *Romeo and Juliet,* I, i, 200; etc.

to irritate by chafing or by inflicting injury.[41] In *Troilus and Cressida,* Nestor calls Thersites a slave whose gall coins slander— slander as prompted by ill-will.[42] Aeneas tells Agamemnon that the Trojans, when they would seem soldiers, have galls, good arms, strong joints, and true swords.[43] At the siege of Orleans, Reignier says that Salisbury may well spend his gall in fretting, for he has neither men nor money with which to make war.[44] Irascibility is in some way connected with gall. As the organ breeds spite and resentment of injury or of insult, it must also yield courage and boldness. Choler, released from the liver in great quantities, inflames man for action, and a gall surcharged with this bitter humor must spend itself. A further reference to the dependence of action upon gall occurs in *Hamlet.* Hamlet rebukes himself for being pigeon-livered and without gall "to make oppression bitter."[45] His self-chastisement is based upon the idea that the liver and the gall are related to, if not the actual seats of, the sensitive appetite. To be pigeon-livered is to be without the irascible instinct.[46] Hamlet knows that he has desire for vengeance, but for the moment he thinks that he lacks the flow of gall necessary to effect this desire; that irascibility will not rally to the support of concupiscence.

The spleen may incline man to a variety of passions. Its function is to draw to itself and purge the melancholy excrement, normally cold and dry, an excrement which breeds fearful passions, checks passageways, and defiles the whole supply of humors. When it performs this task successfully, man is disposed to mirth. The spleen is thus sometimes said to be the seat of laughter.[47] If the spleen flourishes, the body withers; if the spleen withers, the body

---

[41] *1 Henry IV,* I, iii, 229; *2 Henry IV,* I, ii, 166; I, ii, 258; *Measure for Measure,* II, ii, 102; *Hamlet,* I, iii, 39; IV, vii, 148; V, i, 153; etc.

[42] Act I, sc. iii, l. 193. Cf. *Measure for Measure,* III, ii, 199.

[43] *Ibid.,* I, iii, 136-137.

[44] *1 Henry VI,* I, ii, 16-17.

[45] Act II, sc. ii, ll. 605-606.

[46] Such creatures as pigeons, turtles, and sheep possess only a single motion of appetite, concupiscence.—Coeffeteau, *op. cit.,* p. 9.

[47] See Bright, *op. cit.,* p. 220. Coeffeteau (*op. cit.,* pp. 301-302) makes laughter depend upon a sudden motion of the soul, "which desiring to expresse her ioy, excites a greate abundance of hot blood and multiplies the vitall spirits, which agitate and stir vp the muscles which are about the heart, & those stir vp the muscles which are of either side of the mouth." Cf. Huarte, *Examen de Ingenios,* pp. 81-82. Burton (*Anatomy of Melancholy,* Vol. I, p. 174) and Fletcher (*loc. cit.,* p. 47) regard the diaphragm as the seat or instrument of laughter.

flourishes. A spleen "somewhat more drawing to lyttlenesse than
to muchnesse" is therefore a sign of good complexion.[48] Phineas
Fletcher calls the organ the seat of malice and of heaviness rather
than of laughter. He gives the following account of its relation
to the well-being of man:

> And should these waies [from liver to spleen], stopt by ill accident,
> To th' *Hepar* streams turn back their muddie humours;
> The cloudie Isle with hellish dreeriment
> Would soon be fill'd, and thousand fearfull rumours:
> Fear hides him here, lockt deep in earthy cell;
> Dark, dolefull, deadly-dull, a little hell;
> Where with him fright, despair, and thousand horrours dwell.
>
> If this black town in over-growth increases,
> With too much strength his neighbours over-bearing;
> The *Hepar* daily, and whole Isle decreases,
> Like ghastly shade, or ashie ghost appearing:
> But when it pines, th' Isle thrives; its curse, his blessing:
> So when a tyrant raves, his subjects pressing,
> His gaining is their losse, his treasure their distressing.[49]

Shakespeare frequently regards the spleen as an organ which
may modify human behavior. Especially in his comedies he associates it with laughter and mirth.[50] Although the word is not used
to signify melancholy or sadness, a number of passages spring from
the conception of spleen as the storehouse of a humorous excrement.
In such cases spleen interrupts the normal course of action; it
renders the individual subject to sudden impulse, to inclination,
and makes him unfit for deliberative procedure. As the condition
of the liver or the gall may preclude sound judgment, so, too, may
the condition of the spleen; hence it may promote variability of
temper and conduct. To this power such passages as the following refer:

> A thousand spleens bear her a thousand ways.[51]

> . . . . a mad-brain rudesby full of spleen,
> Who woo'd in haste and means to wed at leisure.[52]

Two passages in *King John* associate spleen with impetuosity.[53] In

---

[48] Batman, *op. cit.*, Bk. V, ch. 41. Cf. Fletcher, *loc. cit.*, p. 41.

[49] *Loc. cit.*, p. 41.

[50] *Taming of the Shrew*, Ind., 137; *Measure for Measure*, II, ii, 122; *Love's Labour's Lost*, III, i, 77; V, ii, 117; *Twelfth Night*, III, ii, 72; *Troilus and Cressida*, I, iii, 178.

[51] *Venus and Adonis*, 907.

[52] *Taming of the Shrew*, III, ii, 10-11. Cf. *1 Henry IV*, II, iii, 81; III, ii, 125; V, ii, 19; *As You Like It*, IV, i, 217; *King John*, IV, iii, 97; *Romeo and Juliet*, III, i, 162; *Othello*, IV, i, 89.

[53] Act II, sc. i, l. 448; Act V, sc. vii, l. 50.

agreement with Fletcher, Shakespeare occasionally makes spleen synonymous with malice, or ill nature.[54] And similarly he uses the term to suggest a fit of temper or passion:

> Brief as the lightning in the collied night,
> That, in a spleen, unfolds both heaven and earth, ...[55]

Spleen may serve also as a spur to action—action which springs from hatred or revengeful feelings. Warwick's soldiers, who fail at St. Albans, have been robbed of their heated spleens.[56] Richard III, before making his valiant stand against Richmond, cries out:

> Our ancient word of courage, fair Saint George,
> Inspire us with the spleen of fiery dragons![57]

Exiled from Rome, Coriolanus resolves to fight against his country with the spleen of all the under fiends.[58]

Just why spleen should be associated with heat, ill temper, and irascibility is hard to determine. It is probable that the explanation lies in the nature of melancholy, however, for the spleen, according to Elizabethan theory, serves no other purpose than to collect and purge this humor.[59] In the following passage Burton describes several kinds of melancholy:

". . . . *Melancholy* is either *simple* or *mixed*; offending in *quantity* or *quality*, varying according to his place, where it settleth . . . . and differing according to the mixture of those natural humours amongst themselves, or four unnatural adust humours as they are diversely tempered & mingled. If natural *melancholy* abound in the body, which is cold & dry, *so that it be more than the body is well able to bear, it must needs be distempered* . . . . and so the other, if it be depraved, whether it arise from that other *melancholy* of *choler* adust, or from blood, produceth the like effects, & is . . . . if it come by adustion of humours, most part hot & dry. Some difference I find, whether this *melancholy* matter may be engendered of all four humours, about the colour and temper of it. . . . . From *melancholy* adust ariseth one kind, from *choler* another, which is most brutish : another from *phlegm*, which is dull; and the last from *blood*, which is best. Of these some are cold and dry,

---

[54] *Henry VIII*, I, ii, 174; II, iv, 89; II, iv, 110; *Richard III*, II, iv, 64; *Troilus and Cressida*, II, ii, 128; II, ii, 196; *Timon of Athens*, III, v, 113; *Julius Caesar*, IV, iii, 47.

[55] *Midsummer Night's Dream*, I, i, 145-146.

[56] *3 Henry VI*, II, i, 124.

[57] *Richard III*, V, iii, 349-350. Cf. *King John*, II, i, 68.

[58] *Coriolanus*, IV, v, 97.

[59] See Batman, *op. cit.*, Bk. V, ch. 39.

others hot & dry, varying according to their mixtures as they are intended, & remitted."[60]

Here it is obvious that certain kinds of melancholy possess qualities which are conducive to action. La Primaudaye tells us that a humor may become corrupt through a degeneration of its substance or through a mixture with other humors. In either of these ways melancholy may wax gross and biting; it may burn to the nature of ashes.[61] Melancholy, thus variable in its characteristics, may incline man to almost any passion:

"Of all the other humours Melancholy is fullest of variety of passion, both according to the diuersitie of place where it setleth .... as also through the diuers kinds, as naturall, vnnaturall: naturall eyther of the splene or of the veines, faultie onely by excesse of quantitie, or thicknesse of substance: vnnaturall by corruption, and that eyther of bloud adust, choller, or melancholly naturall, by excessiue distemper of heate, turned in comparison of the naturall, into a sharp lye by force of adustion."[62]

These passages refer, of course, to a general corruption of the humor; yet it is reasonable to conclude that spleen, as the natural receptacle of melancholy, may provoke a number of passions, varying according to the nature of the substance that collects within it. Let us consider a single passage from Shakespeare's plays. To Cassius, who has yielded to anger made violent by testy choler, Brutus says:

By the gods,
You shall digest the venom of your spleen,
Though it do split you.[63]

A spleen filled with the sharp lye of corrupt melancholy—corrupt in this instance through mixture with choler—gives rise to rancor. The venom, unless digested or consumed by nature, must express itself in words or deeds. The valor that comes from a heaving spleen is a valor arising from bitter enmity.

The kind of passion to which man is subject varies not only according to the condition of certain organs but also according to the disposition of his entire body, particularly as regards the humors and the spirits. As the body is well or ill disposed so are the affections. "We see also by experience," writes La Primaudaye;

60 Burton, *op. cit.*, Vol. I, pp. 197-198.
61 *Op. cit.*, pp. 533-534.
62 Bright, *op. cit.*, p. 123.
63 *Julius Caesar*, IV, iii, 46-48.

"that there is great agreement betweene the qualities and temperature of the body, and the affections of the soule: insomuch that as
the bodies of men are compounded of the qualities of heate, colde,
moisture, and drinesse, so among the affections some are hot, others
colde; some moist, others dry, and some mingled of these diuers
qualities."[64] Everyone is subject in a special way to the affections
which agree in nature with the temperature and complexion of
his body. Children, young men, healthy folk, and the idle, for
example, are inclined habitually to joy because their temperature
is hot and moist. Since the humors are subject to constant variation in quantity and in quality, moreover, the same individual may
yield more readily to passion at one time than at another, or he
may even succumb to a passion contrary to his nature:

". . . . sometimes wee feele our selues, we know not why, moued
to mirth, melancholy, or anger: insomuch that any little occasion
were sufficient to incense that Passion: for, as these humors depend vpon the heauens, aire, sleepe, & waking, meat and drinke,
exercise and rest, according to the alteration of these externall
causes, one or other Humour doth more or lesse ouer-rule the body,
and so causeth an alteration of Passions."[65]

The soul and the body are so closely united that whatever affects
the one affects the other. A good complexion may therefore render
man comparatively immune to dangerous passions:

"A bodie of sanguine complexion . . . . the spirits being in their
iust temper in respect of quality, and of such plenty as nature
requireth, not mixed or defiled by any strange spirit or vapor, the
humours in quantity and quality rated in geometrical, and in
iust proportion, the substance of the body, and all the members so
qualified by mixture of elements, as all conspire together in due
proportion breedeth an indifferencie to all passions."[66]

Ill humors may annoy the soul by corrupting the substance of its
instruments. We have already considered the relation of liver, gall,
and spleen to life. The humors interfere further with the operations of the soul as they alter the heart and the brain:

"If the brain is altered, the object is not rightly apprehended
and thus the heart is moved to a disorderly passion; if the heart
is altered, although the report be delivered to the heart sincerely,

---

[64] *Op. cit.*, p. 455.

[65] Wright, *op. cit.*, p. 65.

[66] Bright, *op. cit.*, p. 118. See also the description of the perfect temperament, above, p. 39.

it does not answer in affection as the object requireth but more or lesse, as the distemper misleadeth: if both parts be overcharged of humour, the apprehension and affection both are corrupted, and misse their right action, and so all things mistaken, engender that confused spirit, and those stormes of outragious loue, hatred, hope, or feare, wherewith bodies so passionate are heere and there, tossed with disquiet.''[67]

Likewise the soul is capable of distressing the body, for the passions are always accompanied by physiological changes. Let us note, therefore, the way in which the passions arise and take their course.

When the imagination has judged an impression from the external senses or from memory, animal spirits flock through certain ''secret channels'' from the brain to the heart, where they ''pitch at the dore'' and make known whether the object is good or bad. Immediately the sensitive appetite strives to effect the soul's desire and, through contracting or expanding the heart, either calls in or disperses the humors and the spirits. If the brain is very apprehensive, it sends an abundance of spirits to the heart and thus makes a deep impression upon the organ; if the heart is agreeably disposed, it responds readily and vehemently; and if the humors are agreeably compounded they supply much fuel to feed the passion.[68]

In *Measure for Measure*, Angelo, who has become infatuated with Isabel, says:

> Why does my blood thus muster to my heart,
> Making both it unable for itself,
> And dispossessing all my other parts
> Of necessary fitness?[69]

Here Shakespeare regards passion as producing physical change throughout the body. In *Twelfth Night* he speaks of it as establishing itself in the chief organs of the soul. The Duke wonders how Olivia, who can pay so large a debt of love to a brother, will love,

> when liver, brain, and heart,
> These sovereign thrones, are all suppli'd, and fill'd
> Her sweet perfections with one self king![70]

Psychologists agree that the effects of passion are by no means

---

[67] *Ibid.*, p. 87. Professor Hardin Craig (''Shakespeare's Depiction of Passions,'' *Phil. Quar.*, IV, 1925, p. 293) quotes this passage.

[68] Wright, *op. cit.*, pp. 45-46; Burton, *op. cit.*, Vol. I, p. 290.

[69] Act II, sc. iv, ll. 20-23.

[70] Act I, sc. i, ll. 37-39.

confined to changes produced within the heart, where the sensitive appetite dwells.   Under the impulsion of soul, the entire body responds to a stimulus.   Not only does the heart draw humors—

"but also the same soule that informeth the heart residing in other parts, sendeth the humours vnto the heart, to performe their seruice in such a worthie place: In like maner as when we feele hunger . . . . the same soule which informeth the stomack, resideth in the hand, eyes, and mouth; and in case of hunger, subordinateth them all to serue the stomacke, and satisfie the apetite thereof: Euen so, in the hunger of the heart, the splene, the liuer, the blood, spirits, choller, and melancholly, attend and serue it most diligently."[71]

This broad response of nature to messages from the brain produces epigastric and other physiological changes.   When in operation, the affections of the heart may thus be said to inhabit many parts of the body.   After maintaining that the heart is the dwelling place of the passions and particularly of those that are evoked by objects that are absent, Wright continues:

"Yet I cannot but confesse, that when the obiects are present, and possessed by sense, then the passions inhabite, not only the heart, but also are stirred vp in euery part of the body, whereas any sensitiue operation is exercised; for if we taste delicate meates, smel muske, or heare musicke, we perceiue not onely that the heart is affected; but that also the passion of ioy delighteth those parts of our senses: the like wee proue in paine and griefe for which cause commonly wee say, our teeth ake, our fingers, toes, or legges paine vs: Payne therefore, and pleasure, being Passions of the Minde, and euermore felt in that part of the body, where Sense exerciseth her operations: therfore, as touching is dispersed thorow the whole body, euen so the Passions of pleasure and paine; for in euerie part, if it bee cherished, it reioiceth, if it be hurt, it paineth."[72]

All the affections have their origin within the heart.   Such states

---

[71] Wright, *op. cit.*, pp. 45-46.

[72] *Op. cit.*, p. 34.   Coeffeteau (*op. cit.*, p. 27) presents the same view.   The concupiscible and the irascible inclinations have their chief residence in the heart, he says, but they "disperse themselves" throughout the body. This belief that passion exists in the part affected is based upon the notion that the spirits are capable of giving sensation: ". . . . the *sinewes* . . . . are the *braine* it selfe.   For they are a certaine portion of the *braine*, containing in them *vitall spirits*, and diffusing them throughout the whole body . . . . And wheresoever such a *sensible sinew* is planted, it makes the part wherein it is ingraffed to be partaker of *sense*; and to be so qualified, that it may feele things.   Neither were it improperly spoken to say that not the *passion*, but rather a certaine partaking of the *griefe*, and a denunciation of the same is conveyed up to the *braine*, where all the *sinewes* have their beginning."— Nemesius, *op. cit.*, pp. 310-312.

as joy and hope, in which the soul either embraces or reaches out for a good, expand the organ and other channels through which the spirits and the humors must pass. Joy, if moderate, brings health, for it enables the heart to concoct a goodly store of spirits and to disperse them throughout the body. If vehement, it overheats the heart, and engenders choleric blood; if extreme, it may actually kill the organ by leaving it bloodless. In such passions as sorrow, on the other hand, the heart shrinks, and this shrinking, together with the desire of nature to succor the center of life, draws blood, spirits, and natural heat from the outward parts of the body.[73] The heart trembles and languishes until it is finally dried up and consumed. Grief is much more dangerous to the body than is joy, for it is a malign, cold, and dry passion which wastes the humors and little by little quenches natural heat.[74] The gathering of much melancholy blood about the heart extinguishes or at least dulls the spirits. The heart itself, unable to function properly, is likely to convert blood into melancholy, and this humor withers the body, for its temperature is contrary to heat and moisture, the two qualities most agreeable to life.[75]

The physiological behavior of fear is similar to that of sorrow, for fear is merely sorrow resulting from an evil that seems imminent. In the following passage La Primaudaye enumerates its effects upon the body:

". . . . first of all it draweth in and shutteth vp the heart, and so weakeneth the same. Whereupon nature being desirous to relieue and succour it, sendeth heat vnto it from the vpper parts: and if that be not sufficient, she draweth away that heate also which is in the neather parts. By which doing she suddenly calleth backe the bloud and spirits vnto the heart, and then followeth a generall palenesse and colde in all the outward parts, and chiefly in the face, with a shivering throughout the whole body. . . . . Whereupon it followeth, that by reason of the great beating and panting of the heart, the tongue faltreth and the voice is interrupted. Yea it commeth to passe sometimes, that present death followeth a great and suddein feare, because all the bloud retiring to the heart choaketh it, and vtterly extinguisheth naturall heate and the spirits, so that death must needes ensue thereof."[76]

Trembling of various parts of the body results not merely from

---

[73] John Davies of Hereford, "Microcosmos," loc. cit., p. 35.

[74] See Coeffeteau, op. cit., pp. 332-333.

[75] Wright, op. cit., pp. 61-62.

[76] Op. cit., p. 471.

a sympathy which these parts have with the heart, but also from physiological conditions accompanying passion. By "tonical motion" the spirits produce firmness and erection in the body. When they are withdrawn with blood to the heart, the countenance becomes pale and the relaxation of muscle allows the head to bend forward. In fear or grief the lips tremble because the spirits which should uphold them have departed; the weight of the lip, striving with the weakness of the organ, causes a trembling that is "betwixt erection, and plaine declination." The cheeks contract because nature wishes to discharge a moisture which comes into them with the humidity of tears and because there is an agreement between the muscles of the face and the diaphragm, which, influenced by the shrinking of the heart, contracts the lips and the cheeks.[77]

To account for the fact that fear causes the heart to tremble Coeffeteau tells us that the spirits and heat which come from the outer parts do not remain long within the organ but rather proceed downward:

". . . . in them that *feare*, their spirits grow thicke, and become more heauy by reason of the cold which imagination doth produce . . . . So as the spirits being growne thus heauy, by reason of the cold which this imagination leaues, tends downeward, and remaines not about the heart."[78]

Thus he provides a physiological basis for the figurative statement that one's heart (whence valor comes) may sink to one's heels.

The heart that is unduly contracted with passion has at its disposal certain means of relief. By groaning and sighing it opens slightly as if it would come forth to breathe, "least being wholly shut vp with sorrow it should be stifled."[79] "Sighing," Bright says, "hath no other cause of mouing then to coole and refresh the heart, with fresh breath, and pure ayre, which is the nourishment & food of the vitall Spirits, besides the cooling which the heart it selfe receiueth thereby."[80] Sobbing and sighing, if not vehement, give comfort further by expelling the smoky and sooty vapors that collect within the heart; if vehement, they shake the organ and thus produce soreness.[81]

---

[77] Bright, *op. cit.*, p. 187.
[78] *Op. cit.*, p. 464.
[79] La Primaudaye, *op. cit.*, p. 468.
[80] *Op. cit.*, p. 193.
[81] *Ibid.*, pp. 195-196.

Since grief and fear quench natural heat, it is not altogether obvious why sighing should be considered a means of cooling the heart. Apparently the Elizabethan thought that the cold and dry effects of these passions work from the outward parts to the inward and, according to Coeffeteau, that they finally descend into the abdominal region. Bright speaks of vapors that arise from the heart in sorrow because the heat that flows to the organ works upon moisture.[82] Of the heat which accompanies fear Coeffeteau says:

"They that are surprized with *feare* feele strange alteration; and are wonderfully dry; for that the heate which nature hath drawne about the heart, burnes and filles the bowells with an exceeding heate, which makes him to desire cold and moist things, wherein thirst consists, to quench the troublesome alteration, to refresh the Creature, and to free it from this insupportable heate."[83]

Fear and sorrow are passions that drive spirits and heat to the heart. Since they are fed by melancholy, they dull the spirits, quench and choke natural heat, waste other humors, and finally send the spirits downward. The body and its organs become cold and dry.

From the heat of blood and spirits drawn to the heart in sorrow and fear, vapors arise and ascend to the brain, where they are congealed. When spirits and blood are called from the outward parts, the brain, fuller and hotter than it is under normal conditions, gives off other vapors. To assure safety, nature contracts the organ in such a way that "as one desirous to hold fast that which is apt to flow foorth, looseth by his hard handling and compression, which otherwise might retaine, so it expresseth that which by thinnesse is ready to voyde, and forcing with Spirit, and pressing with contracted substance, signifieth by shower of teares, what storme tosseth the afflicted Heart, and ouercasteth the cheerfull countenance."[84] Man finds comfort in weeping, for passion in some measure assuages when its effects are carried away through the nostrils and the eyes.

---

[82] *Op. cit.*, p. 195.

[83] *Op. cit.*, pp. 464-465.

[84] Bright, *op. cit.*, p. 177-178. Extreme terror or grief does not cause tears, because at such times nature, hiding herself in her own center, draws in the humidities which follow the spirits and blood. Besides, the contraction of pores prevents the flow of tears. This contraction causes the hair to stand on end. Tears may accompany joy, partly because of the enlargement of passageways and partly because of the ready access which spirits have to outward parts.—*Ibid.*, pp. 169 ff.

Nearly every psychologist discusses at length the nature and course of anger. La Primaudaye defines the passion as a vehement motion of the soul arising because a possessed good has been contemned.[85] When the heart is enraged, it becomes swollen and puffed up; blood rises and boils around it; panting and trembling of the breast follow. Since anger is always mingled with sorrow and a desire for revenge, it produces two motions of the soul, the one to avoid evil and the other to pursue with great violence that which brings about provocation. The blood does not wholly withdraw to, and remain in, the heart, as it does in fear and in sorrow—

"but disperses it selfe outwardly. For the heart is as if he stroue to go out of his hoste or campe, not vnlike to a Prince or Captaine that is desirous to march forward in battell array: Whereupon he sendeth forth the bloud and the spirits, as his men of warre, to repell the enemie: which is not done without great mouing and tumult, and much stirring in the heart, which setteth on fire and inflameth the blood and spirits."[86]

Those who become pale with anger are more to be feared than those who become red. In the former case blood and spirits have fled to the heart to succor it, and the organ thus has more fuel to feed the desire for vengeance.[87]

Whatever the passion may be, the heart is always the center of physiological affliction; hence the ease with which an emotion may distress the soul varies according to the natural constitution of the organ. If the heart is soft and tender, it receives impressions easily, for the same reason, one may suppose, that a soft and tender brain receives impressions easily in the ventricle of memory. If it is hard and cold, it responds quickly to grief and retains the impression long; if it is hard and hot, it responds quickly to joy and retains the impression long. In "Wittes Pilgrimage," John Davies of Hereford asks,

---

[85] *Op. cit.*, p. 496. Frequently anger is defined in terms of its effects as a boiling of the blood around the heart. Bright (*op. cit.*, pp. 106-107) protests against such definition. He gives the following explanation of physiological changes: "For first the Heart mooueth, kindled with anger, then the Bloud riseth, which being cholerick increaseth the heate, but addeth nothing to the passion . . . ." The boiling, Bright says, results from contrary motions of the heart—a contraction accompanied by a retreat of blood and spirits to the organ because the soul has been displeased, and an expansion accompanied by an efflux of blood and spirits because the soul desires vengeance.

[86] La Primaudaye, *op. cit.*, pp. 496-497.

[87] *Ibid.*, p. 497.

What *Hart* is of such steely temprament
(Or much more hard:) (for *Steele* the *Magnet* loues)
But gently bowes, when it by Loue is bent?[88]

Shakespeare, in *Henry VIII*, refers to hearts of most hard temper.[89] Hardness, it seems, springs from temper, and this in turn from a conjunction of the four first qualities. Since the proportion of qualities depends upon elements and humors, the hard heart must have been thought of as one actually hard in substance. Similarly the heart may really be heavy, because of the presence in and around the organ of much melancholy blood and dull, heavy spirits. To be light hearted is to have spirits that are well concocted—for spirits vary in weight according to their degree of perfection—and a ready flow of blood and spirits from the organ.

When he kneels to pray, the King in *Hamlet* commands his heart with strings of steel to be as soft as sinews of a new-born babe.[90] Elsewhere it has been pointed out that strings have to do with the movement of the heart.[91] If a heart has strings of steel, it cannot contract or dilate readily to promote passion by controlling humors and spirits. The passage implies further that a substance, soft and tender, may counteract this obduracy and thus render the heart more responsive to impressions than it otherwise would be.

As the passions take their course, their effects upon the heart become increasingly severe. The organ may swell with anger until it is too great for what contains it,[92] or it may actually consume with heat.[93] Similarly it may succumb to the cold and dry influence of grief.[94] In *Richard II*, Ross says:

My heart is great; but it must break with silence,
Ere 't be disburden'd with a liberal tongue.[95]

Under stress of extreme passion, particularly of that which does not find an outlet in words, deeds, or tears and sighing, the heart

---

88 *Loc. cit.*, p. 9.
89 Act II, sc. iii, l. 11.
90 Act III, sc. iii, ll. 70-71.
91 See above, p. 13.
92 *Coriolanus*, V, vi, 103-104. Cf. *1 Henry VI*, I, v, 10; *Antony and Cleopatra*, I, i, 6-8; *Richard III*, IV, i, 34.
93 *Titus Andronicus*, II, iv, 37; *King John*, III, i, 345. Cf. *ibid.*, IV, ii, 103; *Winter's Tale*, II, i, 111; *2 Henry IV*, I, iii, 13; *3 Henry VI*, I, i, 60; etc.
94 *Antony and Cleopatra*, IV, ix, 16-17. Cf. *ibid.*, V, iii, 105; *Romeo and Juliet*, III, v, 59; *Pericles*, IV, i, 24; etc.
95 Act II, sc. i, ll. 228-229. Cf. *Taming of the Shrew*, IV, iii, 77; *Antony and Cleopatra*, IV, xiv, 40; *Hamlet*, I, ii, 159; etc.

may break. Sometimes its strings may snap;[96] and sometimes it may break because of its inability to sustain contrary passions such as joy and sorrow.[97]

All these passages from Shakespeare possess a literal quality which we have not often attributed to them, for in the works of writers whose interests lie definitely in the field of psychology there is abundant reference to the power of passion to overcome the actual substance of the heart. A sonnet in "Wittes Pilgrimage" begins:

> Worke on my Hart, sterne *Griefe*, and do thy worst:
> Draw it togeather till his Strings do crack.[98]

Later, Grief is asked to extend his vigor and crush the heart into the smoke of sighs. The author of *Theatrum Mundi* reports that the hearts of those who have died of love melancholy have been found to be "all burned."[99] Coeffeteau states that in joy and desire the heart melts; in grief it shrinks and freezes; in choler it becomes inflamed; and in fear it pales and trembles.[100] He might have added that the heart may consume away, that it may dry up, or that it may break because of undue expansion or contraction.

With contemporary theory as to the physiological behavior of the passions, Shakespeare was thoroughly familiar, and he utilized this theory as a basis for depicting with concreteness and intensity various types of perturbation. His characters are broadly conscious of physical states to the extent that effects accompanying a passion become synonymous at times with the passion itself. Frequently one comes upon such lines as—

> Dry sorrow drinks our blood;[101]

or

> What, hath thy fiery heart so parch'd thine entrails
> That not a tear can fall for Rutland's death?[102]

In *Richard II*, Gaunt receives chastisement for daring to make pale the kingly cheek and chase the royal blood

---

[96] *King Lear*, V, iii, 216; *Richard III*, IV, iv, 365.

[97] *King Lear*, V, iii, 196-199.

[98] *Loc. cit.*, No. 68, p. 15.

[99] *Theatrum Mundi. The Théatre or Rule of the World* . . . ., Englished by John Alday, London, 1581, p. 192.

[100] *Op. cit.*, pp. 16-17.

[101] *Romeo and Juliet*, III, v, 59.

[102] *3 Henry VI*, I, iv, 87-88.

With fury from his native residence.[103]

After having dismissed her mother and the nurse in order to carry out the scheme of Friar Lawrence, Juliet says:

> I have a faint cold fear thrills through my veins,
> That almost freezes up the heat of life.[104]

The Ghost in *Hamlet*, except that he is forbidden to tell the secrets of his prison house, could unfold a tale

> whose lightest word
> Would harrow up thy soul, freeze thy young blood,
> Make thy two eyes, like stars, start from their spheres,
> Thy knotty and combined locks to part
> And each particular hair to stand on end,
> Like quills upon the fretful porpentine.[105]

One is tempted to cite other passages depicting emotion concretely, but these are enough to show that Shakespeare, like the psychologists of his day, understood mental states in terms of the physical.

Accepting definite theories as to the physiological behavior of the passions, the Elizabethan had of course but little faith in the power of man to conceal emotion. The face he regarded as the map of the microcosm. Flushing and paling, the lustre or dullness of the eye, sobbing and sighing, these and many other outward bodily signs were to him directly revelatory of the inward state of the soul.[106] The psychologist therefore enumerates external phenomena of the passions as zealously as he analyzes inward change. Of anger Charron writes:

"The Signs and Symptoms of this Passion are many, and manifest, more and more visible than those of any other; and so Strange and Strong, that they make a mighty Difference in the Person, alter the whole Temper and Frame both of Body and Mind, transform and turn him into quite another Man. . . . . Some of these Changes and Symptoms, are outward and apparent: Redness and Distortions of the Face, Fieryness of the Eyes, a wild and enraged Look, Deafness and Insensibility in the Ears, Foaming at the Mouth, Palpitation of the Heart; Quickness and Unevenness of the Pulse, Swelling and Bursting Fullness of the Veins, Stammering in the Tongue, Gnashing and Setting of the Teeth, Loudness and Hoarseness in the Voice, The Speech thick and indistinct; and in short, The whole Body is set on Fire, and in a perfect Fever."[107]

---

[103] Act II, sc. i, l. 119.

[104] *Romeo and Juliet*, IV, iii, 15-16.

[105] Act I, sc. v, ll. 15-20.

[106] Craig, ''Shakespeare's Depiction of Passions,'' *loc. cit.*, p. 299.

[107] *Op. cit.*, Bk. I, p. 208. Cf. John Davies of Hereford, ''Microcosmos,'' *loc. cit.*, p. 73.

This emphasis upon symptoms of the passions is paralleled in Shakespeare by a tendency to judge the state of the soul by outward signs. "In thy face I see thy fury," says Gloucester to Cardinal Beaufort in *2 Henry VI*.[108]   Richard III gnaws his lip: he is angry.[109]

> Beaufort's red sparkling eyes blab his heart's malice,
> And Suffolk's cloudy brow his stormy hate.[110]

These are but a few of numerous passages significant of the certainty with which an emotional state reveals itself through observable signs.

In *Julius Caesar*, Brutus says to the conspirators:

> Good gentlemen, look fresh and merrily.
> Let not our looks put on our purposes,
> But bear it as our Roman actors do,
> With untir'd spirits and formal constancy.[111]

With sufficient strength of will, one may of course control the outward signs of passion. Elizabethan theory of the emotions is physiological to such an extent, however, as to provide little ground for a belief in the power of will in ordinary men to prevent outward manifestations of inward states. York says to Margaret in *3 Henry VI*:

> But that thy face is, vizard-like, unchanging,
> Made impudent with use of evil deeds,
> I would assay, proud queen, to make thee blush.[112]

The lines suggest that real disguise—disguise which successfully conceals the soul—is possible only when man has become so accustomed to doing evil as to render himself immune to the many passions—pity, remorse, fear, sorrow, and others—whereby the normal man reveals his motives. In the case of Macbeth, we may observe the process of learning to wear a mask. First, Macbeth's face is as a book wherein men may read strange matters:[113] he is acting contrary to his inner being. At the end of Act I and again in Act III,

---

[108] Act I, sc. i, ll. 143-144.   Cf. *Titus Andronicus*, III, ii, 12; *King John*, IV, ii, 76 ff.; IV, ii, 71-72; *Julius Caesar*, I, ii, 184; *Winter's Tale*, I, ii, 447; etc.

[109] *Richard III*, IV, ii, 27.   Cf. *Henry VIII*, III, ii, 113; *Coriolanus*, I, i, 259; etc.

[110] *2 Henry VI*, III, i, 154-155.

[111] Act II, sc. i, ll. 224-227.

[112] Act I, sc. iv, ll. 116-118.

[113] *Macbeth*, I, v, 63 ff.

scene ii, he resolves to play false, but he is not successful. In the meantime his wife has urged:

> Come on,
> Gentle my lord, sleek o'er your rugged looks;
> Be bright and jovial among your guests to-night.[114]

And in the banquet scene she says:

> O, these flaws and starts,
> Imposters to true fear, would well become
> A woman's story at a winter's fire,
> Authoriz'd by her grandam. Shame itself!
> Why do you make such faces?[115]

Only after Macbeth has "supp'd full with horrors" can he say:

> I have almost forgot the taste of fears. . . . .
> Direness, familiar to my slaughterous thoughts,
> Cannot once start me.[116]

Lady Macbeth dies a victim of thick-coming fancies, a victim of a fruitless effort to belie her soul in words and deeds. Macbeth becomes so thoroughly ingrained with vice that he no longer yields to emotions which betray purposes. His concealment of motives results not from an ability to control outward effects of passion by resolution of the will, but from a soul habituated to evil and therefore imperturbable.

Shakespeare's characters believe so implicitly in a correspondence between outward seeming and the inward state of the soul, indeed, that a revelation of gross disparity is baffling.[117]

> There's no art
> To find the mind's construction in the face.
> He was a gentleman on whom I built
> An absolute trust,[118]

says Duncan of the traitorous Cawdor. Gloucester, full-bent upon the English crown, boasts that he can smile and murder while he smiles; that he can cry "Content" to that which grieves his heart, wet his cheeks with artificial tears, and frame his face to all occasions.[119] Hamlet finds it meet to record in his tables,

---

[114] Act III, sc. ii, ll. 26-28.

[115] Act III, sc. iv, ll. 63-67.

[116] Act V, sc. v, ll. 9-15.

[117] Cf. the greater correspondence between the nature of the body and the normal functioning of the soul, considered below, pp. 114 ff.

[118] *Macbeth*, I, iv, 11-14.

[119] *3 Henry VI*, III, ii, 182-185. His words spoken later to the young Prince Edward—

That one may smile, and smile, and be a villain![120]

Othello's last hope rests upon his confidence in "honest, honest Iago."[121]   According to the psychology of Shakespeare,

> There are no tricks in plain and simple faith.

Men who use an "enforced ceremony"—

> hollow men, like horses hot at hand,
> Make gallant show and promise of their mettle;
> But when they should endure the bloody spur
> They fall their crests, and, like deceitful jades,
> Sink in the trial.[122]

Only men who never feel such stings as those of pity, shame, and remorse completley mask their souls and these eventually are found out.

> "No more can you distinguish of a man
> Than of his outward show; which, God he knows,
> Seldom or never jumpeth with the heart."
> (*Richard III*, III, i, 9-11)—

should not be taken seriously. The Prince is right in his fear of Gloucester. Furthermore, Gloucester is contradicting himself, for he implies elsewhere (*3 Henry VI*, V, vi, 78-79) that he desires to be foul like his body. We have seen already that he takes pride in being able to smile while he murders.

[120] *Hamlet*, I, v, 108.

[121] *Othello*, V, ii, 154.

[122] *Julius Caesar*, IV, ii, 23-27.

CHAPTER VI

THE PASSIONS: THEIR PSYCHOLOGICAL BEHAVIOR

The affections, as they dilate or contract the heart, control the humors and the spirits; they therefore release or withhold energy for action. We have already treated their physiological behavior. To understand further the conception of emotion which underlies Shakespeare's plays—that is, to understand how emotion may enable man to seek the reasonable desires of his soul, or, if inordinate, carry him headlong beyond all bonds of restraint—we must consider certain theories which have to do with what may be termed, perhaps, the psychological characteristics of the passions.

Knowledge, it will be recalled, is intimately dependent upon the external senses, for they are the doors through which all impressions from the world pass to higher faculties of thought and desire. If the eye errs, the mind is likely to err also; reason and the imagination can judge only of what they receive. Minds swayed by eyes, or by any other sense, may indeed be full of turpitude.

The idea that the senses, as porters to the soul, may dominate thought has wide applicability. An interesting use of it occurs in *A Midsummer Night's Dream*; to make the brain full of fantasies Oberon streaks eyes with juice.[1] In *The Comedy of Errors*, Pinch tells Adriana that Antipholus and Dromio of Ephesus are "possessed"; they must be bound and placed in a dark room.[2] Sir Toby has Malvolio bound and left in darkness to regain his wits.[3] Darkness, Batman tells us, is a cure of frenzy or madness; it takes away "the imagination that commeth by the sight."[4] Andrew Boorde urges that madmen be kept in dark rooms; that "there be no paynted clothes, nor no paynted wallys, nor pyctures of man nor woman, or fowle, or beest; for suche thynges maketh them ful of fantasyes."[5] The Elizabethan theory of sensation, brought to play

---

[1] Act II, sc. i, ll. 257-258. Cf. Act II, sc. i, l. 178.
[2] Act IV, sc. iv, ll. 95-97.
[3] *Twelfth Night*, III, iv, 148.
[4] *Batman vppon Bartholome*, Bk. VII, ch. 5.
[5] *A Dyetary of Helth, loc. cit.*, p. 298.

here in the treatment of madness, underlies also Shakespeare's description of conscience. The ready response of mind to reports from the senses makes of conscience a fleeting thing, yielding quickly to a new stimulus. The conscience of the Second Murderer in *Richard III* is a passionate humor, "wont to hold but while one tells twenty."[6] Mention of the word judgment[7] or of a reward,[8] innocent prate,[9] haughty words[10]—all suffice to move conscience. The immediacy of response is so marked that Aufidius, standing over the dead body of Coriolanus, can say,

> My rage is gone;
> And I am struck with sorrow.[11]

Of greater significance for our purpose is the power of sense to arouse the affections. Thomas Wright tells us that the passions are moved not only by their principal objects but also by certain appurtenances, appendices, or scraps of the objects.[12] This statement of an observable fact is one which the Elizabethan made much of. It underlies several passages in Shakespeare in which a picture or a mere description is said to awaken passions of love or grief.[13]

Of the power of sense impressions against reason Charron writes:

"The Ceremony of taking leave, the Idea of some particular Gesture in a parting Friend, strikes us deeper, and gives us more real Trouble, than all the Reasoning in the World, upon Matters of greatest Moment, is able to do. The Sound of a Name repeated, some certain Words and melancholy Accents pronounc'd Pathetically; nay, dumb Sighs, and vehement Exclamations, go to our very Hearts. . . . . And this airy Blast sometimes surprises the most cautious, and transports the most resolved, unless they set a more than common Guard upon themselves."[14]

A present object moves the passions much more vehemently than does perception through recall, "for the imagination in absense,

---

[6] Act I, sc. iv, ll. 120-122.

[7] *Ibid.*, I, iv, 109.

[8] *Ibid.*, I, iv, 126-127.

[9] *King John*, IV, i, 25-27.

[10] *1 Henry VI*, III, iii, 78.

[11] *Coriolanus*, V, vi, 148-149.

[12] *The Passions of the Minde*, pp. 152-153.

[13] *1 Henry VI*, IV, vii, 83; V, v, 1 ff.; *Titus Andronicus*, III, i, 103; *Two Gentlemen of Verona*, II, iv, 209; IV, ii, 122.

[14] *Of Wisdom*, Bk. I, p. 295. Cf. Spenser's description of the attack made upon the soul through the gateways of sense.—*Faerie Queene, loc. cit.*, Bk. II, canto xi, ll. 42 ff.

representeth the pleasure as far off and not prepared, but the thing being present, nothing seemeth to want but execution.''[15]

The psychology of these passages finds expression numerous times in Shakespeare. It renders more plausible such actions as Mark Antony's following the ships of Cleopatra.[16] King John says to Hubert,

> Hadst not thou been by,
> A fellow by the hand of nature mark'd,
> Quoted, and sign'd to do a deed of shame,
> This murder had not come into my mind.[17]

Later the King admits that his rage was blind—that his ''foul, imaginary eyes of blood'' made Hubert seem more hideous than he was—[18] and his reasoning is sound, for when we are wrought by passion we see things not as they are but as we wish them to be. It is interesting to note, however, that in the first instance the King ascribes the culmination of his plan for the murder of Arthur to his seeing a suitable tool; that is, to the power of a present stimulus to direct the mind. Antony, at the body of Caesar, says to Octavius' servant:

> Passion, I see, is catching; for mine eyes,
> Seeing those beads of sorrow stand in thine,
> Began to water.[19]

To the Servant who brings news of the approaching enemy Macbeth urges:

> Go prick thy face, and over-red thy fear,
> Thou lily-liver'd boy. What soldiers, patch?
> Death of thy soul! those linen cheeks of thine
> Are counsellors to fear. What soldiers, whey-face?[20]

Passions become contagious through their outward manifestations; inward faculties respond quickly to impressions from sense.

As an emotion may be aroused through sensation, so it may be perpetuated largely through the presence of favorable objects. When he first begins yielding to that ''horrid image'' which leads to his downfall, Macbeth tells us that present fears are less than horrible imaginings.[21] As the action progresses, however, the extent to

15 Wright, *op. cit.*, p. 158.
16 *Antony and Cleopatra*, III, x, 20-21.
17 *King John*, IV, ii, 220-223.
18 *Ibid.*, IV, ii, 264 ff.
19 *Julius Ceasar*, III, i, 283-285.
20 *Macbeth*, V, iii, 14-17.
21 *Ibid.*, I, iii, 137-138.

which his fear is motivated by concrete obstacles is so apparent that
one need hardly direct attention to such lines as,

> Come, seeling night,
> Scarf up the tender eye of pitiful day,
> And with thy bloody and invisible hand
> Cancel and tear to pieces that great bond
> Which keeps me pale! [22]

or to the immediacy with which self-control asserts itself after the
disappearance of Banquo's ghost:

> Why, so; being gone,
> I am a man again. Pray you, sit still.[23]

Macbeth thinks he can root out fear that shakes him nightly by
striking down every obstacle that confronts him. Likewise the
King in *Hamlet* resolves to put fetters upon his fear, which goes too
free-footed.[24] Hamlet rages like "hectic" in his blood; England
must provide the cure.[25] According to the psychology which
Shakespeare knew and used, the senses exercise no inconsiderable
power over thought and affection.

The sensitive appetite, we have found, possesses a concupiscible
and an irascible inclination. These co-operate in such a way that
the affections of the latter unite with or replace those of the former
whenever the soul is environed with great difficulty. When an
object has been apprehended as good, the passion of love responds,
and from this, in turn, springs a desire to possess the good. If the
object can be procured easily, concupiscence provides sufficient
energy, but if difficulty lies in the way, the irascible inclination
yields hope in support of the concupiscible and thereby enables man
to strive vehemently to effect his purpose.[26] It may release choler
and deprive the soul of contentment until the difficulty has been
removed.[27] Whenever an obstacle is insurmountable, despair arises
to prevent concupiscence from spending itself in vain.[28] Likewise
the two inclinations co-operate in the avoidance of evil. Courage
leads man to combat that which opposes him, and fear prevents his

---

[22] *Ibid.*, III, ii, 46-50.
[23] *Ibid.*, III, iv, 107-108.
[24] Act III, sc. iii, l. 24.
[25] Act IV, sc. iii, l. 68.
[26] Coeffeteau, *A Table of Humane Passions*, pp. 42 ff.
[27] *Ibid.*, pp. 155-156.
[28] *Ibid.*, p. 44.

persisting against great odds.[29]   Whenever difficulty confronts the soul, the irascible instinct supports the concupiscible.

The affections that result from a conjunction of the two inclinations are far more dangerous than those which spring from concupiscence working alone:

"For these first Motions, formed here by the Representation of the Object, are afterwards continued, and communicated to the *Irascible* Part of the Soul, that is, The Place, where the Soul is active, and contriving Means to obtain what she apprehends to be Good; and to deliver her self from that which she apprehends to be Evil.   And then, as a Wheel already in Motion, when a fresh Force pushes it, receives that Addition easily, and whirls about with wonderful Strength, and Swiftness; so the Soul, which is already stirred and warmed with the first Apprehension, when a Second Attempt is made upon it, and the Coals are blown, flames out, and is transported with Rage and Violence, much greater than before.   The *Passions* Then raised, ride higher; are much more furious and ungovernable; for now indeed they are double: The first have come in and joyned them, and thus they back and sustain one another, by this Union, and mutual Consent."[30]

The irascible instinct may induce man to pursue that which is contrary to the concupiscible.   It may lead him, for instance, to hazard his life in seeking revenge.[31]   Thus the very means which nature has devised to insure the comfort of man may prove his undoing: the irascible motions, adding their forces to the power of concupiscence, may fan a passion into a flame that destroys rationality.

Recently Professor Hardin Craig[32] has pointed out that this theory of the two-fold nature of appetite underlies a passage in *Pericles*:

> The passions of the mind,
> That have their first conception by mis-dread,
> Have after-nourishment and life by care;
> And what was first but fear what might be done,
> Grows elder now and cares it be not done. [33]

The passions proceed from a mild state to vehemence.   Desire of a future good kindles hope or despair; the resentment of a future evil kindles fear or courage.   The apprehension of a present evil,

---

[29] *Ibid.,* pp. 45 ff.

[30] Charron, *op. cit.,* Bk. I, pp. 175-176.

[31] Coeffeteau, *op. cit.,* p. 9.

[32] "Shakespeare's Depiction of Passions," *loc. cit.,* p. 290.

[33] Act I, sc. ii, ll. 11-15.

which in the first instance causes grief, may incite anger.[34] Pericles' fear gives way to despair of his being able to contend against Antiochus, for despair is merely a passion by which the soul is made to desist from attempting that which seems impossible.

Frequently in Shakespeare the progress from concupiscence to irascibility is a progress from grief to anger. The latter passion has a double motion: blood flows to the heart because the soul is displeased; it is breathed out again in revenge.[35] The desire of the soul to vanquish its contemner gains force from this fuel that collects in the heart; the efficacy of anger comes from the release of energy when the spirits and blood are dispersed in action. In *3 Henry VI*, Richard says:

> I cannot weep, for all my body's moisture
> Scarce serves to quench my furnace-burning heart;
> Nor can my tongue unload my heart's great burden,
> For self-same wind that I should speak withal
> Is kindling coals that fires all my breast,
> And burns me up with flames that tears would quench.
> To weep is to make less the depth of grief.
> Tears then for babes; blows and revenge for me.[36]

His heart, which should have grown cold with grief at the news of York's death, is being heated by the fires of vengeance. He resolves not to weep out his grief, the method of concupiscence, but to eradicate it by means of revenging anger. A knowledge of the relation between irascibility and concupiscence seems to underlie also a passage in *Titus Andronicus*. Marcus says to Lavinia:

> Shall I speak for thee? Shall I say 'tis so?
> O, that I knew thy heart; and knew the beast,
> That I might rail at him to ease my mind!
> Sorrow concealed, like an oven stopp'd,
> Doth burn the heart to cinders where it is.[37]

Although the Elizabethan regarded sorrow as a passion which in its initial stage actually heats the heart, it is probable that Marcus is here thinking of Lavinia's helplessness to seek revenge; of her helplessness to put into words the fires of vengeance which must burn her soul.[38] A later passage in the same play builds clearly

---

[34] Charron, *op. cit.*, Bk. I, p. 176.
[35] See above, p. 85.
[36] Act II, sc. i, ll. 79-86.
[37] Act II, sc. iv, ll. 33-37.
[38] Cf. *Venus and Adonis*, 331-336:
> "An oven that is stopp'd, or river stay'd,
> Burneth more hotly, swelleth with more rage;
> So of concealed sorrow may be said;

upon the theory of two kinds of passion. When asked why he
laughs at calamity, Titus replies:

> Why, I have not another tear to shed.
> Besides, this sorrow is an enemy,
> And would usurp upon my watery eyes
> And make them blind with tributary tears;
> Then which way shall I find Revenge's cave?[39]

It is this recognition of the proper relation between sorrow and
revenge which enables Titus to rise above his grief and say:

> Come, let me see what task I have to do. [40]

King Lear is less fortunate in distress. To the gods he cries:

> If it be you that stirs these daughters' hearts
> Against their father, fool me not so much
> To bear it tamely; touch me with noble anger,
> And let not women's weapons, water-drops,
> Stain my man's cheeks! No, you unnatural hags,
> I will have revenges on you both
> That all the world shall — I will do such things, —
> What they are, yet I know not; but they shall be
> The terrors of the earth. You think I'll weep:
> No, I'll not weep.
> I have full cause of weeping; but this heart
> Shall break into a hundred thousand flaws,
> Or ere I'll weep. O, Fool! I shall go mad! [41]

Here Shakespeare depicts with remarkable clarity one of the most
intense struggles any of his characters endures. The old King attempts to rise from grief to a revenging anger—from concupiscence
to irascibility—but age and utter helplessness prevent his effecting
his purpose. His noble resolve not to ease his heart by weeping,

> Free vent of words love's fire doth assuage;
> But when the heart's attorney once is mute,
> The client breaks, as desperate in his suit.''

In *The Winter's Tale* (II, i, 107-111) Hermione, having assured Leontes
that she is not prone to weep, goes on to say:

> ''. . . .but I have
> That honourable grief lodg'd here which burns
> Worse than tears drown.''

Hermione is unwilling to yield to concupiscent tears; she can hardly ease
her heart through revenge of wrong; hence it must burn. Shakespeare's
references to sorrow as a passion which burns are bound up in some way
with the theory of concupiscence and irascibility. They are derived in part,
of course, from the notion we have already considered, that grief drives to
the heart blood and spirits bearing heat and that this heat, if not breathed
out in revenge, is quenched gradually as the spirits become dulled with melancholy and sink lower.

[39] Act III, sc. i, ll. 267-271.

[40] Act III, sc. i, l. 276.

[41] *King Lear*, II, iv, 277 ff.

when he is incapable of revenge, hastens the dissolution of his mind.
In Shakespeare and in Elizabethan psychology, to weep one's "sad
bosom empty" is to make less the fuel of revenge. If that which
offends the soul can be overcome, grief must

> Convert to anger; blunt not the heart, enrage it.[42]

And the passion that results is one of tremendous power, dangerous of course if it overthrows reason:

> Cold *feare* and *griefe* then *Reason* so benumme,
> ʼThat it feeles nothing but cold *griefe* and *feare*.
> This *colde* made hot by *Ire*, which it doth steere
> Becomes *hell fire*, which like a quenchlesse *flame*
> Consumeth all it toucheth or comes neere,
> And leaues nought els behind but lasting *blame*,
> So, *Feare* turn'd *Fury*, *Man* doth all vnframe.
>
> For, as in *nature*, *things* that are most *cold*
> Made *hot*, are most extreame *hot*, like the *Fires:*
> So *Feare*, most *cold* by kind, yet if it should
> Bee chas'd vncessantly with *Hate* and *Ire*,
> ʼT would be more *hot*, then all *fires* made intire.
> For, *Man* is more out-ragious, wilde, and wood
> In *Passion's* heate, then *Passion* can desire;
> No *Beast* is half so fell, in maddest moode,
> As *Man*, when *Furie* sets on fire his *bloud*. [43]

As the passions become inordinate they blind the understanding.
Like green spectacles, through which everything appears green, a
passion causes man to judge whatever promotes it as good and
agreeable to reason, and by exhausting the forces of the soul prevents the apprehension from restoring a normal state. The imagination, perverted through physiological changes, presents objects
to the intellect with intensity, and the intellect, upon looking into
the court of imagination, discovers nothing but the "mother and
nurse" of the passion.[44] Here we find the psychology which prompts
Bushy to say to the Queen in *Richard II*, who insists that she is
grieving for something more than the parting from her lord the
King:

> Each substance of a grief hath twenty shadows,
> Which shows like grief itself, but is not so;
> For sorrow's eyes, glazed with blinding tears,
> Divides one thing entire to many objects,
> Like perspectives, which rightly gaz'd upon

---

[42] *Macbeth*, IV, iii, 229. Cf. *ibid.*, IV, iii, 1-4.

[43] John Davies of Hereford, "Microcosmos," *loc. cit.*, pp. 72-73. This
psychology provides "a natural reason of rebels' civill fury."—*Ibid.*, p. 72,
n. 5.

[44] Wright, *op. cit.*, pp. 48 ff.

> Show nothing but confusion, ey'd awry
> Distinguish form; . . . . [45]

In addition to the power of passion to cause reason and imagination to see things after the color of itself, Wright lists as characteristics of emotional response contradiction, contrariety, insatiability, importunity, and impossibility. The first and second have to do with rebellion against reason and among the passions themselves. When man least suspects it, the affections may completely undermine rationality, for while the wits are careless or engaged in thought, there may creep into the heart a motion so strong as to transport the soul beyond all bonds of control. At other times, contrary passions may arise and force one or another to give way. Then, too, as covetousness increases with riches, so the passions in general are insatiable—hardly to be satisfied. Those that are inordinate either prevent judgment or result from a judgment already corrupt; consequently one may say that the passions do not regard either time or place but rather leap into action upon every occasion and with great importunity. Finally they lead man to seek the impossible; the desires of passion keep "neyther sense, order, nor measure."[46]

Of the conflict of passions among themselves Wright says:

"The Egyptians fought against the Egyptians, the East wind riseth often against the West, the South against the North, the Winde against the tyde, & one Passion fighteth with another. The cholericke Caualier would with death reuenge an iniurie, but feare of killing or hanging opposeth it selfe against this Passion. Gluttonie would haue dainties, but Couetousness prescribeth parsimonie. Lecherie would raigne and dominier, but dreadfulnesse of infamie, and feare of diseases draw in the reines of this inordinate affection. By which opposition we may easily perceiue, how vnquiet is the heart of a passionate man, tossed like the Sea with contrary windes, euen at the same time and moment."[47]

This doctrine that one passion may lead to or restrain another is a familiar part of Elizabethan thought. Take, for instance, the following from La Primaudaye:

"And as the affections are quickly bred one of another, so some of them are brideled & restrained by others . . . . If a man loue any thing, hee wisheth it would come, and hopeth also that hee shall

---

[45] Act II, sc. ii, ll. 14-20.
[46] *Op. cit.*, pp. 68 ff.
[47] *Op. cit.*, pp. 70-71.

enioy it : and contrariwise hee feareth that it will not come to passe. If it come to passe, he reioyceth. If it come not to passe when he thinketh it will, or when he expecteth it, he is grieued. In like manner, great ioy is lessened through griefe, and enuy through mercy, or through feare. And one griefe altereth another, when it is greater : and feare maketh griefe to be forgotten, and causeth the lame to runne . . . . in the fight of the affections there is no respect had to that which is most iust, but onely to that which is strongest and most violent, and which hath gotten such power ouer the soul that it hath wholy subdued her to it selfe . . . . ''[48]

In Shakespeare the theory that one passion yields readily to another finds expression through the immediacy with which grief converts to anger and through the depiction of a struggle for supremacy between two or more passions. In *The Winter's Tale* the Third Gentleman speaks of the noble conflict fought in Paulina between joy for the discovery of Perdita and sorrow for the loss of her husband.[49]   Here the conflict is waged evenly. The Duke in *Twelfth Night* has in mind the kind of passion that swallows up all other motions and takes possession of the entire soul, when he says of Olivia :

> How will she love when the rich golden shaft
> Hath kill'd the flock of all affections else
> That live in her ; when liver, brain, and heart,
> These sovereign thrones, are all suppli'd, and fill'd
> Her sweet perfections with one self king! [50]

Brabantio is so distressed by the elopement of Desdemona with Othello that he does not feel the general care of the state ; his particular grief

> Is of so flood-gate and o'erbearing nature
> That it engluts and swallows other sorrows
> And it is still itself. [51]

And in *The Merchant of Venice,* Portia's love for Bassanio, a love which has been struggling with other motions—despair, fear, and jealousy—gains full mastery of the soul when Bassanio chooses the lead casket. Portia knows the danger to which this excess of love may lead :

> How all the other passions fleet to air,
> As doubtful thoughts, and rash-embrac'd despair,

[48] *The French Academie,* p. 465. Cf. John Davies of Hereford, ''Micrososmos,'' *loc. cit.,* pp. 39-40.

[49] Act V, sc. ii, l. 78.

[50] Act I, sc. i, ll. 35-39.

[51] *Othello,* I, iii, 56-58. Cf. *Macbeth,* I, iii, 139 ff.

And shuddering fear, and green-ey'd jealousy!
O love,
Be moderate; allay thy ecstacy;
In measure rein thy joy; scant this excess!
I feel too much thy blessing; make it less,
For fear I surfeit. [52]

Shakespeare was sensitive in unusual degree to the emotional states of his characters, and fortunately he had at his command a science which enabled him to render these states peculiarly vivid to his audience. The joys and sorrows of his characters are still powerful in their appeal, of course, for they are but the incarnation of universal affections of the human heart. Viewed from the standpoint of Elizabethan thinking they are portrayed more sharply than much analysis of emotion in more recent literature, for Shakespeare's science, crude and now in many respects antiquated, was not at all abstruse.

The passions, it will be remembered, produce an alteration in the body. So long as the change is confined to the heart, man suffers no great danger, for the motions are still subject to reason. The difficulty comes when physiological effects invade the brain: "For how hot soeuer the heart and breast are or may be, yet man abideth alwaies still and quiet if the heate pearce not vp to the braine."[53] One is reminded of Lear's attempt to still his rising heart,[54] and of his earlier resolve to prevent melancholy from ascending even to the heart.[55] Evidently the power of a strong emotion to disturb the soul is commensurate with the extent to which it alters the instruments of thought.

The passions, once having entered the brain, gradually gain control of the mind. In a passage which has to do with distemperature of the body—and passion always leads to distemperature—Timothy Bright speaks of melancholy vapors that arise to the brain and obscure the clearness with which the spirits are endued. The effect upon thought is not so apparent at first—

"as in processe of time, when the substance of the braine hath plentifully drunke of that spleneticke fogge, whereby his nature is become of the same quality, and the pure and bright spirits so defiled, and eclipsed, that there indifferency alike to all sensible things,

[52] Act III, sc. ii, ll. 108 ff.
[53] La Primaudaye, op. cit., pp. 497-498. Cf. John Davies of Hereford, "Microcosmos," loc. cit., p. 73.
[54] King Lear, II, iv, 122.
[55] Ibid., II, iv, 56-58.

is now drawne to a partialitie, and inclination, as by melancholy they are inforced.''[56]

Later he refers to the presence in the brain of a "substanciall obscuritie" which extends its operation through the cells of common sense, fantasy, and memory:

"This [obscurity] taking hold of the braine by processe of time giueth it an habite of depraued conceite, whereby it fancieth not according to truth: but as the nature of that humour leadeth it, altogether gastly and fearefull. This causeth not onely phantasticall apparitions wrought by apprehension only of common sense, but fantasie .... compoundeth and forgeth disguised shapes, which giue terrour vnto the heart .... Neyther onely is common sense, and fantasie thus ouertaken with delusion, but memory also receiueth a wound therewith ....[57]

The passage offers a close parallel to Ben Jonson's description of jealousy, which, like a pestilence, infects

> The houses of the brain. First, it begins
> Solely to work upon the phantasy,
> Filling her seat with such pestiferous air,
> As soon corrupts the judgment; and from thence,
> Sends like contagion to the memory;
> Still each to other giving the infection.
> Which, as a subtle vapour, spreads itself
> Confusedly through every sensitive part,
> Till not a thought, or motion in the mind
> Be free from the black poison of suspect. [58]

A similar psychology must underlie Hamlet's reference to the "dram of eale," which

> Doth all the noble substance of a doubt
> To his own scandal. [59]

From what has just been said it is obvious that, as they continue, the passions are cumulative in their power both to control the humors and the spirits and to distress the mind. Nemesius distinguishes three degrees of anger. The first heat or beginning of the motion he calls choler, or angry displeasure; the second he calls a continuing or inveterate anger, and the third a revenging anger.[60]

---

[56] *A Treatise of Melancholy*, pp. 124-125.
[57] *Ibid.*, pp. 126-127.
[58] *Every Man in his Humour*, Mermaid Series, II, i. Professor Bundy ("Shakespeare and Elizabethan Psychology," *loc. cit.*, p. 525) quotes this passage.
[59] *Hamlet*, I, iv, 37-38. Quoted from Q₂.
[60] *The Nature of Man*, p. 395.

Similarly Burton describes the progress of melancholy as it disrupts the quietude of the soul:

"Generally thus much we may conclude of melancholy; that it is most pleasant at first . . . . but at the last *laesa imaginatio,* his phantasy is crazed, &, now habituated to such toys, cannot but work still like a fate; the Scene alters upon a sudden, Fear and Sorrow supplant those pleasing thoughts, suspicion, discontent, and perpetual anxiety succeed in their places; and so by little and little, by that shoeing-horn of idleness, and voluntary solitariness, Melancholy . . . . is drawn on . . . . it was not so delicious at first, as now it is bitter and harsh: a cankered soul macerated with cares and discontents, *taedium vitae* . . . . impatience, agony, inconstancy, irresolution, precipitate them unto unspeakable miseries."[61]

From a study of the origin and psychic growth of specific emotions as they are described in Elizabethan treatises, one may learn much regarding Shakespeare's depiction of the passions. Take, for example, the disease of madness, a disease which, in Elizabethan thinking, meant either a temporary dethronement of reason in heightened passion, or the more permanent affliction, insanity, but one which, in either case, was understood in terms of the principles operative in almost any perturbation. Madness is merely the extremity of distemperature, and as such, it may be studied with reference to theories of the passions.

At the grave of Ophelia, Laertes prays that a treble woe may fall upon the head of him who deprived his sister of her "most ingenious sense."[62] He probably refers to the imagination. In *King Lear,* Cordelia calls upon the gods to wind up the untuned and jarring senses of her father.[63] Physiologically, madness springs from a defect of the brain. Batman calls it an infection of the foremost cell (in which he localizes the imagination), with a deprivation of the imagination.[64] Burton, in describing the kind of madness to which students and lovers succumb, speaks of the spirits that ascend to the brain and with their heat dissolve the inner senses.[65] As the passages from Shakespeare imply, the intellect is unimpaired. Its power seems distraught only because the external and the internal senses minister false reports:

---

61 *Anatomy of Melancholy,* Vol. I, p. 467.

62 *Hamlet,* V, i, 269-272.

63 Act IV, sc. vii, l. 16.

64 *Op. cit.,* Bk. V, ch. 6.

65 *Op. cit.,* Vol. I, p. 485.

"For the mad man of what kinde soeuer he bee of, as truly concludeth of that which fantasie ministereth of conceit, as the wisest: only therein lieth the abuse and the defect, that the organicall parts which are ordained embassadours, and notaries vnto the minde in these cases, falsifie the report, and deliuer corrupt records."[66]

In discussing the cure of melancholy, a passion which is not always differentiated from madness,[67] Burton urges that one must withstand and expel the vain, false, and frivolous imaginations, the absurd conceits, the feigned fears and sorrows from which the disease primarily develops; one must strive with the utmost endeavor not to "cherish those fond imaginations which so covertly creep into his mind, most pleasing and amiable at first, but bitter as gall at last, and so headstrong, that by no reason, art, counsel, or persuasion, they may be shaken off."[68] Ultimately, vehement and continual meditation may lead to madness. This fact Lady Macbeth knows; she repeatedly warns her husband against continuing an image in the mind.[69] At last, however, she herself succumbs to the power of "thick-coming fancies," for neither she nor the Doctor can pluck from the memory the rooted sorrow, which pursues her to death. King Lear, also, knows the power of a mental image to undermine reason. He breaks off thinking about the cruelty of his daughters—"that way madness lies"[70] —and thus for a time saves himself from insanity. The theory that a fond imagination may creep covertly into the brain and disrupt the quietude of the soul is significant, we shall find, in the psychology of almost any passion. It is, indeed, quite modern except in so far as the Elizabethan regarded the "figures" in the brain as having a materiality that recent science does not warrant.

Any violent passion blinds rationality. The organs of the external and the internal senses undergo alteration and thus the latter senses evolve distorted ideas. One sees everything according to the color of the passion. In Shakespeare madness in any form causes one to view the world with "other eyes" and with jarring senses. The temperate see the world as an organized universe in which divine and human law operate. They may know that "Something is rotten in the state of Denmark," but they know also that

[66] Bright, op. cit., p. 137.
[67] See Burton, op. cit., Vol. I, p. 160.
[68] Op. cit., Vol. II, p. 120.
[69] Macbeth, II, ii, 33-34; II, ii, 45-46; III, ii, 8 ff.
[70] King Lear, III, iv, 21.

the evil may be cured: "Heaven will direct it." Only the distempered regard the earth as a "sterile promontory," the firmament
as a "pestilent congregation of vapours," and life as a tale—

> Told by an idiot, full of sound and fury,
> Signifying nothing.

Of Desdemona, Othello says, when he has begun to lose faith in her
chastity,

> Perdition catch my soul,
> But I do love thee! and when I love thee not,
> Chaos is come again. [71]

"Chaos" may refer, of course, to perturbation of the soul but it
also may be significant of Othello's view of life, for chaos in the
microcosm causes man to find a corresponding chaos in the macrocosm, varying in extent according to the violence of the passion.

In the case of actual madness the world becomes a disorganized
state in which the principles of justice and morality no longer hold.
To King Lear it becomes a stage of fools. Chastity, love, gratitude,
and sincerity disappear from society.[72] Similarly, after his dis-
illusionment, Timon of Athens regards life as universal confusion.
He prays to the gods that no assembly of twenty men may be without a score of villains.[73] Note the extent of his railing outside the
walls of Athens:

> Matrons, turn incontinent!
> Obedience fail in children! Slaves and fools,
> Pluck the grave wrinkled Senate from the bench,
> And minister in their steads! To general filths
> Convert o' the instant, green virginity! . . . .
> Son of sixteen,
> Pluck the lin'd crutch from thy old limping sire;
> With it beat out his brains! Piety and fear,
> Religion to the gods, peace, justice, truth,
> Domestic awe, night-rest, and neighbourhood,
> Instruction, manners, mysteries, and trades,
> Degrees, observances, customs, and laws,
> Decline to your confounding contraries,
> And let confusion live! . . . . [74]

Not only does Timon lose faith in humanity, but he also sees the
world of nature through the color of his affliction. The sun, the
moon, the sea, the earth—"each thing's a thief."[75]

---

[71] *Othello*, III, iii, 90-92.

[72] *King Lear*, IV, vi, 111 ff. Cf. Craig, "The Ethics of *King Lear*," loc.
cit., pp. 106, 108.

[73] *Timon of Athens*, III, vi, 86.

[74] *Ibid.*, IV, i.

[75] *Ibid.*, IV, iii, 438 ff.

There was current in Elizabethan thinking the notion that nature in man sometimes takes the form of a wayward, erring tendency, which, when unregulated by law, results in the confusion of all that makes for stability and happiness in life, and it would seem as if the world to the madman is a world in which this tendency is allowed its rights. It is a place in which man has forgotten the original teaching of Nature, to take the way of justice and to follow the Golden Rule; a place in which the "wisedome of Princes, and the feare of Gods threate" no longer force man "both to allowe things confirmed by nature, and to beare with old custome." The world to the madman, as Shakespeare represents it, has indeed suffered the dissolution of those natural virtues—"religion and acknowledging of God; naturall loue to our children, and other; thankfulnesse to all men; stoutnesse, both to withstand and to reuenge; reuerence to the superior; assured and constant trueth in things"—which, when practised in control of this erring tendency in human life, yield civilization.[76]

Let us revert now to the theory that a fond imagination may creep covertly into the brain and undermine rationality. This doctrine, the truth of which one can readily attest, has wide applicability in Elizabethan thinking, and it is illustrated many times in Shakespeare's plays. It accounts for Hamlet's melancholy, following upon his mother's rash marriage.[77]

> Thou hast no figures nor no fantasies
> Which busy care draws in the brains of men;
> Therefore thou sleep'st so sound, [78]

says Brutus when he finds his boy, Lucius, asleep. Iago, in his practices against Othello, relies upon the power of a mental image to nourish a passion:

> The Moor already changes with my poison.
> Dangerous conceits are, in their natures, poisons,
> Which at the first are scarce found to distaste,
> But with a little act upon the blood,
> Burn like the mines of sulphur. [79]

---

[76] For a statement of this conception of mankind in relation to nature, see Wilson's *Arte of Rhetorique*, 1560 (G. H. Mair, ed., Clarendon Press, 1909), p. 32. Professor Craig cites the passage in his "Ethics of *King Lear*," *loc. cit.*, p. 101. Excerpts from it are quoted above.

[77] Note his first soliloquy, in which he questions, "Must I remember?"

[78] *Julius Caesar*, II, i, 231-233.

[79] *Othello*, III, iii, 325 ff. Cf. Craig, "Shakespeare's Depiction of Passions," *loc. cit.*, p. 291.

The poison has begun to work upon the Moor: Iago needs only to keep alive the dangerous conceit of Desdemona's infidelity, which he has implanted in the mind of his victim. A study of jealousy as it is described in Elizabethan treatises will indicate further how thoroughly Shakespeare understood the means by which an emotion insinuates itself into the mind, and the power it gains over the soul. Let us begin with a passage from Charron:

"Jealousie is a Disease of the Soul; an argument of great Weakness; an evil and a foolish Disease, but withal a furious and terrible one: It rages and tyrranizes over the Mind; insinuates it self under the pretence of extraordinary Friendship and Tenderness: But when it hath gotten Head, and taken Possession, it builds a mortal Hatred upon the foundation of Kindness. Vertue, and Health, and Beauty, and Desert, and Reputation, which are the Attractives of our Love and Affection, are likewise the Motives and Incendiaries of this Passion; they kindle and minister fresh Fewel to both these Fires."[80]

At the outset Othello presses Iago with questions because he is sure of himself and because he believes in Desdemona's chastity. He clutches the villain's suggestions without foreseeing the tremendous agony in store for him:

> And on the proof, there is no more but this, —
> Away at once with love or jealousy! [81]

Later, when he tells Iago how happy he would have been if he had known nothing[82] and voices his suffering in the lines which begin,

> O, now, for ever
> Farewell the tranquil mind! farewell content! [83]

Othello realizes how strong a structure passion may build upon a foundation of apparent kindness. Virtue, health, beauty, desert, and reputation, all qualities of Desdemona and all the attractives of love, serve as fuel to the passion originally enkindled by a

---

[80] *Op. cit.*, Bk. I, p. 216. James Ferrand (Ἐρωτομανία, *or a Treatise Discoursing of the Essence, Causes, Symptomes, Prognosticks, and Cure of Love*, 2d ed., Oxford, 1645, p. 189) gives an account of jealousy so similar in phraseology as to suggest borrowing.

[81] *Othello*, III, iii, 191-192. Professor E. E. Stoll (*"Othello*: An Historical and Comparative Study," *University of Minnesota Studies in Language and Literature*, No. 2, 1915, p. 12) considers these lines "classically presumptuous words." They should be compared with Charron's description (quoted above) of the way in which jealousy takes its hold.

[82] *Ibid.*, III, iii, 335 ff.

[83] *Ibid.*, III, iii, 347 ff.

"dangerous conceit" and fanned into flame through the machina-
tions of Iago in his constant effort to perpetuate and enlarge the
original concept for which he is responsible.[84]

Of the extent to which matters of little consequence disturb the
soul Charron says:

"Our soul is frequently thrown into violent Disorders, by little
Whimsies, a meer Fansie, a Dream, a Shadow and empty Amuse-
ment, without Substance, without Ground; and works it self up to
all the Excesses of Anger and Revenge, Joy and Grief, and Confusion; and all This with building Castles in the Air. The Ceremony of taking leave, the Idea of some particular Gesture in a parting Friend, strikes us deeper, and gives us more real Trouble than
all the Reasoning in the World, upon Matters of great Moment, is
able to do."[85]

Iago's knowledge of human conduct is so thorough that he knows
the force of trifles to move the soul.   He catches upon any word
or action which may arouse suspicion and repeatedly, through subtle
argument, suggests "whimsies" which he knows Othello will take
hold of.[86]   The psychology of this practice he reveals in the lines:

> Trifles light as air
> Are to the jealous confirmations strong
> As proofs of holy writ. [87]

Iago knows that a passion once aroused will feed itself; he knows
that Othello, under the influence of jealousy, will seek to confirm
suspicion and judge everything that occurs as favorable to the passion.   Thus he is free to command:

> Look to your wife; observe her well with Cassio;
> Wear your eyes thus, not jealous nor secure. [88]

Othello soon urges:

> If more thou dost perceive, let me know more;
> Set on thy wife to observe.[89]

The characteristic of the passions expressed here is one which
Shakespeare might have noted from observation; but it is also a

---

[84] Craig, "Shakespeare's Depiction of Passions," *loc. cit.*, pp. 290-291.

[85] *Op. cit.*, Bk. I, p. 295.

[86] Note, for example, the subtlety of argument he uses in Act IV, sc. i,
ll. 10 ff. to keep alive and enlarge upon a "meer Fansie"—that of the
handkerchief—which he has awakened in Othello's mind.

[87] *Ibid.*, III, iii, 321-323.

[88] *Ibid.*, III, iii, 197-198.

[89] *Ibid.*, III, iii, 239-240.

characteristic discussed frequently in connection with jealousy.
Charron says of the passion:

"This is *Wormwood* and *Gall* to us: It depraves and embitters
all the Sweets of life . . . . It turns Love into Hatred, Respect into
Disdain, Assurance into Distrust: It breeds a most unhappy Curiosity; Makes us busie and inquisitive to our own Ruin; desirous and
impatient to know what nothing but the Ignorance of, can keep us
tolerably easie under; and what, when we do know, there is no Cure
for, but such as makes the Misfortune worse, and more painful."[90]

He who is jealous "*hunts after every word he hears, every whisper,
and amplifies it to himself . . . . with a most unjust calumny of
others, he misinterprets every thing is said or done, most apt to
mistake or misconstrue,* he pries into every corner, follows close, ob-
serves to an hair."[91]

In Act IV, scene i (to take a single illustration), a most unhappy
curiosity prompts Othello to ply Iago with questions: his passion
is feeding itself. Iago knows his victim and he knows the power of
passion to blind apprehension. Thus he arranges to speak with
Cassio of Bianca in the presence of Othello. As Cassio smiles,

> Othello shall go mad;
> And his unbookish jealousy must construe
> Poor Cassio's smiles, gestures, and light behaviors
> Quite in the wrong. [92]

As the interview proceeds Othello misinterprets everything that
is said and done.

"Those which are jealous," writes Burton, "most part, if they
be not otherwise relieved, *proceed from suspicion to hatred, from
hatred to frenzy, madness, injury, murder, and despair.*"[93] Here
the way in which jealousy leads to catastrophe is set for us. Through
hunting after evidence, amplifying, and misinterpreting, Othello
proceeds from suspicion, to frenzy, to madness, to murder, and to
despair which eventuates in self-destruction. With remarkable in-
sight into human behavior and with an accurate knowledge of contemporary psychology, Shakespeare has described the culmination
of a dreadful passion in the heart of one "not easily jealous."

Nature has placed the affections in the heart as a means by which
the soul may accomplish its purposes, but she has also given them

---

90 *Op. cit.*, Bk. I, pp. 216-217.
91 Burton, *op. cit.*, Vol. III, p. 322.
92 *Othello*, IV, i, 101-104.
93 *Op. cit.*, Vol. III, p. 329.

power to rise above reason and lead man to his own destruction. Obviously the intellect—life itself—is in constant danger; man must know how to regulate wild and restive emotion, at once his friend and his foe. An exhaustive account of the methods he may use would prove tedious and unprofitable to our purpose; only those common to Elizabethan treatises and to Shakespeare need consideration here.

We have already seen in connection with madness that a person should be removed from objects which may provoke distemperature.[94] One may prevent the growth of passion by avoiding anything which may stimulate it through sense. When Othello learns of midnight brawling among his subordinate officers, he says:

> Now, by heaven,
> My blood begins my safer guides to rule;
> And passion, having my best judgement collied,
> Assays to lead the way. If I once stir
> Or do but lift this arm, the best of you
> Shall sink in my rebuke. [95]

The principle he puts into practice is one which Charron advises: when confronted by provocation to anger one should refrain from movement of the body, "for any sort of agitation of our Limbs, Hands, Feet, but especially of the Tongue, sets the blood and humours presently into a ferment, and kindles a fire in the Soul."[96]

One of the ways in which prudence may be exercised against passion, Wright says, is—

"not to vex and trouble thy selfe too much when a passion seizeth vpon thee, but diverting thy mind from it, and restraining thy consent aswell as thou canst from yielding vnto it; and in short time thou shalt see it vanish away . . . . either because the humor which was moued, returneth to his former seat, or the impression made in the imagination diminisheth, or the attention of the soule distracted with other matter, faileth, or some other passion expelleth it, or the deuill ceaseth to tempt, either . . . . all these, or most of them mitigate, consume, and wholly subuert that passion which before so troubled us, and seemed insuperable."[97]

Some such reasoning as this lies back of Henry IV's advice to Clarence concerning Prince Hal:

---

[94] See above, p. 92.
[95] *Othello*, II, iii, 204-209.
[96] *Op. cit.*, Bk. III, p. 664.
[97] *Op. cit.*, p. 94.

> Chide him for faults, and do it reverently,
> When you perceive his blood inclin'd to mirth;
> But, being moody, give him time and scope,
> Till that his passions, like a whale on ground,
> Confound themselves with working. [98]

Important also is the theory that one passion may drive out another. As a remedy against the attack of "a most vehement rebellious motion," Wright suggests that one should resolutely turn the force of his soul to a contrary passion and "with one naile driue out another."[99]   In Shakespeare, Pericles urges:

> O Helicanus, strike me, honoured sir;
> Give me a gash, put me to present pain;
> Lest this great sea of joys rushing upon me
> O'erbear the shores of my mortality,
> And drown me with their sweetness. [100]

One need not always stifle a passion with a contrary passion, however. A greater grief will quench a lesser grief, and a greater love a lesser love. "For the Passions are never equally poized, but one or other of them will always cast the Scales."[101]   The extent to which one passion may be used against another Shakespeare develops as fully as does the psychologist:

> Tut, man, one fire burns out another's burning,
> One pain is less'ned by another's anguish;
> Turn giddy, and be holp by backward turning;
> One desperate grief cures with another's languish.
> Take thou some new infection to the eye,
> And the rank poison of the old will die. [102]

The devices we have considered are only makeshifts against the tremendous power of passion. Man must possess fortitude, firmness of mind, and resolution of will—patience—if he wishes actually to withstand the onslaught of emotion. In "Wittes Pilgrimage," John Davies of Hereford writes,

> If Hope and Patience did not hold the Hart
> From being squiz'd to nought with gripes of griefe,
> It could not bee by Nature, nor by Arte,
> But Death would hold that Seate of Life in chiefe: . . . .
> So that in patience, only wee possesse
> The Soules we haue, which haue the Liues we hold;

---

[98] *2 Henry IV*, IV, iv, 37-41.

[99] *Op. cit.*, p. 84.

[100] *Pericles*, V, i, 192-196.

[101] Charron, *op. cit.*, Bk. II, p. 11.

[102] *Romeo and Juliet*, I, ii, 46-51. Benvolio has reference to Romeo's love for Rosaline. For a further application of the theory to the cure of love, see below, pp. 120-121.

> And Hope sustaines the Soule in heauynesse:
> So patient hope is fraile Lifes strongest Hold.
> If both these vertues then in one must ioyne
> To make our Soules, and Bodies, ioyne in one . . . .
> Wee must inuoke the Heaun's to giue vs Hope
> Well arm'd with Patience, sith we liue thereby
> Secur'd in Dolors, which to Death lie ope,
> And make vs liue, when Death and Dolors die. 103

As sorrow grows upon him, King Lear cries to the heavens for patience;[104] the Queen in *Hamlet* implores her son to sprinkle cool patience upon his distemperature.[105] In Shakespeare and in psychological treatises there is a repeated urging to patience as the only sure safeguard against the enemy within the heart, an enemy dangerous in its power both to destroy the substance of the body and to usurp the place of reason.

---

103 *Loc. cit.*, p. 42.

104 *King Lear*, II, iv, 274. Cf. *ibid.*, II, iv, 233; *Troilus and Cressida*, V, ii, 68; *Julius Caesar*, IV, iii, 192; V, i, 106; *Measure for Measure*, V, i, 116.

105 Act III, sc. iv, ll. 122-124. Cf. *Romeo and Juliet*, I, v. 73; III, iii, 16; V, i, 27; *Julius Caesar*, III, ii, 145; III, ii, 250; *Coriolanus*, III, i, 191; etc.

CHAPTER VII

THE BODY AS AN INDEX TO THE SOUL: LOVE

According to an important doctrine inherited by the Renaissance from Plato[1] and the medieval psychologists, there should be correspondence between outer lineaments of the body and the nature of the soul: fair features presage a noble mind. "Now this outward *Gracefulness* of the *Body*, and more particularly that of the *Face*," writes Charron, "ought in all reason to be an Indication, and certain Evidence of the inward *Beauties* of the Soul. . . . . For surely nothing is more agreeable to Nature, than the mutual Relation and Conformity of the Body and the Mind."[2] Followers of Plato believed that beauty of the body is an image not only of the infinite and divine beauty of God but also of the beauty of the soul. Outward excellence proceeds from the internal bounty or goodness of the mind, just as the lustre of gems springs from a perfect mixture of the four elements, as flowers draw their beauty from roots, or as the countenance of a beast owes its fairness to a good interior constitution.[3] The doctrine is developed at length in Castiglione's *Courtier*:

". . . . beauty cometh of God and is like a circle, the goodness whereof is the center. And therefore, as there can be no circle without a center, no more can beauty be without goodness. Whereupon doth very seldom an ill soul dwell in a beautiful body. And therefore is the outward beauty a true sign of the inward goodness, and in bodies this comeliness is imprinted, as it were, for a mark of the soul, whereby she is outwardly known. . . . . The foul therefore for the most part be also evil, and the beautiful good. Therefore it may be said that beauty is a face pleasant, merry, comely, and to be de-

---

1 Note, for example, the following: "Everything that is good is fair, and the fair is not without measure, and the animal who is fair may be supposed to have measure. . . . . there is no symmetry or want of symmetry greater than that of the soul to the body: and this we do not perceive or ever reflect that when a weaker or lesser frame is the vehicle of a great and mighty soul, or conversely, when they are united in the opposite way, then the whole animal is not fair, for it is defective in the most important of all symmetries; but the fair mind in the fair body will be the fairest and loveliest of all sights to him who has the seeing eye."—*Timaeus, Dialogues of Plato*, 4 vols., B. Jowett, tr., Jefferson Press, Vol. II, 88, p. 578.

2 *Of Wisdom*, Bk. I, p. 39.

3 Coeffeteau, *A Table of Humane Passions*, p. 93 ff.

114

sired for goodness; and foulness a face dark, uglesome, unpleasant, and to be shunned for ill . . . . And it may be said that good and beautiful be after a sort one self thing, especially in the bodies of men; of the beauty whereof the nighest cause . . . . is the beauty of the soul . . . ."[4]

Similarly, La Primaudaye tells us that God created all things in such a way that He commonly joined beauty and goodness. In the following passage he suggests that, in so far as the activity of the soul depends upon the composition of the organs of the body and upon temperature, the correspondence has a definitely physical basis:

"For first, the beauty which appeareth without in any body, is as it were a witnesse and testimony of the beauty in the soule, according to that which wee haue already spoken of the agreement of the powers and affections thereof with the temperature of the bodie."[5]

There is a natural affinity between a well-formed body and virtue.[6]

In the world which Shakespeare creates, this doctrine becomes a basis of judging character. When Marina declares that her history, if recounted, would seem like untruths, disdained in the reporting, Pericles replies,

> Falseness cannot come from thee; for thou look'st
> Modest as Justice, and thou seem'st a palace
> For the crown'd Truth to dwell in. [7]

In *King John*, Constance tells us that had her son been ugly and malformed, she would not have cherished him; nor would she have expected of and for him great things. Since he is fair and princely, she cannot find contentment:

> If thou that bid'st me be content wert grim,
> Ugly, and sland'rous to thy mother's womb,

---

4 Quoted from Thomas Hoby's translation, reprinted in *The Literature of Italy* (1265-1907), 16 unnumbered vols., edited by Rossiter Johnson and Dora Knowlton Ranous, New York, 1907, pp. 347-349. I have omitted Castiglione's argument (p. 348) that in the macrocosm beauty is always joined with that which is good and profitable.

5 *The French Academie*, p. 481.

6 See Ludovicus Vives, *Introdvction to Wisedome*, bound with Sir Thomas Elyot's *Banket of Sapience*, and *Preceptes of Agapetus*, London, 1550, without pagination, sig. B iiii; John Davies of Hereford, "Microcosmos," *loc. cit.*, p. 65; Bacon, *Of the Advancement of Learning, loc. cit.*, Vol. III, p. 368. Burton (*Anatomy of Melancholy*, Vol. II, p. 154) is skeptical of the relationship.

7 *Pericles*, V, i, 121-123. Cf. *Measure for Measure*, III, i, 184 ff; *Tempest*, I, ii, 457.

> Full of unpleasing blots and sightless stains,
> Lame, foolish, crooked, swart, prodigious,
> Patch'd with foul moles and eye-offending marks,
> I would not care, I then would be content;
> For then I should not love thee, no, nor thou
> Become thy great birth nor deserve a crown.
> But thou art fair, and at thy birth, dear boy,
> Nature and Fortune join'd to make thee great. [8]

The notion of correspondence between body and soul lies back of several passages in *2 Henry VI*[9] and in *Richard III*.[10] It appears again in *Hamlet*. The Prince cannot understand how his mother could choose as a second husband the "counterfeit presentment" of his father, who was

> A combination and a form indeed,
> Where every god did seem to set his seal,
> To give the world assurance of a man. [11]

Since his mother is no longer young, her folly cannot be attributed to the heat of blood. The faculties of the brain, when overpowered by ecstasy, reserve some quantity of choice. Neither madness nor the sickly part of one true sense, acting alone, could err as grossly as his mother has erred. Hamlet concludes, therefore, that her sense has been apoplexed—that the sinews have been filled with vapors or fumes which prevent the flow of spirits that carry reports from the outer organs to the brain and there perform the work of the internal senses. He suggests further that his mother's gross judgment may have been instigated by a devil.[12] The normal order of creation, as the dramatist presents it, is to join beauty with goodness to such a degree that one who sees clearly may estimate character in terms of the correspondence.

This Platonic conception of beauty as a symbol of virtue became, during the Middle Ages and the Renaissance, a fundamental principle in the psychology of love. There developed a cult of beauty in which physical features were extolled and catalogued according to conventional patterns.[13] The hair, for example, should be yellow.

---

[8] Act III, sc. i, ll. 43 ff.

[9] Act V, sc. i, l. 157.

[10] Act I, sc. i, ll. 14 ff; Act I, sc. iii, ll. 228-230; Act I, sc. iii, l. 293. For the relation of this doctrine to villainy, see below, pp. 142 ff.

[11] Act III, sc. iv, ll. 60-62.

[12] Act III, sc. iv, ll. 68 ff.

[13] Professor Walter Clyde Curry has made a study of the ideal of personal beauty in Middle English literature: *The Middle English Ideal of Personal Beauty; as Found in the Metrical Romances, Chronicles, and Legends of the XIII, XIV, and XV Centuries*, Baltimore, 1916. For a description of the

Castor and Pollux, Paris, Menelaus, in fact most amorous young men of all preceding ages, and even Venus and Cupid were yellow-haired.[14] Upon the testimony of Peter Morales, the Virgin Mary had hair of wheat color.[15] The hair is Cupid's net;[16] the eyes are love's fowlers, the hooks of love—lode-stars Shakespeare calls them —that in a moment cure madmen and make sane folk mad.[17] Of all eyes black are the most amiable and enticing.[18] Burton writes further of a high brow, white and smooth like the polished alabaster, vermillion cheeks, coral lips, a white and round neck, dimples, white and even teeth, black eyebrows, a little soft hand, and of many other conventional features said to be provocative of love.[19] He calls beauty a goddess whom the very gods adore; love's harbinger, love's lode-stone, a witch and a charm. Beauty is a dower in itself; it deserves a kingdom and immortality.[20] There was still during the Renaissance a "religion of beauty" and some of its devotees worshipped mere beauty, but the "religion" itself was grounded upon the principle that beauty is truth. "True and Native Beauty," according to Ferrand's interpretation of Galenic theory, consists not in fair and soft features, but in "the just composure, and Symmetry of the Parts of the Body, a due proportion of flesh, & the goodnesse of the Colour"[21]—in a body well tempered to the needs of the soul.

One is not surprised, then, to find that in Shakespeare beauty— not altogether mere beauty, but beauty as a symbol of virtue—is the chief provocative of love. Juliet teaches the torches to burn bright; she is

> Beauty too rich for use, for earth too dear![22]

Hero, Portia (*Merchant of Venice*), Desdemona, Imogen, and other noble women are all extolled for their beauty. And it is not only the lover who finds his lady fair: Othello achieves a maid

---

ideally beautiful woman of the Renaissance, see J. B. Fletcher, *The Religion of Beauty in Woman*, New York, 1911, p. 11.

[14] Burton, *op. cit.*, Vol. III, p. 91.
[15] *Ibid.*, p. 97.
[16] *Ibid.*, p. 92.
[17] *Ibid.*, p. 93.
[18] *Ibid.*, p. 95.
[19] *Op. cit.*, pp. 90-91.
[20] *Ibid.*, p. 76.
[21] James Ferrand, Ἐρωτομανία, p. 225.
[22] *Romeo and Juliet*, I, v, 49.

That paragons description and wild fame;
One that excels the quirks of blazoning pens,
And in the essential vesture of creation
Does tire the ingener. [23]

In their adherence to the principle of correspondence between
outer seeming and inner being, Shakespeare and his contemporaries
were not entirely blind to the fact that in actual life men and
women whose bodies have been well disposed by nature are sometimes evil. The fair Cressida proves false. This disparity, Castiglione says, in no way contradicts the theory that beauty inclines
man to goodness:

"I will not now deny that it is possible also to find in the world
beautiful women unchaste; yet not because beauty inclineth them
to unchaste living, for it rather plucketh them from it, and leadeth
them into the way of virtuous conditions, through the affinity that
beauty hath with goodness; but otherwhile ill bringing up, the continual provocations of lovers' tokens, poverty, hope, deceits, fear,
and a thousand other matters, overcome the steadfastness, yea, of
beautiful and good women; and for these and like causes may also
beautiful men become wicked."[24]

La Primaudaye assumes that God sometimes disjoins nobility of
mind from beauty to show that all good things are from His grace,
rather than from nature. Since God commonly offsets one thing
by another, He may provide the foul body with a fair mind, or
vice versa. Because many abuse the gift of beauty, He sometimes
lets men fall into vices so great that the deformity of their souls
brings disgrace upon their beauty.[25] Normally, however, lineaments
of the body indicate the nature of the soul.

To the Elizabethan, who believed that the soul is definitely instrumentalized and that a proper mixture of the elements within
a body affords a good constitution, gross disparity between outward
seeming and inward being was startling. Several times in Shakespeare, when the realization that beauty may shelter an unchaste
soul comes to a lover who thinks his lady false, the poignancy of
grief is heightened. In *Much Ado* the expression of Claudio's grief
is burdened with the lack of correspondence between Hero's fair
features and her deeds as Don John has represented them:

O Hero, what a Hero hadst thou been,
If half thy outward graces had been plac'd

---

[23] *Othello*, II, i, 61-64.
[24] *Loc. cit.*, p. 350. Cf. Charron, *op. cit.*, Bk. I, pp. 39-40.
[25] *Op. cit.*, p. 481.

> About the thoughts and counsels of thy heart!
> But fare thee well, most foul, most fair! farewell,
> Thou pure impiety and impious purity. [26]

The contrast between appearance and conduct is so monstrous that Claudio resolves to hang conjecture upon his eyelids to convert all beauty into thoughts of evil. The beauty of Desdemona, so fair and yet so foul, stings Othello to the quick:

> If she be false, O, then heaven mocks itself! [27]

From persons who are ugly or deformed one may expect evil deeds. Foul souls in such persons as Hero or Desdemona, women who paragon description, are so contrary to nature that upon discovering them one may well lose faith in humanity.

There is another theory important in the study of love, one which we have found significant for other passions—the theory that the senses are the doors of the soul through which knowledge must come and that the affections are stirred most readily through their mediation. The objectivity of Elizabethan thinking is indeed nowhere more apparent than in the psychology of love. Affection normally enters the soul through the eye. By often gazing, according to Burton's quotation from Ficinus, men drink or suck in love between them. Whoever has a clear eye, even though he may be in some respects deformed, by often looking upon a person will make him mad and *"tie him fast to him by the eye."*[28] Love may come through other senses: "The evident cause of Love, according to the doctrine of the Morall Philosophers, & Platonists, are five; to wit, the five senses: which the Poet understood by the five golden shafts of Cupid."[29] Heliodorus, Burton says, proves that love is a witchcraft that enters through the eyes, the pores, and the nostrils and engenders the same qualities and affections in man as were in the person whence it came.[30] Love may enter through the ears, "for there is a grace cometh from hearing . . . . as *well as from sight; and the species of love are received into the phantasy by relation alone."*[31] In Shakespeare, King Henry VI falls in love with Margaret of Anjou through Suffolk's report of her beauty and virtues;[32]

---

[26] Act IV, sc. i, ll. 101-105.
[27] *Othello*, III, iii, 278. Cf. *Cymbeline*, II, iv, 108-112.
[28] *Op. cit.*, Vol. III, pp. 96-97.
[29] Ferrand, *op. cit.*, p. 41.
[30] Burton, *op. cit.*, Vol. III, p. 96.
[31] *Ibid.*, pp. 72-73.
[32] *1 Henry VI*, V, v, 1 ff.

Desdemona is won by a tale.[33] The youth in *Venus and Adonis*
arms his heart against his ear.[34] But nearly always the eye is the
gateway of love.

> Did my heart love till now? Forswear it, sight!
> For I ne'er saw true beauty till this night, [35]

says Romeo when for the first time he sees the fair Juliet. The
Elizabethan hero falls in love with the maid who in his eye is the
sweetest lady that ever he looked upon;[36] and she proves worthy
of his love, for outward grace signifies inward grace. The Renaissance followed Plato's teaching that love takes its growth in the
soul through the medium of the eye.[37]

Love, thus entering through the eye, is likely to prove changeful,
for with the sight of a more beautiful person than the object of the
first love, the eye may receive an image which may drive out and
even replace a former passion. Shakespeare describes affection in
Love's Labour's Lost as being

> Form'd by the eye and therefore, like the eye,
> Full of strange shapes, of habits and of forms,
> Varying in subjects as the eye doth roll
> To every varied object in his glance. [38]

And in *The Two Gentlemen of Verona* he compares "the weak
impress of love" derived through sense to a figure

> Trenched in ice, which with an hour's heat
> Dissolves to water and doth lose his form. [39]

Upon the basis of this psychology Burton urges anyone suffering
from the affliction of love to compare his lady with other women;
to confer "hand to hand, body to body, face to face, eye to eye, nose
to nose, neck to neck . . . ." He suggests further that one should

---

[33] *Othello*, I, iii, 150 ff.
[34] Ll. 779-780. Cf. the sonnet upon love entering through the ears (Davison's *Poetical Rhapsody*, A. H. Bullen, ed., p. 100):
"Oft did I hear our eyes the passage were
By which Love entered to assail our hearts;
Therefore I guarded them, and, void of fear,
Neglected the defence of other parts.
Love, knowing this, the usual way forsook,
And, seeking, found a by-way by mine ear."
[35] *Romeo and Juliet*, I, v, 54-55.
[36] See *Much Ado*, I, i, 189.
[37] See *Phaedrus, loc. cit.*, Vol. I, 251, p. 556.
[38] Act V, sc. ii, ll. 772-775.
[39] Act III, sc. ii, ll. 7-8. Cf. Act II, sc. iv, ll. 200-202.

imagine his beloved in varying circumstances; for example, in coarse raiment, or dirty and besmeared with soot.[40] One should attempt to cure a friend who has become a slave to affection by persuading him that his beloved lacks conditions requisite in an "Absolute Beauty."[41] Benvolio is a good physician, therefore, when he urges Romeo to attend the feast of the Capulets: at this feast will sup the fair Rosaline and all the "admired beauties" of Verona; Romeo should go thither and with an "unattainted eye" compare the object of his love with other women. Romeo thinks Rosaline fair, because he saw her poised against herself, "none else being by."[42] He should forget to think of Rosaline by giving liberty to his eyes, by examining other beauties.[43] The power of one love to drive out another is expressed also in *The Two Gentlemen of Verona*:

> Even as one heat another heat expels,
> Or as one nail by strength drives out another,
> So the remembrance of my former love
> Is by a newer object quite forgotten. [44]

According to Elizabethan psychology, there are three degrees of knowledge and three correspondent inclinations of desire.[45] This theory is of the utmost importance in our study of love. Recently Professor Charles Read Baskervill[46] has related it to Shakespeare's conception of the suitors in *The Merchant of Venice*. He quotes a passage from Hoby's translation of the *Courtier*, in which the theory becomes the basis for differentiating three types of love. The details are so explicit that we may well consider an abridgment[47] of the passage here:

". . . . love is nothing else but a certain coveting to enjoy beauty; and forsomuch as coveting longeth for nothing but for things known, it is requisite that knowledge go evermore before coveting, which of his own nature willeth the good, but of himself is blind, and knoweth it not. Therefore hath Nature so ordained that to every virtue of knowledge there is annexed a virtue of longing. And be-

---

[40] *Op. cit.*, Vol. III, p. 239.

[41] Ferrand, *op. cit.*, pp. 221 ff.

[42] *Romeo and Juliet*, I, ii, 86 ff.

[43] Act I, sc. i, ll. 233-234. Cf. Lady Capulet's advice to Juliet: "Read o'er the volume of young' Paris' face."— Act I, sc. iii, l. 81.

[44] Act II, sc. iv, ll. 192-195.

[45] See above, pp. 24-25.

[46] "Bassanio as an Ideal Lover," *Manly Anniversary Studies in Language and Literature*, University of Chicago Press, 1923, pp. 90-103.

[47] My abridgment is made from the reprint in *The Literature of Italy*. In the discussion which follows, I am, of course, indebted to Professor Baskervill.

cause in our soul there be three manner ways to know, namely, by sense, reason, and understanding: of sense ariseth appetite or longing, which is common to us with brute beasts; of reason ariseth election or choice, which is proper to man; of understanding, by the which man may be partner with angels, ariseth will. Even as therefore the sense knoweth not but sensible matters and that which may be felt, so the appetite or coveting only desireth the same; and even as the understanding is bent but to behold things that may be understood, so is that will only fed with spiritual goods. Man of nature endowed with reason, placed, as it were, in the middle between these two extremities, may, through his choice inclining to sense or reaching to understanding, come nigh to the coveting, sometime of the one, sometime of the other part."—pp. 343-344.

Castiglione goes on to describe the three kinds of love. He emphasizes the vast difference between affection dominated by sense and affection controlled by the intellect:

"When the soul then is taken with coveting to enjoy this beauty as a good thing, in case she suffer herself to be guided with the judgment of sense, she falleth into most deep errors, and judgeth the body in which beauty is discerned, to be the principal cause thereof .... moved .... not with true knowledge by the choice of reason, but with false opinion by the longing of sense. Whereupon the pleasure that followeth it is also false and of necessity full of errors [pp. 344-345] .... and to enjoy beauty without passion, the Courtier by the help of reason must full and wholly call back again the coveting of the body to beauty alone, and, in what he can, behold it in itself simple and pure, and frame it within his imagination sundered from all matter, and so make it friendly and loving to his soul, and there enjoy it [p. 358] .... And besides, through the virtue of imagination, he shall fashion within himself that beauty much more fair than it is indeed. But among commodities the lover will find another yet far greater, in case he will take this love for a stair, as it were, to climb up to another far higher than it. .... And therefore, to come out of this so narrow a room, he shall gather in his thoughts by little and little so many ornaments that mingling all beauties together he shall make a universal concept .... This stair of love, though it be very noble and such as few arrive at it, yet is it not in this sort to be called perfect, forsomuch as where the imagination is of force to make conveyance and hath no knowledge but through those beginnings that the senses help her withal, she is not clean purged from gross darkness; and therefore, though she do consider that universal beauty in sunder and in itself alone, yet doth she not well and clearly discern it, nor without some doubtfulness, by reason of the agreement that the fancies have with the body. .... When our Courtier, therefore, shall be come to this point, although he may be called a good and happy lover, in respect of them that be drowned in the misery of

sensual love, yet will I not have him to set his heart at rest, but boldly proceed farther, following the highway after his guide, that leadeth him to the point of true happiness. And thus, instead of going out of his wit with thought, as he must do that will consider the bodily beauty, he may come into his wit to behold the beauty that is seen with the eyes of the mind, which then begin to be sharp and thorough seeing, when the eyes of the body lose the flower of their sightliness [pp. 359-360] . . . ."

Turned to account in *The Merchant of Venice*, this philosophy of love renders plausible the outcome of the lottery of caskets. Judgment, rising as it does from the dictates of sense, from imagination, or from understanding, is indicative of character. Love is as noble as the judgment from which it proceeds. Portia's father has arranged a device whereby the character of a suitor is tested in a twofold way: by his reaction to the substance of the caskets and by his interpretation of the inscriptions they bear. Only one who looks with the eyes of the mind can judge rightly upon these matters; only a true lover can win the hand of Portia. Thus the three suitors may be differentiated in character according to the bases of their choice.

Morocco passes over the lead casket, unwilling to hazard except for that which offers "fair advantages." For a moment he is about to assume desert. Then he is ensnared by the hope of gaining "what many men desire." To him the second inscription promises Portia, and apparently he thinks of beauty only as an appeal to sense, for he says nothing of virtue. His choice rests finally on the relative excellence of the metals before him: "Never so rich a gem Was set in worse than gold."[48] Morocco, who opens the golden casket only to learn that

All that glisters is not gold; . . . .
Gilded tombs do worms infold,[49]

relies upon sense. Had he been "old in judgement" his answer would have been embodied in fair Portia's picture. Aragon reasons with sufficient clarity to avoid the surface appeal of gold and to understand the implication of sensual satisfaction in the line,

Who chooseth me shall gain what many men desire.[50]

His judgment, however, is not "clean purged from gross darkness,"

48 Act II, sc. vii, ll. 54-55.
49 Act II, sc. vii, ll. 65-69.
50 Act II, sc. ix, l. 24.

as is the judgment of an ideal courtier. "By reason of the agreement that the fancies have with the body," he cannot pass the subtlest test of wisdom: lead must look fairer ere he will give or hazard. Aragon knows nothing of the humility essential to genuine affection;[51] hence he cannot ascend the stair which leads from sense through imagination to intellect, with its right judgment and perfect love. Bassanio has learned that mere beauty is but a "seeming truth."[52] Following the sure light of understanding, he knows that to be worthy of his love he must give and hazard all. Through self-abnegation, he passes beyond sense and imagination to the "point of true happiness." The inscription he finds suggests a contrast between the two extremes—love of sense and love of mind:

> You that choose not by the view,
> Chance as fair and choose as true![53]

The casket scenes build upon a theory of knowledge and desire current among Shakespeare's contemporaries. Upon the basis of this theory, lottery becomes a successful and plausible method of selecting a husband for Portia. Character expresses itself in judgment.

The imagination inclines either to sense or to reason; it communicates with the affections of the heart. Love may therefore be irrational, following sense, or rational, following reason. There appears in literature, accordingly, a frequent contrast not among three kinds of love but between love of the heart or mind, on the one hand, and love of the senses—desire, fancy, or frenzy—on the other.

> Love in the bosom is begot,
> Not in the eyes,

says Thomas Campion.[54] The contrast is stated clearly in two of Shakespeare's earliest plays:

> Love looks not with the eyes, but with the mind.[55]

> Young men's love then lies
> Not truly in their hearts, but in their eyes.[56]

---

[51] Professor Baskervill (*loc. cit.*, pp. 101-102) suggests the importance of humility and self-abnegation as characteristics of a true lover.

[52] Act III, sc. ii, ll. 88 ff.

[53] Act III, sc. ii, ll. 132-133.

[54] *Songs and Masques*, Muses' Library, p. 123. Quoted by Professor Baskervill, together with similar passages and references, *loc. cit.*, pp. 97-98. The contrast is, of course, a part of the larger theme of conflict between body and soul, reason and heart.

[55] *Midsummer Night's Dream*, I, i, 234.

[56] *Romeo and Juliet*, II, iii, 67-68.

It is implied in the well known lyric, "Tell me where is fancy bred."[57] Irrational affection is truly engendered in the eyes and fed with gazing; it takes the reason prisoner and causes man to pay his heart "for what his eyes eat only." It dies in the cradle of sense, as a result either of satiation or of a new impression by which one fire drives out another. Rational love is common to men and divine beings. It is a chaste and noble affection guided by the intellect.

> The will of man is by his reason sway'd;
> And reason says you are the worthier maid,[58]

says Lysander, who, although his eyes have been streaked with the juice of "love-in-idleness," knows the relationship that should be maintained among the faculties of the soul. At the opposite extreme is the ludicrous doting of Titania upon a mortal:

> Mine ear is much enamour'd of thy note;
> So is mine eye enthralled to thy shape;
> And thy fair virtues, force perforce, doth move me
> On the first view to say, to swear, I love thee;[59]

or the sensual passion of such characters as Edmund in *King Lear* and the Youth in *The Rape of Lucrece,* whose heart shall never countermand his eye.[60] The true lover must be on guard against sense.

Love, as a violent passion that enthralls one's whole being, is often regarded as a furious evil. Sometimes it is said to proceed from correspondent qualities of the blood or from complexions so constituted as to engender mutual affection; sometimes it is said to develop when two people have one mind, or when, through astral influence, they are constrained to love. According to an opinion which seems to have been rather widely current, love takes its hold through a process which is definitely physiological. The most explicit statement of this theory I have found is the following from *Theatrum Mundi*:

"[Philosophers have said] that when we cast our sight vpon that which we desire, sodainly certaine spirits that are engendered of the most perfectest parte of bloud, proceedeth from the heart of the partie which we doe loue, and promptly ascendeth euen vp to the eyes, and afterward conuerteth into vapours inuisible, and en-

---

[57] *Merchant of Venice*, III, ii, 62 ff.
[58] *Midsummer Night's Dream*, II, ii, 115-116.
[59] *Ibid.*, III, i, 141-144.
[60] L. 276.

treth into our eyes which are bent to receiue them, euen so as in looking in a glasse there remaineth therin some spot of breathing, and so from the eyes it penetrateth to the heart, euen so by lyttle and lyttle it spreadeth all about, & therefore the miserable Louer being drawen to, by the new spirits, the which desire alwaies to ioyne and drawe neere, with theyr principall and naturall habitation, is constrained to mourne and lament his lost libertie.''[61]

In mutual love there is a transference between two persons of beams and spirits, and afterwards one inclines to the other because *"his heart would have his spirits"*; the infection may come "at the twinkling of an eye,"[62] as it does to many of Shakespeare's characters.

Elizabethan writers generally concede that the heart is troubled in love, but they disagree regarding the chief dwelling place of the passion. The concupiscible appetite, according to Platonic theory, was sometimes said to reside in the liver; hence that organ came to be associated with affection. Burton tells us that rational love resides in the brain and irrational love in the liver. Both disturb the heart and carry it "a thousand ways by consent."[63] After citing various theories as to the source of love melancholy, he concludes that the malady is a passion of the brain, arising from a corrupt imagination.[64] With this opinion Ferrand agrees. The part affected by a passion, he says, is sometimes regarded as the seat and sometimes also as the cause of the disease. In love melancholy the brain is the part affected and the heart the seat of the cause, as in love the liver is a cause. The heart is the true seat of the affliction of passionate love.[65] Further on he states that rational love is an affection of the brain and irrational love an affection of the liver, but neither of the heart, "which suffers no whit at all in Love, but only by Sympathy."[66] It would seem, according to Ferrand and Burton, that the motion of desire resides in the liver but that, inasmuch as in rational love reason must judge and the will elect, this passion may be said to dwell in the brain and inasmuch as the mind, particularly the imagination, through creating many

---

61 Pierre Boaistuau, *Theatrum Mundi, the Theatre or Rule of the World*, John Alday, tr., London, 1581, pp. 192-193.

62 Burton, *op. cit.*, Vol. III, pp. 98-99. Cf. Ferrand, *op. cit.*, p. 220.

63 *Op. cit.*, Vol. III, p. 18.

64 *Ibid.*, pp. 63-64.

65 *Op. cit.*, p. 77 ff.

66 Pp. 115-116.

conceits fills the lover with either fear or hope, passionate love may be considered a disease of the brain. The heart is always a center of affliction; through promoting bodily changes which alter temperature and even undermine the substance of the brain, it may act as a cause of love melancholy.[67] Coeffeteau, on the other hand, states that an abundance of blood inclines men to love, not because the concupiscible appetite resides in the liver, where blood is made, but because the qualities of the sanguine temperament are also the qualities of love. Coeffeteau,[68] Wright,[69] and Bright[70] agree that all affections dwell in the heart.

Since Shakespeare sometimes refers love to the liver and sometimes to the heart, one cannot be certain which of the organs of the soul he considered the seat of the passion. Undoubtedly he believed that love is in some way dependent upon the liver; for even writers who confine all passions to the heart admit that the liver, in that it concocts blood and the other humors from which temperature very largely springs, may dispose one to or against love. If the organ is "burning hot" one will be inclined to love violently. A passage in *Twelfth Night* suggests that Shakespeare may have agreed with those contemporaries who name the liver as the seat of the impulse to love: the Duke says of women,

> Alas, their love may be call'd appetite,
> No motion of the liver, but the palate.[71]

Whatever may have been his opinion as to the seat of the first motion of love, one may reasonably conclude that the dramatist thought of love as enthroning itself in the heart and thus as being finally a matter of the heart, responding of course to an impression that comes through the brain from the senses:

> Young men's love then lies
> Not truly in their hearts, but in their eyes.[72]

Imogen calls her heart the mansion of her love.[73]

---

[67] Similarly, Fletcher, ("The Purple Island," *loc. cit.*, p. 39, n. h) prefers to regard love as seated in the liver and the moderate heat of that organ as more agreeable to the passion than are the fires of the heart, where anger dwells.

[68] *Op. cit.*, pp. 21 ff.

[69] *The Passions of the Minde*, p. 32 ff.

[70] *A Treatise of Melancholy*, p. 103.

[71] Act II, sc. iv, ll. 100-101. Cf. Act II, sc. v, l. 106; *Much Ado*, IV, i, 233; etc.

[72] *Romeo and Juliet*, II, iii, 67-68. Cf. Act I, sc. v, l. 54.

[73] *Cymbeline*, III, iv, 70.

Like any other passion, love gains its hold upon an individual by dispersing its effects throughout the body and particularly in the chief organs of the soul:

"Love, having first entred at the Eyes, which are the Faithfull spies and intelligencers of the soule, steales gently through those sluces, and so passing insensibly through the veines to the Liver, it there presently imprinteth an ardent desire of the Object, which is either really lovely, or at least appeares to be so. Now this desire, once enflamed, is the beginning and mover of all the sedition. . . . . But distrusting its owne strength, and fearing that it is not able to overthrow the Reason; it presently layeth siege to the Heart: of which having once fully possest it selfe, as being the strongest fort of all, it assaulteth so violently the Reason, and all the noble forces of the Braine, that they are suddenly forced to yeeld themselues up to its subjection."[74]

The influence of love, according to Ferrand's interpretation of Ficinus, is carried readily to all parts of the body by means of the spirits:

". . . . the Animall spirits being sent forth by the Lover to the person beloved, and from thence retorted back againe on the Lover; by reason of their wonderful subtilenesse and thinnesse, they are easily transmitted into the inward parts, and so communicating themselves to all the parts of the body through the veines and Arteries, they trouble the blood, and so cause this disease of Love . . . ."[75]

When love begets contemplation, the withdrawal of heat to the brain produces great distemperature, "which corrupting and consuming the whole bloud, makes the face grow pale & wanne, causeth the trembling of the heart, breeds strange convulsions, and retires the spirits in such sort, as he [the lover] seemes rather an image of death, then of a living creature."[76] In its extremity love may actually destroy the chief organs of the soul and thus man himself:

"I haue seene a Natomie made of some of those that haue dyed of this malady, that had their bowels shrunke, their poore heart all burned, their Liuer and Lightes all vaded and consumed, their Braines endamaged, and I thinke that their poore soule was burned by the vehement and excessiue heat that they did endure, when that the rage of loue had ouercome them."[77]

[74] Ferrand, *op. cit.*, pp. 67-68.
[75] *Op. cit.*, pp. 68-69.
[76] Coeffeteau, *op. cit.*, pp. 170-171.
[77] *Theatrum Mundi*, p. 192. Cf. Burton, *op. cit.*, Vol. III, p. 173.

The psychological effects of love are numerous and more variable than for any other passion. Through the quality of heat love acts as a vivifying power. It sharpens the imagination and lends subtlety to the wit; even the most stupid person upon falling in love may become poetic. Love instills courage and hardiness. Burton tells us that there is no man so pusillanimous, so very much a dastard, whom it would not incense, make of a divine temper and an heroical spirit.[78]

He adds further:

"As it makes wise men fools, so many times it makes *fools become wise; it makes base fellows become generous, cowards courageous .... covetous, liberal and magnificent; clowns, civil; cruel, gentle; wicked profane persons, to become religious; slovens, neat; churls, merciful; and dumb dogs, eloquent; your lazy drones, quick and nimble.*"[79]

Love has also its malign influence. When the heart and mind yield to its power,

"All's utterly lost .... the Senses are all out of order, the Reason is disturbed, the Imagination depraved, the discourses are all impertinent, and the poor *Inamorato* thinkes of nothing but his dearly beloved Mistresse. All the Actions of his Body are in like manner quite out of tune, he growes pale withall, leane, distracted, has no appetite, his eyes are hollow and quite sunke into his head. Then shall you have him ever and anon weeping, sobbing, and sighing by himselfe, and in perpetual anxiety, avoiding all company, and choosing solitarinesse; that so he may entertaine his melancholy thoughts with the greater freedome. Now Feare assaults him on one side; and then presently Despaire encounters him on the other."[80]

Burton gives a similar account of the behavior of those suffering from love. Although the lover may at times be merry, his passion is, for the most part, a plague and a torture:

".... the beginning, middle, end of Love is nought else but *sorrow, vexation, agony, torment, irksomeness, wearisomeness, so that to be squalid, ugly, miserable, solitary, discontent, dejected, to wish for death, to complain, rave, and to be peevish, are the certain signs and ordinary actions of a Love-sick person.*"[81]

[78] *Op. cit.*, Vol. III, p. 198.
[79] *Op. cit.*, Vol. III, pp. 197-198.
[80] Ferrand, *op. cit.*, p. 67.
[81] *Op. cit.*, Vol. III, p. 173.

"Love is little better then meere Madnesse," says Ferrand.[82]

This view of love as a passion that variously disturbs the soul was perpetuated and extended as much through literature, perhaps, as through works on the subject of mind. Burton cites many passages from classical writers in which are set forth the "vices" of love:

> Suspicions,
> Peace, war, and impudence, detractions,
> Dreams, cares, and errors, terrors and affrights,
> Immodest pranks, devices, sleights and flights,
> Heart-burnings, wants, neglects, desire of wrong,
> Loss-continual, expense, and hurt among.[83]

Among the poets of the Renaissance the sufferings attendant upon love were developed into many fanciful definitions of the passion.[84] Conventionally, the lover is represented as being torn between contradictory "properties" such as hope and fear, heat and cold, joy and sorrow.[85]

In some of his earliest plays Shakespeare incorporates conceits based on this semi-scientific and semi-poetic conception of love. In *Romeo and Juliet* there is Romeo's fanciful definition of love as a smoke

> made with the fume of sighs;
> Being purg'd, a fire sparkling in lover's eyes;
> Being vex'd, a sea nourish'd with lovers tears.
> What is it else? A madness most discreet,
> A choking gall, and a preserving sweet.[86]

Sylvius in *As You Like It* tells Orlando what it is to love.[87] Rosalind shows a knowledge of the signs of love melancholy—a lean cheek, a blue and sunken eye, an unquestionable spirit, a beard neglected, ungartered hose, a bonnet unbanded, sleeves unbuttoned, shoes untied, and a general appearance that demonstrates a careless desolation[88]—which would have proved creditable to a "Doctor of Physicke" such as James Ferrand. In *Love's Labour's Lost*, on the other hand, Shakespeare treats not of melancholy but of hopeful love; he gives an elaborate description of the power of love to

---

82 *Op. cit.*, p. 230.

83 *Op. cit.*, Vol. III, p. 163.

84 See, for example, Davison's *Poetical Rhapsody*, Vol. II, pp. 24, 59-60, 129, etc.

85 See *ibid.*, pp. 72, 56-57, 58, 59, 64, etc.

86 Act I, sc. i, ll. 196-200.

87 Act V, sc. ii, ll. 90 ff.

88 *Ibid.*, III, ii, 392 ff.

course through the body and vitalize all the faculties of the soul:
Love

> Lives not alone immured in the brain;
> But, with the motion of all elements,
> Courses as swift as thought in every power,
> And gives to every power a double power,
> Above their functions and their offices.
> It adds a precious seeing to the eye;
> A lover's eyes will gaze an eagle blind;
> A lover's ear will hear the lowest sound,
> When the suspicious head of theft is stopp'd;
> Love's feeling is more soft and sensible
> Than are the tender horns of cockled snails;
> Love's tongue proves dainty Bacchus gross in taste.
> For valour, is not Love a Hercules,
> Still climbing trees in the Hesperides?
> Subtle as Sphinx; as sweet and musical
> As bright Apollo's lute, strung with his hair;
> And when Love speaks, the voice of all the gods
> Make heaven drowsy with the harmony.[89]

Shakespeare's conception of love was fundamentally an incarnation of contemporary thought. It was a conception to which the philosopher, the moralist, the physician, the astrologer, and the poet had all contributed. With the passing of centuries many of its principles have been discarded, but that fact is of little consequence; they served in the creation of varied forms of love, ranging from the illicit passion of Edmund for Goneril and Regan to ideal devotion expressed in the lines,

> Love is not love
> Which alters when it alteration finds,
> Or bends with the remover to remove.[90]

[89] Act IV, sc. iii, ll. 328 ff.
[90] *Sonnet*, No. 116.

CHAPTER VIII

CONFLICT AMONG THE FACULTIES OF THE SOUL

Plato tells us that when the offspring of the Creator fashioned man they provided him with an immortal and a mortal soul. The latter they made subject to terrible and irresistible affections: pleasure, which incites him to evil, and pain, which deters from good; rashness and fear, foolish counselors; implacable anger, and hope, which may be deceived easily by sense and by all-daring love. Fearing to pollute the "divine principle" any more than was necessary, they placed it in the head and constructed the neck as an isthmus and boundary line between it and the mortal nature. Since one part of the mortal nature is superior to the other, they divided the trunk of the body into two compartments separated by the diaphragm. That part of the inferior soul which gives courage and spirit they placed nearer the head, between the diaphragm and the neck, that it might be directed by reason and join with it in restraining desires "when they are no longer willing of their own accord to obey the command of reason issuing from the citadel." That part of the soul which desires food and drink for the body they placed below the diaphragm; in this region, as far away from the council chamber as possible, they bound the desires "as a wild animal which was chained up with man and must be nourished if man was to exist."[1] In the *Phaedrus* the soul with its powers thus separated is represented as a charioteer with two horses not easily managed:

"Now the winged horses and the charioteer of the gods are all of them noble, and of noble breed, while ours are mixed; and we have a charioteer who drives them in a pair, and one of them is noble and of noble origin, and the other is ignoble and of ignoble origin; and, as might be expected, there is a great deal of trouble in managing them."[2]

Plato here suggests that sensitive faculties of the soul are likely to rebel against reason.

This notion of strife among the powers of the soul, retained and

---

[1] *Timaeus, loc. cit.*, Vol. II, 70, p. 561.
[2] *Loc. cit.*, Vol. I, 246, p. 551.

enlarged upon by the medieval philosopher, was, during the Renaissance, an important doctrine. Writers point out that conflict is inherent in the very nature of man, for he is allied through mind to celestial beings and through flesh to inferior creatures. The soul is illuminated or debased as it allows one or the other of the two forces to gain mastery. God placed the heart between the head and the belly, the vital virtue between the animal and nutritive virtues, and the will between the understanding and sensual faculties. Continuously the heart and the will must look upward that they may join themselves to reason rather than to sensuality; they are in the body as if they had been placed between heaven and earth, with power to turn in either direction.[3] The various faculties are so constituted, moreover, that they may readily dissent from the governance of reason. The external senses, it will be recalled,[4] are capable of a degree of knowledge and of pleasure and pain. Since they cannot comprehend the full meaning of objects presented to them, they report to the soul merely outward images, and in their reports emphasize qualities agreeable to sense rather than to the general welfare of man. As sentinels in an army sometimes err because they are not acquainted with the designs of the general, the senses, not knowing all that takes place in imagination and in reason, may accept enemies as friends.[5] Through their power to arouse the imagination they may provoke serious disturbances in the state of man:

"And when they go giddily to work upon this Imagination, and without ever expecting Orders from the *Understanding*, fall on immediately, and alarm the *Concupiscible*, and *Irascible* Faculties; then they raise Tumults, and Mutinies in the Soul; and while these last, there is nothing but Clamour and Violence; the Voice of *Reason* cannot be heard, nor the Commands of the *Understanding* be at all obeyed."[6]

External sense is man's first instructor. Instead of freeing him from deceit, however, it "deceiues him most."[7]

Imagination, also, is likely to become a foe to reason; in fact,

[3] La Primaudaye, *The French Academie*, p. 633.

[4] See above, p. 14.

[5] Charron, *Of Wisdom*, Bk. I, pp. 172-174.

[6] *Ibid.*, p. 174.

[7] Fulke Greville, "A Treatie of Humane Learning," *The Works . . . . of the Right Honourable Fulke Greville, Lord Brooke*, 4 vols., ed. Grosart, 1870, Vol. II, p. 7.

Elizabethan writers agree in describing this faculty as the general source of all our evils and disorderly passions.[8] Since it is near the outer senses, it may allure the soul to love that which is bodily and thus, as an intermediary between the senses and the affections, establish a coalition contrary to reason.[9] Opinion, or rash judgment, strengthens itself in the imagination, arouses the affections, and overthrows reason. It is a very dangerous guide:

". . . . a very hot and hasty Mistress; for as soon as ever we entertain it . . . . it seizes upon the Imagination; and there standing upon its Defence, strengthens it self as in a Castle, Mans all the Works, and holds it out against Reason; then it comes down to the Heart, and there stirs and agitates the Affections, with the violent Resentments of Hope and Fear, and Joy and Grief. In a Word, it is a perfect Incendiary in the State, looks out all the Fools, and Disaffected in the Soul, and blows them up into Sedition; raises the *Mobb*, that is, the Passions, and sets all in an Uproar and Confusion. And all this by taking wrong Methods, going Headlong to work, and not submitting the Matter to the *Understanding* . . . ."[10]

One should note especially that the imagination holds a crucial position among the faculties of the soul: it not only evolves ideas and, under normal behavior, recommends to the consideration of reason those that are of sufficient magnitude, but it also communicates with the heart, where the affections reside. This faculty thus has to do with both thought and action. "It is true," writes Bacon, "that the Imagination is an agent or *nuncius* in both provinces, both the judicial and the ministerial. For Sense sendeth over to Imagination before the Decree can be acted; for Imagination ever precedeth Voluntary Motion."[11] Nor is the faculty simply a messenger: the mind has over the body that commandment which a lord has over a bondman, but reason has over the imagination only that commandment which a magistrate has over a free citizen. The faculty has, or at least usurps, considerable authority.[12] Because of its freedom and its dualistic relation to reason and to the affections, it exercises a vital influence upon conduct.[13]

---

[8] See, for example, Charron, *op. cit.*, Bk. I, p. 160; Burton, *Anatomy of Melancholy*, Vol. I, pp. 291 ff.

[9] La Primaudaye, *op. cit.*, p. 423; John Davies of Hereford, "Mirum in Modum," *loc. cit.*, pp. 9-10.

[10] Charron, *op. cit.*, Bk. I, pp. 172-173.

[11] *Of the Advancement of Learning, loc. cit.*, p. 382.

[12] *Ibid.*, p. 382.

[13] Bundy, "Shakespeare and Elizabethan Psychology," *loc. cit.*, p. 522.

The powers of action—the affections and the will—are even more precarious to reason than is imagination. Although according to the law of nature they should remain subordinate to the intellect, the affections show an inclination to follow inferior powers of apprehension: the passions and the external senses are like naughty servants who bear more love to one another than they yield obedience to their master. This amity Wright attributes in part to the fact that the passions and the senses are submerged in organs of the body, whereas reason is independent of corporeality. The senses and the passions respond immediately to an object; reason deliberates.[14] The affections desire the good, as reason loves it, but they behold merely the present, which fills the imagination more largely than does the future; therefore reason is commonly vanquished.[15] Finally, the affections incline toward the outer wits because they were united to them before the intellect developed:

"... . for all the time of our infancy and child-hood, our senses were ioint-friends in such sort with Passions, that whatsoeuer delighted sense, pleased the passions; and whatsoeuer was hurtfull to the one, was an enemy to the other; and so, by long agreement and familiarity, the passions had so engaged themselués to sense, and with such bonds and seales of sensual habits confirmed their friendship, that as soone as reason came to possession of her kingdome, they began presently to make rebellion; for right reason oftentimes depriued sense of those pleasures he had of long time enioyed, as by commanding continencie, and fasting, which sense most abhorred: then passions repugned, and very often haled her by force, to condescend to that they demanded ... . "[16]

Reason, once having entered into league with the passions, becomes a better friend of sensuality than the passions were before; straightway it invents ten thousand kinds of delights which the passions, without the support of reason, could not have desired.[17]

Superior to the affections, and thus ultimately responsible for conduct, is the will, a faculty joined to the understanding as the affections are joined to the imagination. Through this power reason should be able to direct action, but there is an inferior kind of thought and action, that of the imagination and the affections, faculties that are often too impatient to stay in matters of great

---

[14] *The Passions of the Minde*, pp. 8-9.
[15] Bacon, *Of the Advancement of Learning*, loc. cit., pp. 410-411.
[16] Wright, *op. cit.*, p. 9.
[17] *Ibid.*, p. 10.

moment for mature judgment and choice, and often too powerful to allow the intellect to exercise right control. The success of this sensitive nature against reason depends in part upon the disposition of the will. Since the will is blind, it is often misled; no object, however evil, is without some means of insinuating itself into the liking of will.[18] Furthermore will is to an extent naturally inclined to yield to the affections. Thus Wright argues:

"Besides, the sensitiue appetite being rooted in the same soule with the Wil, if it be drawne, or flieth from any obiect, consequently, the other must follow; euen so, the obiect that haleth the sensitiue appetite, draweth withall, the Will; and inclining her more to one part than to another, diminisheth her libertie and freedome.

"Moreouer, the Will, by yeelding to the Passion, receiueth some little bribe of pleasure, the which moueth her, to let the bridle loose, vnto inordinate appetites, because she hath ingrafted in her, two inclinations, the one to follow Reason, the other to content the Senses: and this inclination (the other being blinded by the corrupt iudgement, caused by inordinate Passions) here she feeleth satisfied."[19]

Wright suggests also that the will, governess of the soul, loathes dissension; as an uncareful magistrate neglects the good of his own commonwealth to avoid a particular evil, it fears to displease the senses and consequently refrains from exercising over them the care which by nature it ought to use.

Elizabethan writers accept unreservedly the metaphysical theory of the freedom of the will. They agree that reason and judgment are joined to will not to govern and command but to direct and admonish through counsel. Regarding this freedom La Primaudaye says:

"After whilest the matter is in deliberation, she may command either to prosecute the same, or to deferre it to some other time, or to giue it ouer quite, and to turne the mind to some other thing, as it were a Prince among his Councell. And if the consultation be finished, and sentence giuen by iudgement, yet may the Will stay it selfe from desiring and following after that which is counselled and iudged to be good by reason. So that the whole consultation lieth in the liberty and choice of Will."[20]

The will may sanction the enactment of whatever seems pleasing

---

18 Hooker, *Of the Laws of Ecclesiastical Polity,* Vol. I (I, vii, 6), p. 172.
19 *Op. cit.,* p. 58.
20 *Op. cit.,* p. 445.

and often may refuse all counsel merely to show that it is mistress of the soul. Having liked a good, it may proceed to execution, stay execution, or even cease operation after the work has begun. It follows accordingly that the will, as Charron puts it, "hath the most commanding Influence upon a Man's Condition; and his whole Happiness in a manner depends upon it alone . . . . This draws the whole Man after it, and carries him whithersoever it self is determin'd; for he that conquers the *Will*, hath subdu'd the Person."[21] Understanding is merely a guide; will "finishes the Action, and determines the whole Matter; and in that respect the *Will* is superior even to the *Understanding* it self."[22]

This "most exquisite" piece of human nature, will, then, is subject to a depravity which extends itself to all the forces of man. Will may be depraved by the senses, for "Sensible Goodness is most apparent, near, and present; which causeth the Appetite [and through appetite, will] to be therewith strongly provoked;"[23] it may be depraved through false reasoning or through its own waywardness, arising in part from blindness, unrestrained freedom, and an inclination to content the senses. When will turns from understanding, there is nothing the soul can do except to exercise its power in agreement with sensitive faculties:

"[Will] loseth hir dignite, *and* becommith ministre unto the sences, which before were hir slaves, who usurpyng the pre-eminence, *and* having the affectis *and* Wylle holly at their commaundment, do possede the body as theyr propre mancion, leavynge nothynge to the soule, but to use onely hir powers after their sensuall appetites."[24]

There is nothing in the mind that must not obey will, "if she stande at strife, and wylle yeld no parte of hir right to hir aduersarie."[25] To retrieve a perverted will is almost impossible:

As easie wer't the *Ocian* drie to lave. [26]

This theory of the power of will is identical with the description Shakespeare gives through the mouth of Iago:

---

[21] *Op. cit.*, Bk. I, p. 163.

[22] *Ibid.*, p. 164.

[23] Hooker, *op. cit.*, Vol. I (I, vii, 6), p. 172.

[24] Sir Thomas Elyot, *Of the Knowledg which Maketh a Wise Man. A disputacion Platonike* (London, 1533), *Palaestra*, LXXXIII (1920), 57.

[25] Vives, *Introduction to Wisedome*, sig. D v.

[26] John Davies of Hereford, "Microcosmos," *loc. cit.*, p. 47.

" 'Tis in ourselves that we are thus or thus. Our bodies are our gardens, to the which our wills are gardeners; so that if we will plant nettles, or sow lettuce, set hyssop and weed up thyme, supply it with one gender of herbs, or distract it with many, either to have it sterile with idleness, or manured with industry, why, the power and corrigible authority of this lies in our wills.''[27]

It is implied in York's generalization based upon the folly of Richard II:

> Then all too late comes counsel to be heard,
> Where will doth mutiny with wit's regard; [28]

and illustrated superbly in the life of Mark Antony, who, indisputably wise in captainship when reason was at the helm, allowed his will to become "lord of his reason,''[29] and dallied away an empire at the feet of an Egyptian queen.

The doctrine that the faculties of the soul are likely both by arrangement and by nature to rebel against reason is fundamental in Elizabethan thinking. One finds it in nearly all the writings on the subjects of mind and ethics.[30] La Primaudaye, for example, points out that as man holds a middle ground between angels and brutes, so the heart and the will are drawn "betweene the head and the belly, and betweene reason with that part which is capable thereof, and the sensible part which is without reason." If the will unites with reason it will be able easily to resist sensuality and to remain mistress of the soul; but if will turns from the counsel of reason, it must serve instead of command, and consequently becomes "altogether brutish.''[31] If the will should keep its natural

---

[27] *Othello*, I, iii, 322 ff.

[28] *Richard II*, II, i, 27-28.

[29] *Antony and Cleopatra*, III, xiii, 4.

[30] The extent to which the idea of conflict among the faculties of the soul pervaded thought during the Middle Ages and the Renaissance is not to be estimated solely by its widespread expression in philosophical treatises. It appeared as a motive in Christian literature as early as A. D. 400 in Prudentius' *Psychomachia*, an allegorical epic consisting of a series of single combats between such characters as *Ira* and *Patientia*. It formed the basis of Middle English debates between the body and the soul, between the eye and the heart, and of Lydgate's *Reason and Sensuality*. The predominant theme of the moral plays is a strife between the good and the bad powers for the control of man. In Sydney's *Arcadia* (ed. Feuillerat, Cambridge Press, 1912, Vol. I, p. 339-340) there is an account of a "skirmish betwixt *Reason* and *Passion*" in which seven "reasonable" shepherds engage in an argumentative skirmish with seven "appassionated" shepherds. The idea of conflict underlies the second book of Spenser's *Faerie Queene*, John Davies of Hereford's "Humours Heauen on Earth" (*loc. cit.*, Vol. I), and many other works of the period.

[31] *Op. cit.*, p. 633.

estate—that is, if will should accept reason as councilor, the affections as servants, and the senses as drudges or slaves—men would be as gods:

"But if manne do forgette to set Wyll under the governaunce of rayson, and with a circumspect deliberation, to appoint unto hir limites and bondes . . . . After the bodie is eskaped from adversyte, or is delyvered of vehement peine and anguisshe, forth with the senses do prepare themselfes eftsones to rebell. And affectes, whiche as wanton girles be flexible or redye to inclyne to every motion, do prepare them with wanton countenaunce and pleasaunt promyses to allure eftesones Will to their appetite . . . ."[32]

So one might continue to multiply descriptions of the conflict between man's higher and his lower nature. Suffice it to point out, however, that the maintenance of rational supremacy is no inconsiderable task, inasmuch as reason must work through inferior faculties. The ideas upon which it deliberates come from the imagination, and this faculty may function in proper subordination or it may unite with the affections against the intellect. The affections may choose to follow sense and rash imagination. Reason has power to control action only through will, and will, we have seen, frequently yields to appetite. In the final analysis strife is largely a matter of conflict between reason and the powers of action, more specifically, between reason and the affections; for the senses and the imagination work disaster particularly through their power to command the affections, and the affections entice will from following reason. There should be a lasting union between heart and mind.[33]

Nearly always, however, the faculties of the soul dissent from reason. John Davies of Hereford says,

> The totall *frame* of *man's* divinest *part*,
> By *light* divine we see is out of frame;

---

[32] Elyot, *loc. cit.*, p. 61.

[33] See John Davies of Hereford, "Microcosmos," *loc. cit.*, p. 26. Professor Bundy (*loc. cit.*, p. 520) states that knowledge was generally thought of as a matter of the rational soul, while action was essentially a concern of the lower. A more exact interpretation of Elizabethan doctrine would be that there is a sensitive level of thought as well as a sensitive level of action. Right thinking and right doing spring alike from the supremacy of the intellect, understanding and will, but usually imagination determines thought and the affections control action. In other words, the intellect, both in the field of knowledge and in its capacity to direct action, must work through sensitive faculties. As the imagination is the source of material for thought, the heart is the source of energy for action.

> Th' antipathie betwixt the *Minde* and *Hart*,
> Giues but too good assurance of the same.[34]

In the same poem he adds,

> But, so farre off are we from curbing *Passion*,
> That wilfully we mount it, and so ride
> On it ε gallopp (spurr'd with *Indignation*)
> To all *Extreames*, where *Vices* all abide.[35]

This is the typical attitude: that the senses over-rule reason and desires lead the will; "the body commandeth the soule, and the cart is before the horse."[36]

Sometimes it approaches a conception of the total depravity of man:

> "But in spiritual things we will no good, prone to evil . . . . we are egged on by our natural concupiscence, and there is . . . . a confusion in our powers, *our whole will is averse from God and his law*, not in natural things only, as to eat and drink, lust, to which we are led headlong by our temperature and inordinate appetite . . . . our concupiscence is originally bad, our heart evil, the seat of our affections captivates and enforceth our will; so that in voluntary things we are averse from God and goodness, bad by nature, by ignorance worse, by art, discipline, custom, we get many bad habits; suffering them to domineer and tyrannize over us . . . ."[37]

Although he thus describes man as a creature generally yielding to the heart, the Elizabethan moralist does not question the ultimate responsibility of the intellect for action. Except when the instruments of the soul have become diseased, will may control the affections, if it so desires.[38] Treatises on the subject of mind are directed, in fact, to the end that man may know himself—for wisdom and virtue are matters of self-knowledge—and thereby exercise his reason in the proper regulation of sense.

> The knowledge of the *Soule*, and of her *Powres*,
> Is the *well*-head of *morrall-Wisdome's* flood,[39]

says John Davies of Hereford. Bacon relates the aim of rhetoric and logic to the problem of control through the supremacy of

---

[34] "Microcosmos," *loc. cit.*, p. 26.

[35] *Loc. cit.*, p. 39.

[36] Sr. R. Barckley, *The Felicitie of Man or his Summum Bonum*, London, 1631, pp. 662-663. Cf. *Merchant of Venice* (I, ii, 19-20): "The brain may devise laws for the blood, but a hot temper leaps o'er a cold decree."

[37] Burton, *op. cit.*, Vol. I, pp. 190-191.

[38] Craig, "Shakespeare's Depiction of Passions," *loc. cit.*, p. 293.

[39] "Microcosmos," *loc. cit.*, p. 38.

reason. "The duty and office of Rhetoric," he says, "is *to apply Reason to Imagination* for the better moving of the will." The end of rhetoric is "to fill the imagination to second reason, and not to oppress it"; the end of logic is "to teach a form of argument to secure reason, and not to entrap it." "The end of Morality," Bacon adds, "is to procure the affections to obey reason, and not to invade it."[40]

Moralists agree that the state of well-being, so far as it may be attained in this world, consists in the proper restraint of the imagination and the affections. Charron, in discussing the meaning of wisdom, says,

"And that Order [of our creation] consists in this, That the meaner and more gross Appetites should be kept in due Subjection, and that which is the most excellent part of our Nature, should controul and bear sway. That is, When Reason governs Sense, and Truth is preferred before false and empty Appearances."[41]

Man is never in his proper course when he disregards this "Universal Law of Nature." Accordingly, one is urged to cultivate temperance as a means of bringing about this *summum bonum*, a quiet mind. Virtue, temperance, and wisdom are all defined in terms of a well regulated soul:

"Vertue . . . . is a disposition and power of the reasonable part of the soule, which bringeth into order and decencie the vnreasonable part, by causing it to propound a conuenient end to it own affections and passions, whereby the soule abideth in a comely and decent habit, executing that which ought to be done, according to reason."[42]

"Temperance (saith *Plato*) is a mutuall consent of the soule . . . . causing all disordered and vnbridled desires to take reason for a rule and direction. . . . . This vertue then of temperance is a stedfast and moderate rule of reason ouer concupiscence, and ouer other vehement motions of the mind."[43]

"This [temperance] is the authority and superintendance of Reason over those eager and violent Affections, which carry our Wills towards Pleasures and sensual Delights. The curb of our Soul, the instrument to scumm off those Ebullitions, which by the Heat and Intemperance of the Blood are apt to boyl over; that so the mind may be preserved uniform, and in consistence with

[40] *Of the Advancement of Learning, loc. cit.*, pp. 409-410.
[41] *Op. cit.*, Bk. II, p. 82.
[42] La Primaudaye, *op. cit.*, 1586, p. 52.
[43] *Ibid.*, p. 181.

Reason: And not debase it self, by submitting, and accomodating its measures to sensible Objects, but preserve its rightful Superiority; and force them to serve and sute themselves to the Dictates of the Mind.''[44]

Wisdom Charron describes as a regular conduct of the soul, a pleasing harmony of judgment and will, and a well proportioned disposition; the passions, on the other hand, he calls the ague-fits of a distempered soul, the boundings and reboundings of folly, the wild skips and wanton sallies, the impetuous emotions, the rash, unguided flights of man, without any aim, order, or measure.[45]

Significant in this conception of temperance as the proper restraint of sensitive faculties, is a theory that man has a propensity either to virtue or to vice, natural in part and in part subject to such material influences as diet and climate; a theory which for the Elizabethan, who believed implicitly in a doctrine of elements, humors, and tempers as forming an intricate physiological correlation between body and soul, must have been significant in a way seldom appreciated today. "But sens of so many men as nowe we be, have bene, and shall be in the worlde," says Elyot in describing the power of will, "the bodyes in the principal humours, wherof they be compacte . . . . be of dyvers temperatures. Therfore be they in sondry wyse inclyned in the operation of theyr sences or wyttes.''[46] We are dealing with a theory which minimizes educational and environmental influences, with a theory elaborately physiological but never quite absolute in Elizabethan thinking.

> Who has a breast so pure,
> But some uncleanly apprehensions
> Keep leets and law-days and in sessions sit
> With meditations lawful? [47]

is a question Iago puts to Othello. Shakespeare and his contemporaries would have answered that none is proof against evil. There is no perfect temperament among mortal beings, but there is an infinite variety of temperaments and a varying temperament for each individual; and there is an infinite variety of conducts and a varying conduct for each individual. Something may be gained from a study of the instrumentalization of the soul in relation to good and evil. Let us note first the temper conducive to natural

---

[44] Charron, op. cit., Bk. III, p. 676.
[45] Ibid., Bk. II, p. 9.
[46] Loc. cit., pp. 56-57.
[47] Othello, III, iii, 138-141.

goodness, for the notion of villainy involves additional consider-ations.

Right conduct is a matter of the proper restraint of the affections and the imagination. But the ease with which temperance may be maintained varies according to the constitution of the individual and particularly according to the constitution of the more important bodily organs. When the instruments of the soul "are not crowded or over-burdened, but filled in such Proportions as sute well with their ordinary Custom and Capacity, and such as are convenient for a due discharge of their respective Duties, then all the Opera-tions of the Soul are gentle and mild, sedate and regular. But, on the other side, when any of these Parts are either put into a swifter or more violent Motion, or are heated above their ordinary and proper Temper, then they immediately feel a considerable Change, to the great Prejudice and Disorder of the Soul."[48] Likewise the sanguine temperament is a defense against the passions.[49]

A body in which there is an ill proportion of elements and humors, on the other hand, inclines the soul to evil. Regarding the intem-perance of love Plato says: "And in general, all that which is termed the intemperance of pleasure is unjustly charged upon those who do wrong, as if they did wrong voluntarily." In the same discussion he continues:

"For no man is voluntarily bad; but the bad become bad by reason of an ill disposition of the body and bad education: every man finds these things to be an evil and a mischief; and in like manner the soul is often vicious through the bodily influence of pain. For where the sharp and briny phlegm and other bitter and bilious humors wander over the body, and find no exit or escape, but are compressed within and mingle their own vapors with the motions of the soul, and are blended with them, they produce an infinite variety of diseases in all sorts of degrees, and being carried to the three places of the soul on which any of them may severally chance to alight, they create infinite varieties of trouble and melan-choly, of tempers rash and cowardly, and also of forgetfullness and stupidity. Further when men's bodies are thus made ill, and evil forms of governments are super-added . . . . here is another source of evil; and these are the two ways in which all of us who are bad become bad, through two things which are wholly out of our power."[50]

---

[48] Charron, op. cit., Bk. I, p. 169.
[49] Bright, A Treatise of Melancholy, p. 118.   Quoted above, p. 79.
[50] Timaeus, loc. cit., 87, p. 577.

The Renaissance still held this view: through the disposition of his body man may be inclined to evil; and his inclination is likely to be fostered by wrong education. Even under normal conditions truth and goodness are usually vanquished.

This belief that the body may dispose one to evil finds expression also in a theory presented in an earlier chapter, that there is a close correspondence between outer seeming and inner being. God created all things in such a way that he commonly joined beauty and goodness.[51] A lack of correspondence may arise from accident or from divine purpose; but generally bodily beauty signifies more good of the soul than does deformity. "For the Lineaments of the body do disclose the disposition and inclination of the mind in general,"' is Bacon's dictum.[52]

The notion of correspondence, although thus generally accepted, was not made to contradict the theory of the freedom of the will. By more than one author we are reminded that Socrates acknowledged that physical deformity gave witness rightly to the deformity of his soul, but that through persistent effort he amended his mind. "For use almost can change the stamp of nature,"[53] says Hamlet to his mother, and we may credit his statement, for Shakespeare was not a bad psychologist. " 'Tis in ourselves that we are thus or thus,"[54] is the pronouncement of another Shakespearean character, who, in spite of villainy, is a keen moralist. Take the words of one whose purpose it was to expound the workings of the mind: of habituation La Primaudaye says,

"Thus the actions of the Wil and power of desire in the soule.... when they are often reiterated, so that they grow to bee firme and stedfast, are called habits, because the Wil is so accustomed thereunto, that it becommeth more constant either in desiring one certaine thing, or in eschewing the same. Therfore as affections are more or lesse forward, more seldome or often vsed, more weake or strong, so they are called eyther inclinations or actions, or habits."[55]

Nemesius clearly places the ultimate responsibility for evil upon will, rather than upon any physiological weakness: "For vices consist not in our faculties; but in habits; and our habits depend

---

[51] La Primaudaye, op. cit., p. 481. See above, pp. 114 ff.
[52] Of the Advancement of Learning, loc. cit., p. 368.
[53] Hamlet, III, iv, 168.
[54] Othello, I, iii, 322.
[55] Op. cit., p. 461.

upon our *will*; and it is therefore the fault of our *will*, that we are evill, and not (*originally*) of our *nature*."[56]

These passages leave no doubt as to the ultimate responsibility of will for action; but one may safely say that the Elizabethan regarded as extremely difficult the task of overcoming a natural tendency to do evil. Complexion is "a fixed thing, ingenerate by nature, and not ouerthrowne but by some venimous quality directly opposit against it, or long custome of other disorder, whereby nature is supplanted in time, & growing in acquaintance with which first it misliked, and is ouermatched with a counterfet nature, gotten by vse of that otherwise is vnnaturall."[57] Burton admits that good discipline, education, philosophy, and divinity may mitigate and restrain the passions in some few men at some time, but he insists that, for the most part, the passions domineer and are so violent that, as a torrent which bears down all before it, they overwhelm reason and judgment, and pervert the temperature of the body.[58]

Villainy in Shakespeare, if it is to be rightly understood, must be viewed in the light of contemporary thought about the problem of evil. There are, to begin with, in the works of the dramatist certain characters whose evil deeds spring from external influences. To this class belong Iachimo, whose practices are ascribed to the effect of the airs of England upon his Italian brain,[59] and Scroop, who conspired against Henry V. The latter was tempered against villainy, not given to swerving with the blood. The king suggests that he must have been wrought upon by fiends,[60] and this for the Elizabethan would have been a sufficient explanation of treason. Evil spirits work readily upon the fantasy and the will; they know the course of the humors and attack us when we are least on guard.[61] Other characters possess an inherent tendency to do evil; they but follow the course to which nature has addicted them. Such, in general, are the bastards. Thersites in *Troilus and Cressida*, whom Achilles calls a crusty batch of nature,[62] declares himself in everything illegitimate;[63] the bastard half-brother of Faulconbridge

---

[56] *The Nature of Man*, pp. 573-574.
[57] Bright, *op cit.*, p. 104.
[58] *Op. cit.*, Vol. I, p. 289.
[59] See above, pp. 52-53.
[60] *Henry V*, II, ii, 111 ff.
[61] See La Primaudaye, *op. cit.*, p. 415.
[62] Act V, sc. i, l. 5.
[63] Act V, sc. vii, ll. 16 ff.

(*King John*) makes a similar confession,[64] but since he had a king
to his father, even though he is a bastard, he can boast of his composition.[65]   Don John is "compos'd and fram'd of treachery";[66]
his spirits "toil in frame of villainies."[67]   Of his mode of action
he says, "And it better fits my blood to be disdain'd of all than
to fashion a carriage to rob love from any."[68]   Similarly, Edmund
in *King Lear* allows an evil "complexion" to take its course; too
late he resolves to do a good deed despite his own "nature."[69]

Evil is of course natural to Aaron and Richard III.   The former
has a will irrevocably bent in the pursuit of evil.   He is fatted by
the very thoughts of villainy;[70] and when he is finally trapped,
confesses that he would do ten thousand evils worse than any he
has yet performed if only he might have his will.[71]   Once Shakespeare suggests the doctrine of correspondence between body and
soul: in an aside Aaron says,

> Let fools do good, and fair men call for grace,
> Aaron will have his soul black like his face. [72]

Repeatedly the doctrine is urged against Richard III.   He is like
neither his father nor his mother, but like a mis-shapen stigmatic,
marked by the destinies to be avoided;[73] he is a foul indigested
lump, as crooked in his manners as his shape;[74] an elvish-marked,
abortive, rooting hog, sealed in his nativity the slave of nature and
the son of hell; upon him sin, death, and hell have set their marks.[75]
"Why, love forswore me in my mother's womb!"[76] says Richard
of himself.   Further we are told that the circumstances and por-
tents attending his birth presaged no good.[77]   Evidently the dramatist had in mind the principle that the normal order of creation

---

64 *King John*, I, i, 209 ff.
65 *Ibid.*, I, i, 262 ff.
66 *Much Ado*, V, i, 257.
67 *Ibid.*, IV, i, 191.
68 *Ibid.*, I, iii, 29-31.
69 *King Lear*, V, iii, 244.
70 *Titus Andronicus*, III, i, 203.
71 *Ibid.*, V, iii, 187-190.
72 *Ibid.*, III, i, 205-206.
73 *3 Henry VI*, II, ii, 135-138.
74 *2 Henry VI*, V, i, 157-158.
75 *Richard III*, I, iii, 228 ff. and 293.
76 *3 Henry VI*, III, ii, 153.
77 *3 Henry VI*, V, vi, 44 ff. and 70 ff.

is to provide correspondence between body and soul; a principle
so widely held that his audience must have felt a relationship between Richard's foul body and his villainy.

Shakespeare does not make the practices of this victim of nature
absolutely foreordained, however. He gives us, in the first soliloquy
of *Richard III,* a remarkable instance of the wilful choice of evil.
Richard III argues that he is not shaped for "sportive tricks" or
for the "amorous looking-glass." In the "weak piping time of
peace," he has no delight except to see his shadow in the sun and
to descant on his own deformity. This is poor thinking, to be sure,
but we have no reason to doubt that Richard is sincere, or that
Shakespeare intended us to accept the lines at their full value. Instead of overcoming his inherent propensity to evil, Richard determines to gain recognition by procuring the English crown, and
he goes on to reveal his plot against Clarence. At the close of the
soliloquy he adds, "Dive, thoughts, down to my soul," words which
represent the final perversion of will. In the light of Elizabethan
thinking, they probably mean the wilful subjection of intellect to
a mode of thought and action guided by the desires of the heart.
Will chooses a course to which inferior faculties (because of the
disposition of their instruments) are very strongly bent. Here
Richard reasons himself into villainy and acquaints us with his
immediate plans. He gives us all that we need to know in order
to understand his character. And if one had asked the dramatist
how will, which loves only the good, can yield to so vile a course,
he might have replied that since Richard feels himself, and actually
is, deprived of many joys common to men who are like one another,
since his body is foul and naturally disposed to lead the soul in
evil ways, Richard finds no joy except to command, to check, to
overbear such as are of better person than himself. He makes his
heaven to dream upon the crown.[78] Will sets up a good which
should compensate for handicaps and disgrace. Thenceforth Richard judges as right everything which leads to his goal.

In the case of Iago there is no reference to the principle of correspondence between body and soul. Iago states some motives for
his actions regarding the validity of which much has been said.[79]

---

[78] *3 Henry VI,* III, ii, 147 ff.
[79] See Professor A. C. Bradley, *Shakespearean Tragedy,* 2d ed., London,
1922, pp. 222 ff.; Professor E. E. Stoll, "Hamlet and Iago," *Kittredge Anniversary Papers,* Ginn and Co., 1913, pp. 261-272.

With these motives there seems to be at least a partial psychological reasoning of the action, and this critics have generally failed to consider. In the first scene of *Othello,* Iago describes two classes of men who serve their superiors. The second, he says,

> trimm'd in forms and visages of duty,
> Keep yet their hearts attending on themselves,
> And, throwing but shows of service on their lords,
> Do well thrive by them, and when they have lin'd their coats
> Do themselves homage. These fellows have some soul. [80]

Such a one Iago professes himself to be. In following Othello he follows but himself;[81] his cause is hearted.[82] Thus far, Iago has been speaking to Roderigo, whom he is trying to bleed; he has been speaking, therefore, with a purpose, and we should not press the significance of his words too far. In soliloquy he declares that the thought that Othello may have seduced Emelia—a suspicion which was held abroad[83] and one which had troubled him enough to make him accuse his wife—[84] gnaws like poison at his inwards. Nothing can or shall content his soul until he is evened with the Moor. He suspects Cassio, too.[85] Here Iago is revealing himself to the audience, after the fashion of other Shakespearean characters who speak to us in soliloquy. He is reasoning himself into villainy just as Richard III reasons himself into villainy—that the audience may understand. His argument is flimsy—even to some extent an afterthought, if you will—[86] but on Iago's part it is sincere. It is the argument of a mind whose faculties have been perverted. To Roderigo, Iago says he has never found a man who knew how to love himself.[87] Self-love a psychologist contemporary with Shakespeare defines as the law of the flesh, sensuality, the enemy of God, the spring of vice, the root of impiety, the bane of Godly conversation, the object of mortification, the sink of sin, ever craving, never content, tyrannizing over the greatest, and overthrowing the least.[88] Iago implies that he has this self-love in a high degree. The psy-

---

[80] Ll. 50-54.
[81] Act I, sc. i, l. 58.
[82] Act I, sc. iii, l. 373.
[83] Act I, sc. iii, l. 393.
[84] Act IV, sc. ii, l. 147.
[85] Act II, sc. i, 304 ff.
[86] Bradley, *op. cit.,* p. 225.
[87] Act I, sc. iii, l. 315.
[88] Wright, *op. cit.,* pp. 14-15.

chology of Iago's conduct, it would seem, is grounded upon his self-love, upon a heart attending upon itself; and the good his will chooses is that which contents baser nature, often expressed by the Elizabethan in terms of heart, blood, or sense. His villainy springs from the functioning of a soul guided by what Hooker calls Secondary laws, laws grounded not upon sincere but upon depraved nature.[89] Reason, thus perverted to a mode of thinking urged by sensitive faculties, finds out a thousand ways of doing evil unknown to inferior powers. Iniquity yields service without bringing any qualms of conscience, and we should not be startled at Iago's imperturbability, superhuman though it may seem. Deeds are judged by their relation to the desires of the intellect, and Iago's intellect is in league with sensitive faculties. Great men in the way of truth know how to control emotion; otherwise they could not be great. Othello, Brutus, and Antony prosper so long as they are men whom passion cannot move. Similarly, great men who delight in evil curb emotion. They are actually immune to feelings of remorse.[90] The moral code of Iago and of other villains in Shakespeare—Aaron, Richard III, Edmund, and Don John—whose action is guided by Secondary laws, is,

> All with me's meet that I can fashion fit. [91]

Such a code, coupled with vigorous intellect, precludes display of passion.

Twice at least Shakespeare suggests that the villain in following his inclination to do evil declares himself to be beyond the pale of divine and human law.

> Thou, Nature, art my goddess; to thy law
> My services are bound, [92]

says Edmund in *King Lear*. Later he denies all influence of the stars, a thing no honest man would have done even though he knew that through the resolution of will one may resist the malignity of the stars as well as the evil effects of the body upon the soul. Richard III says,

---

[89] *Op. cit.*, Vol. I (I, x, 13), p. 199. Cf. Craig, ''The Ethics of *King Lear*,'' *loc. cit.*, p. 104.

[90] Cf. Macbeth's effort (ultimately successful) to gain this imperturbability, considered above, pp. 89-90.

[91] *King Lear*, I, ii, 200.

[92] *Ibid.*, I, ii, 1-2.

I have no brother, I am like no brother;
And this word ''love,'' which graybeards call divine,
Be resident in men like one another
And not in me, I am myself alone. [93]

According to Elizabethan psychology man loves because he can see the image of himself in others. Richard renounces kinship with other men and thus surely he renounces subservience to the laws of man. Self becomes the center of his world as it does of Iago's and perhaps of all habitual villainy.

The following is a description of three types of wicked men, taken from Charron's *Of Wisdom*. It contains much which is applicable to what has been said of evil characters in Shakespeare:

''Some, *first*, are perfectly incorporated with Evil, they Reason themselves into it; their Resolutions and the whole Bent of their Wills are fixed entirely in its Interests; or else long Custom hath got such a perfect Mastery over them, that they cannot Disengage themselves. These miserable Wretches are utterly abandoned; their very Understanding is vitiated, sees, consents to, and approves the Evil: And This usually is the Case, when Vice and Debauchery meets with a Strong and Vigorous Mind, and hath taken such deep root in it, that it comes at last to be naturalized, and of a piece with it; all the Faculties are tinctured, it is corrupted throughout, and Vice so closely interwoven, as to become a part of its Temper and Constitution. Others, *secondly*, have their Intervals of Folly only; They are wicked now and then by fits, just as any violent Gush of a Temptation disturbs or puts them out of their Course; or some impetuous Passion drives them headlong upon the Rocks; so that these Men are surprized, and carried away forcibly, by a Current too strong for them to stem. The *Third* sort are betwixt these two Extremes: They have a right Notion of Vice, consider'd in it self; and when they reflect upon their Fault abstractedly, do severely accuse and condemn themselves for it; and thus they differ from the First Sort, who are advanced even to the desperate degree of a good liking of Wickedness: But then they have not the violence or surprize of Passions or Temptations to qualify and extenuate their Crime; and in this respect they differ from the Second sort too. But these Men go to work in cold blood, and with great deliberation; they weigh Circumstances, and drive a Bargain as it were; observe well the Heinousness of the Sin; and then put the Pleasure or Profit it brings, into the contrary Scale; and thus they barter away their Souls, and are content to be wicked at a certain Price, and for such as they think a valuable Consideration.''[94]

Shakespeare, the reader will readily observe, has evil doers repre-

[93] *3 Henry VI*, V, vi, 80-83.
[94] Bk. II, pp. 97-98.

be pardoned and retain the effects.[102]   In Shakespeare only men who succumb to "Intervals of Folly" are truly penitent.

Shakespeare, of course, does not classify his characters.   Probably he never thought consciously of their being kinds of evil doers. All that I wish to point out is the extent to which his characters embody contemporary thought, and their greater reality when we know them as did the Elizabethans.

---

[102] Act III, sc. iii, ll. 53 ff.

CHAPTER IX
THE RELATION OF ELIZABETHAN PSYCHOLOGY TO ACTION AND CHARACTER

Shakespeare thought with his contemporaries on subjects of mind and ethics. His psychology was a crude explanation of observable facts, based on the science of the Middle Ages and motivated in its development by a desire to understand the functioning of the soul for the better regulation of conduct. In the preceding chapters we have found that a knowledge of the theories to which the dramatist subscribed, illuminates many passages in his plays. This knowledge is also pertinent in a right conception of action and character.

The affections, it will be recalled, are the means of action. Thought can be executed only when they, through their command of the humors and the spirits, provide sufficient energy for the deed. This theory that action depends upon the heart (where the affections dwell) seems to underlie Hamlet's words when he resolves to speak daggers to his mother, but use none:

> How in my words soever she be shent
> To give them seals never, my soul, consent! [1]

Frequently in Shakespeare it accounts for a language which to the Elizabethan must have been extremely vivid: the emotional state of a character and the efficacy of action are expressed in terms of the heart. "A thousand hearts are great within my bosom!"[2] says Richard III in his final rally of courage, which prompts him to set his life upon a cast. After the battle against Richmond has been waged a while, Catesby remarks,

> The King enacts more wonders than a man,
> Daring an opposite to every danger. [3]

Similarly, anger is represented as a passion which swells the heart until physical distress can be endured no longer:

> Break off the parley: for scarce can I refrain
> The execution of my big, swoln heart
> Upon that Clifford, that cruel child-killer. [4]

[1] *Hamlet*, III, ii, 416-417.
[2] *Richard III*, V, iii, 347.
[3] *Ibid.*, V, iv, 2-3.
[4] *3 Henry VI*, II, ii, 110-112. Cf. *Coriolanus*, V, vi, 103-104.

And in *Antony and Cleopatra* transformation in character is expressed in terms of heart. Of Antony, Philo says,

> His captain's heart
> Which in the scuffles of great fights hath burst
> The buckles on his breast, reneges all temper,
> And is become the bellows and the fan
> To cool a gypsy's lust. [5]

A knowledge of the importance of heart in executing and even (through powerful emotion) in directing thought renders more significant the injunction Macbeth sends to his wife regarding the first prophecy of the witches: "Lay it to thy heart."[6]

The relation of the affections to action is apparent also in several passages that have to do with the spirits. When Hamlet resolves to follow the Ghost, his arteries become so charged with spirits that they are as hardy as the Nemean lion's nerve. Later he cries,

> Hold, my heart,
> And you, my sinews, grow not instant old,
> But bear me stiffly up. [7]

To Banquo's Ghost, Macbeth says,

> Take any shape but that, and my firm nerves
> Shall never tremble. [8]

In making his last stand against Caesar, Antony will be "treble-sinewed, hearted, breath'd"; he will fight "maliciously."[9] Spirits lend erection to the body; they are fuel for action. When the heart contracts and withdraws the spirits to the center of life, the nerves tremble, and one loses the power to resist evil.

One's purpose, then, cannot be executed unless there be an emotional response sufficient to carry the soul to its desires. Accordingly, there is in Shakespeare a tendency to strike while the passion lasts, or even to work oneself into a state conducive to effective action.[10]

> If I talk to him, with his innocent prate
> He will awake my mercy which lies dead;
> Therefore I will be sudden and dispatch,

---

[5] Act I, sc. i, ll. 6-10.
[6] *Macbeth*, I, v, 14.
[7] *Hamlet*, I, v, 93-95.
[8] *Macbeth*, III, iv, 102-103.
[9] *Antony and Cleopatra*, III, xiii, 178-179.
[10] Craig, "Shakespeare's Depiction of Passions," *loc. cit.*, p. 294.

determines Hubert in *King John*, regarding the murder of Arthur.
A moment later he adds,

> I must be brief, lest resolution drop
> Out of mine eyes in tender womanish tears.[11]

But the young Prince is given time to prate, and Hubert's murder-
ous passion consumes itself. On the other hand, Lady Macbeth
feels the need of passion sufficient to

> Stop up the access and passage to remorse,
> That no compunctious visitings of nature
> Shake my fell purpose, nor keep pace between
> The effect and it![12]

Antony, before the dead body of Caesar, plays upon the emotions
of the mob until he is sure his purpose will be accomplished.[13] Before Harfluer, King Henry addresses his soldiers in a plea for effective passion, to be summoned, it would seem, through the resolution of will;[14] soldiers must be nerved to the fight.

The relation of the affections to action is particularly evident in
the psychology of despair, a passion by which the soul should be
made to desist from following after that which is impossible. In
its birth, according to Senault, despair is weak, but in its progress
it becomes bold; and whenever it sees that by withdrawing from a
difficult good the soul receives great injury, it takes courage and
puts forth all its strength to carry off the thing whose assured loss it
estimates. Inasmuch as despair has in it elements of both fear and
hope, it may proceed to the extreme either of cowardice or of
temerity. It proceeds to the former extreme when, in order not
to recognize its own strength, it withdraws from a good which can
be acquired; and to the latter when, in order not to admit its own
weakness, it engages in an affair which can be followed only by
an unfortunate end. Reason should decide when man may flee
without infamy and attack without temerity.[15] Despair, Burton
says, should not always be discommended, for many times, as in
wars, it produces extraordinary valor. It makes men "improve

---

[11] Act IV, sc. i, ll. 25 ff.

[12] *Macbeth*, I, v, 45-48.

[13] *Julius Caesar*, III, ii, 265-266.

[14] *Henry V*, III, i, 3 ff. Cf. York's resolution spoken with reference to his
desire for the English crown: "Now, York, or never, steel thy fearful
thoughts, etc."—*2 Henry VI*, III, i, 331 ff.

[15] *De l'Usage des Passions*, pp. 373-374.

their worth beyond itself, and of a forlorn impotent Company become Conquerors in a moment.''[16]

One sees readily that this reasoning accounts for tremendous outbursts of valor against insuperable odds. In the case of Macbeth,
despair is at first cowardly. As the English forces approach, Macbeth grows sick at heart, for he knows that he receives only mouth
honor from his followers.[17] With the approach of Birnam Wood
he ''gins'' to be aweary of the sun,[18] and finally the report concerning the nature of Macduff's birth brings a climax of coward-
liness; it cows the better part of his nature: he will not fight.[19]
Then comes the turning point. When the soul discovers that by
yielding to Macduff it must take part in an infamous evil—that of
living to be exhibited as ''our rarer monsters are''—despair lends
strength. Although the prophecies of the witches have fallen away,
Macbeth tries the last. Before his body he throws his warlike shield
and urges,

> Lay on, Macduff,
> And damn'd be him that first cries, ''Hold, enough!''[20]

The psychology of despair probably underlies Cleopatra's words
to Seleucus, who has dared to humiliate her before Caesar by speaking the truth about the treasures she has withheld:

> Prithee, go hence;
> Or I shall show the cinders of my spirits
> Through the ashes of my chance. [21]

We shall find that it also clarifies Enobarbus' remark[22] concerning
the folly of Antony's resolution to oppose Caesar at Alexandria.

In *2 Henry IV*, Morton attributes the defeat of Hotspur's soldiers
at Shrewesbury to a lack of heart, and goes on to characterize the
Archbishop of York as one who binds his followers in double surety.
Hotspur

> had only but the corpse,
> But shadows and the shows of men, to fight;
> For that same word, rebellion, did divide
> The actions of their bodies from their souls;
> And they did fight with queasiness, constrain'd,
> As men drink potions, that their weapons only

---

[16] *Anatomy of Melancholy*, Vol. III, p. 450.
[17] *Macbeth*, V, iii, 19 ff.
[18] *Ibid.*, V, v, 49.
[19] *Ibid.*, V, viii, 17 ff.
[20] *Ibid.*, V, viii, 33-34.
[21] *Antony and Cleopatra*, V, ii, 172-174.
[22] *Ibid.*, III, xiii, 195-200.

> Seem'd on our side; but, for their spirits and souls,
> This word, rebellion, it had froze them up,
> As fish are in a pond.[23]

The Archbishop is followed both with body and with mind. Similarly, in anticipation of Macbeth's defeat, we are told,

> And none serve with him but constrained things
> Whose hearts are absent too. [24]

The doctrine expressed here—that successful action depends upon the orderly functioning of the sensitive and rational faculties of the soul, upon the co-operation of head and heart, reason and the affections with the proper restraint of the imagination—is of the utmost importance in Elizabethan psychology. It was fundamental, also, in Shakespeare's thinking, if one may take the evidence of his plays.

Antiochus clearly has the doctrine in mind when he says, after the riddle that for a long time has concealed his infamy has been solved,

> Till Pericles be dead,
> My heart can lend no succour to my head.[25]

His heart, in its hunger for the death of Pericles, has no regard for other matters that require attention. In *Troilus and Cressida*, Ulysses says of Achilles,

> Imagin'd wrath
> Holds in his blood such swoln and hot discourse
> That 'twixt his mental and his active parts
> Kingdom'd Achilles in commotion rages
> And batters 'gainst itself. [26]

Both passages imply that any departure from the rule of wisdom is likely to bring discomfiture, if not actually to prove one's undoing. Upon the basis of this principle, we shall find, are made some vital distinctions of character.

In the case of Hotspur the unhealthy force of inferior faculties is particularly evident. Of the King's final demand for the prisoners brought from Holmedon, Hotspur says,

> And if the devil come and roar for them,
> I will not send them. I will after straight
> And tell him so; for I will ease my heart,
> Albeit I make a hazard of my head. [27]

---

[23] Act I, sc. i, ll. 192 ff.
[24] *Macbeth*, V, iv, 13-14.
[25] *Pericles*, I, i, 170-171.
[26] Act II, sc. iii, ll. 182-186.
[27] *1 Henry IV*, I, iii, 125-128.

His father questions,

> What, drunk with choler? Stay and pause a while.

One recalls also such passages as the following, spoken under the influence of emotion:

> By heaven, methinks it were an easy leap
> To pluck bright Honour from the pale-fac'd moon,
> Or dive into the bottom of the deep,
> Where fathom-line could never touch the ground,
> And pluck up drowned Honour by the locks;
> So he that doth redeem her thence might wear
> Without corrival all her dignities. [28]

Of some of these utterances Northumberland says,

> Imagination of some great exploit
> Drives him beyond the bounds of patience. [29]

Worcester remarks,

> He apprehends a world of figures here,
> But not the form of what he should attend. [30]

Hotspur is the victim of imagination; and a powerful imagination, according to Elizabethan psychology, is likely to enroll the heart against reason. "With great imagination proper to madmen," he leads his powers to death and, "winking," leaps into destruction.[31] He goes down in defeat made glorious by his very boldness, but to a defeat imminent at the outset because of his inherent tendency to yield to sensitive faculties. Of this weakness in character his friends have been aware.

In *Coriolanus* a similar frailty assumes greater magnitude: the hero is by nature a tragic character in that he lacks the capacity to maintain a proper relation between the head and the heart. He is noble, to be sure, too noble for the world, and we with Aufidius[32] should rather condone what cannot be amended than denounce the whole man; yet the shortcoming proves fatal. The reason for the tragedy is clear:

> His heart's his mouth;
> What his breast forges, that his tongue must vent;
> And, being angry, does forget that ever
> He heard the name of death. [33]

---

[28] *Ibid.*, I, iii, 201 ff.
[29] Act I, sc. iii, ll. 199-200.
[30] Act I, sc. iii, ll. 209-210.
[31] See Lord Bardolph's comment, *2 Henry IV*, I, iii, 27 ff.
[32] Act IV, sc. vii, ll. 8-12.
[33] Act III, sc. i, ll. 257-260.

Volumnia knows her son; she knows that in all points but one he is like unto herself and that the difference is his weakness:

> I have a heart as little apt as yours,
> But yet a brain that leads my use of anger
> To better vantage. [34]

Reason should teach Coriolanus to control his proud heart in submitting to the common people. Under normal circumstances a man whose heart is his mouth prospers; but when a crisis confronts him, he is, as was Coriolanus, "too absolute." Consider Volumnia's argument upon the matter:

> You are too absolute;
> Though therein you can never be too noble,
> But when extremities speak. I have heard you say
> Honour and policy, like unsever'd friends,
> I' the war do grow together. Grant that, and tell me
> In peace what each of them by the other lose
> That they combine not there. . . . .
> If it be honour in your wars to seem
> The same you are not, which, for your best ends,
> You adopt your policy, how is it less or worse
> That it should hold companionship in peace
> With honour, as in war, since that to both
> It stands in like request? [35]

In war Coriolanus can make a politic subjection of heart to head, but when he is dealing with the common herd, he has too much pride. If, like his mother, he had possessed a capacity always to lead his heart to vantage, he would have placated the citizens and moved in triumph to the consulship.

In *Antony and Cleopatra*, Shakespeare had, a short time before, presented another great figure, who, in the struggle between his "mental" and his "active" parts, allows the latter to triumph and thus batters against himself. One may note at the outset that Antony is aware of his shortcoming, for he says to a messenger from Rome, whom he urges to rail with full license:

> O, then we bring forth weeds
> When our quick minds lie still; and our ills told us
> Is as our earing. [36]

---

[34] Act III, sc. ii, ll. 29-31.

[35] Act III, sc. ii, ll. 39 ff.

[36] Act I, sc. ii, ll. 113-115. Cf. Antony's words to Cleopatra (Act III, sc. xiii, ll. 110-114):

> "And when we in our viciousness grow hard—
> O misery on't! —the wise gods seel our eyes;
> In our own filth drop our clear judgements; make us
> Adore our errors; laugh at's, while we strut
> To our confusion."

Again, to Caesar, he confesses having swerved from the rule of wisdom: he did not deny arms, but

> Neglected, rather;
> And that when poisoned hours had bound me up
> From mine own knowledge. [37]

The Elizabethan knew that to be bound up from one's own knowledge is to tread dangerous ground. Antony knows, when he is himself, and he expects Cleopatra to know, that his sword, made weak by his affection, obeys affection on all cause. [38]

Furthermore, Enobarbus understands the nature of his hero's shortcoming. "Is Antony or we in fault for this?" asks Cleopatra regarding the ignominious flight at sea.

> Antony only, that would make his will
> Lord of his reason, [39]

is the prompt reply. In the same scene Enobarbus suggests again the psychology of Antony's action, this time of his resolve to challenge Caesar to single combat:

> I see men's judgements are
> A parcel of their fortunes; and things outward
> Do draw the inward quality after them,
> To suffer all alike. . . . .
> Caesar, thou hast subdu'd
> His judgement too.[40]

Once more, before the final stand against Caesar, this voice of reason speaks:

> Now he'll outstare the lightning. To be furious,
> Is to be frighted out of fear; and in that mood
> The dove will peck the estridge; and I see still,
> A diminution in our captain's brain
> Restores his heart. When valour preys on reason,
> It eats the sword it fights with. [41]

His words are probably based upon the psychology of despair. Whereas Antony has just predicted his own downfall (Act III, sc. xiii, l. 54) he now, in lines immediately preceding this passage, summons courage and resolves to fight until he makes Death love him. A normal reason may recommend that fear turn fury, and

---

[37] Act II, sc. ii, ll. 89-91.

[38] Act III, sc. xi, ll. 56 ff.

[39] Act III, sc. xiii, ll. 3-4.

[40] Ll. 31-37.

[41] Act III, sc. xiii, ll. 195-200. Cf. John Davies of Hereford's description of "*Feare* turn'd *Fury*," quoted above, p. 99.

control the passion which develops. Antony has already given way to emotion, however, and so he has been thinking weakly. With this "diminution" in his power to think, he is less able to resist the growth of passion. The return of tremendous courage continues the overthrow of his reason. Blind to his own weakness and to the peril confronting him, he thus engages in an affair which can be "followed only by an unfortunate end." There is in Antony a marked tendency of inferior faculties to dominate thought and action; this tendency at length proves fatal.

The theory that successful action depends upon a well regulated soul and that any departure from the governance of reason is dangerous, holds good, as Professor Bundy has shown,[42] for other tragic heroes. We need not pause to examine the evidence of a confederacy against reason as it operates in each character; let us consider, however, the problem of *Hamlet* to see whether we can bring together factors which may have a bearing upon its solution. Critics of dramatic technique have discovered the relation of the play to its antecedents, and their conclusions have set us right about many points. We may agree with Professor E. E. Stoll, upon the evidence of the *Fratricide Punished* and the *Spanish Tragedy*, that Kyd attempted to justify Hamlet's delay by introducing guards about the king, by turning feigned madness to account to make access easier, and by giving an appropriate character to the hero. Shakespeare dispenses with the guards, and so employs only the last method, characterization.[43] We are thus brought back to a study of character; and here of course a knowledge of other revenge tragedies is valuable. Character should be considered also with reference to psychology. If we read *Hamlet* in the light of Elizabethan theories about action, we shall find, with Professor Bundy,[44] that the moral problem of its hero is not very different from the moral problem of Shakespeare's other tragic heroes. Hamlet is a noble and vigorous character, but he possesses a tragic weakness, the tendency of the heart and the imagination to blind the intellect.

Hamlet's imaginative and passionate state of mind is made clear in the first scenes of the play; and the impression one gets at the outset, according to Shakespeare's dramatic technique, is seldom,

---

[42] "Shakespeare and Elizabethan Psychology," *loc. cit.*, pp. 530 ff.

[43] "*Hamlet*: an Historical and Comparative Study," *University of Minnesota Studies in Language and Literature*, No. 7 (1919), p. 14.

[44] *Loc. cit.*, p. 540.

if ever, gainsaid. When questioned, Hamlet acknowledges that he
has that within which passes show.[45] In his first soliloquy we find
him weary of life, brooding over his mother's rash marriage, and
finally resolving to stifle grief even though his heart may break.
When he talks with Horatio about the funeral and the marriage,
he thinks he sees his father in his mind's eye, but as yet he has heard
nothing of the Ghost.[46] In Shakespeare only characters who are
perturbed are subject to hallucinations. Hamlet is depressed when
the play begins. His melancholy, like any other passion, results
in conflict among the faculties of the soul — in a tendency of the
imagination and the affections to rebel against reason.[47]

In several cases Hamlet seems to undergo a real struggle to keep
passion or a too free imagination from subduing reason. "Till then
sit still, my soul," he says, anticipating the nightly return of his
father's spirit.[48] When the Ghost actually does appear, and Hamlet
follows it, Horatio (at all times master of himself) says of his
friend: "He waxes desperate with imagination."[49] Having heard
the revelation of the Ghost, Hamlet again attempts to still his heart.
While memory holds a seat in his *distracted* globe, he will remember
the apparition.[50] Visited a second time by the Ghost, Hamlet cries
out,

---

[45] *Hamlet*, I, ii, 85.

[46] Act I, sc. ii, l. 184.

[47] Professor E. E. Stoll ("Shakespeare, Marston, and the Malcontent Type,"
Mod. Phil., III, 1906, 289 ff.) believes that Hamlet is in some respects a
descendant of Marston's Malvole. Professor Levin L. Schücking (*Character
Problems in Shakespeare's Plays*, Henry Holt and Co., 1922, pp. 157 ff.)
shows that Hamlet possesses many characteristics of the melancholy type
described in the character books of the period. Psychologists, also, consider
these characteristics, and, since we have found that Shakespeare was conver-
sant with their theories, it is probable that he drew from them here. Miss
Mary Isabelle O'Sullivan ("Hamlet and Dr. Timothy Bright," *P. M. L. A.*,
XLI, 1926, 667-679) believes that he actually used Timothy Bright's *Treatise of Melancholy*.
Dr. Josef Wihan (*Die Hamletfrage, Leipziger Beiträge zur englischen
Philologie, Heft III*, 1921, pp. 32-33) points out that Hamlet's melancholy
is not a disease caused by the predominance of a humor, but a psychic state
arising from events which antedate the play. (Cf. Stoll, "*Hamlet*: an Historical and Comparative Study," *loc. cit.*, p. 72.) Hamlet's depression is but
a reaction of the kind which causes Claudio and Posthumus to suspect all
women, Othello to curse marriage, and Timon and Lear to rail against humanity. It is a melancholy which has sprung from perturbation of the mind;
as such, it expresses itself to some extent in behavior similar to that ascribed
to a person habitually afflicted.

[48] Act I, sc. ii, l. 257.

[49] Act I, sc. iv, l. 87.

[50] Act I, sc. v, ll. 93 ff.

> Save me, and hover o'er me with your wings,
> You heavenly guards! [51]

Later he adds,

> Do not look upon me,
> Lest with this piteous action you convert
> My stern effects; then what I have to do
> Will want true colour, tears perchance for blood. [52]

Hamlet realizes here that the last shred of rational supremacy is about to give way to inferior faculties. Finally, when he sets out to contend with Laertes, Hamlet acknowledges a troublesome heart: "But thou wouldst not think how ill all's here about my heart."[53] This last probably indicates merely a premonitory feeling. It is significant, however, that Horatio urges his friend to obey his *mind*, if it dislike anything. Still reason does not take cognizance of the illness about the heart; Hamlet defies augury and relies upon the special providence that rules even the fall of a sparrow. References to the heart and to the imagination and passionate utterances such as Hamlet several times gives vent to, were more significant for the Elizabethan than they are for us. Surely there is, then, in some of these passages, an indication of tragic frailty. But let us revert to the first communication from the Ghost.

Here Hamlet is warned not to taint his *mind* or to let his *soul* contrive aught against his mother.[54] The mind (frequently used of rationality) may be tainted by a too free imagination, or through vehement passion. The soul (frequently used of the heart—affections) may contrive only when it transcends reason. We know, from Hamlet's own testimony, that all is not well within him; we know, from the testimony of other plays, that only when man is not himself does he see the world as a "sterile promontory." The Ghost, therefore, strikes the crux of the matter when he charges Hamlet not to let inferior faculties outrun reason in the struggle between heart and head.

Several times, nevertheless, Hamlet becomes the victim of intense passion. After the First Player's speech he is carried away by powerful emotion. His outbursts against Ophelia and his mother are not prompted by reason. The latter feels his danger and urges patience; her words indicate the extremity of his passion:

[51] Act III, sc. iv, ll. 103-104.
[52] Act III, sc. iv, ll. 127-130.
[53] Act V, sc. ii, l. 222.
[54] Act I, sc. v, ll. 85-86.

> Alas, how is't with you,
> That you do bend your eye on vacancy
> And with the incorporal air do hold discourse?
> Forth at your eyes your spirits wildly peep,
> And, as the sleeping soldiers in the alarm,
> Your bedded hair, like life in excrements,
> Start up, and stand on end.   O gentle son,
> Upon the heat and flame of thy distemper
> Sprinkle cool patience. [55]

At the grave of Ophelia towering passion again subdues reason, and again the queen understands her son's frailty. She looks upon the display of feeling as a customary fit of madness, and knows the course it will take:

> This is mere madness,
> And thus a while the fit will work on him.
> Anon, as patient as the female dove,
> When that her golden couplets are disclos'd,
> His silence will sit drooping. [56]

After his emotion has subsided, Hamlet is sorry that to Laertes he forgot himself.[57] He is probably sincere when he tells Laertes that madness—certainly not real insanity, but the kind that comes from a heart at war with reason—is "poor Hamlet's enemy."[58] Hamlet acknowledges a weakness, the same weakness upon which the Queen has several times commented. Impatience under one set of circumstances argues a proneness to impatience.[59] Yielding to the heart, in Elizabethan thinking, does not mean an incapacity for action, but it does mean an incapacity to carry through uninterruptedly a rational plan of action.

Because of his distemperature Hamlet fails at times to understand the course revenge should take, a course directed by the head and put into execution by the heart. Note his reasoning following the First Player's speech:

> What would he do,
> Had he the motive and the cue for passion
> That I have? He would drown the stage with tears
> And cleave the general ear with horrid speech,
> Make mad the guilty and appall the free,

[55] Act III, sc. iv, ll. 116 ff.

[56] Act V, sc. i, ll. 307-311.

[57] Act V, sc. ii, ll. 75-76.

[58] Act V, sc. ii, ll. 241 ff.

[59] This interpretation is, of course, contrary to Professor Stoll's theory ("*Hamlet*: an Historical and Comparative Study," *loc. cit.*, pp. 22-23) that Hamlet has no tragic defect. Giving way to emotion, as Hamlet upon several occasions indisputably does, was for the Elizabethan indicative of grave frailty.

> Confound the ignorant, and amaze indeed
> The very faculty of eyes and ears. [60]

If we study this passage in the light of what other characters say in similar circumstances, we shall find that Hamlet here describes a procedure contrary to the normal way of seeking revenge. In Shakespeare—and in psychological treatises—"To weep is to make less the depth of grief."[61] Rather than drown the stage with tears, one consecrated to revenge should

> let grief
> Convert to anger; blunt not the heart, enrage it. [62]

Or he should follow the example of Titus Andronicus, who, although urged to take a course similar to that which Hamlet has in mind, to rend off his silver hair and gnaw his other hand with his teeth, has not another tear to shed:

> Why, I have not another tear to shed.
> Besides, this sorrow is an enemy,
> And would usurp upon my watery eyes
> And make them blind with tributary tears;
> Then which way shall I find Revenge's cave? . . . .
> Come, let me see what task I have to do. [63]

After a moment of self-chastisement, Hamlet realizes that he has been drawn "beyond the knowledge of himself": "About, my brain!"[64] He becomes aware of his shortcoming as he becomes aware of it in a later scene, when the Ghost returns to whet the "almost blunted purpose":

> Do you not come your tardy son to chide,
> That, laps'd in time and passion, lets go by
> The important acting of your dread command? [65]

Perhaps now we are in a position to consider Hamlet's action. There can be no question about the abuse of his mother and Ophelia,

---

[60] Act II, sc. ii, ll. 586-592. Professor Craig ("Shakespeare's Depiction of Passions," loc. cit., pp. 294-295) places a somewhat different interpretation upon these lines.

[61] 3 Henry VI, II, i, 85.

[62] Macbeth, IV, iii, 228-229.

[63] Titus Andronicus, III, i, 267 ff.

[64] In considering some lines from this soliloquy, Professor Bernard R. Conrad ("The Problem of Hamlet's Delay," P. M. L. A., XLI, 1926, 680-687) says that Hamlet's tendency to unpack his heart in words is at once the outcome and evidence of his disposition to think rather than to act. The fact that Hamlet turns his brain about (through resolution of will) is ample proof that here his "commerce" in words is not the result of rational thinking but of the supremacy of inferior faculties.

[65] Act III, sc. iv, ll. 106-108. Bundy, loc. cit., p. 543.

or about his grappling with Laertes in the grave: these spring from uncurbed passion. The killing of Polonius probably should be accounted for as action issuing from quick impulse; that is, from thought in which the imagination has not stayed for the verdict of reason. Hamlet took Polonius for the King. Having committed the deed, however, he is uncertain as to its nature. To his mother's question, "What hast thou done?" he replies:

> Nay, I know not.
> Is it the king? [66]

In Act V Laertes accepts Hamlet's apology for wrongs which might awaken his "nature, honour, and exception." He is satisfied *in nature*, and will stand aloof only in terms of honor.[67] If Laertes is sincere,[68] we must consider Hamlet's killing of Polonius a rash act. Nor is his procedure against Rosencrantz and Guildenstern the result of deliberation. In recounting the affair to Horatio, Hamlet says:

> Sir, in my heart there was a kind of fighting,
> That would not let me sleep. Methought I lay
> Worse than the mutines in the bilboes. Rashly,—
> And prais'd be rashness for it; let us know
> Our indiscretion sometimes serves us well,
> When our deep plots do pall.

Of his substituting a new commission he adds:

> Being thus be-netted round with villainies,—
> Ere I could make a prologue to my brains,
> They had begun the play . . . .[69]

Both passages imply that there was an element of rashness in Hamlet's method of thwarting the King's plot against his life.

But not all of Hamlet's action is rash, for Hamlet, like Antony, is at times master of his soul. When he is himself, he makes fools of Polonius and of his two school companions. As a rational being bent upon revenge, he makes arrangements for the play, not because he wishes an excuse, but because reason tells him what every sensible

---

[66] Act III, sc. iv, ll. 25-26.

[67] Act V, sc. ii, ll. 255 ff.

[68] Since Laertes makes use of the envenomed foil, one may rightfully doubt his sincerity. The progress of the duel shows, however, that he has some scruples of conscience. He wounds Hamlet only after he has been provoked by the words,

"I am afeard you make a wanton of me."
It would seem that "the King's to blame."

[69] Act V, sc. ii, ll. 4 ff.

Elizabethan knew—that the spirit he saw might have been the devil.
Hamlet is not hedging, as many critics, including Professor Bundy,[70]
still think, when he argues:

> The spirit that I have seen
> May be the devil; and the devil hath power
> To assume a pleasing shape; yea, and perhaps
> Out of my weakness and my melancholy,
> As he is very potent with such spirits,
> Abuses me to damn me. [71]

That the devil is very potent with melancholy spirits is good Elizabethan doctrine.[72] Furthermore, this final decision upon the play
comes after Hamlet has unpacked his heart in words, when he turns
his brain about for saner action. Again rationality asserts itself,
when he comes upon the King at prayer.

> He took my father grossly, full of bread,
> With all his crimes broad blown, as flush as May, [73]

is sound reasoning for a character in a tragedy of revenge, and
reasoning which served to stay the sudden impulse to strike. True
revenge demands an eye for an eye.[74] Finally it should be noted
that the soliloquy in Act IV ends in a resolution to act.[75] The King
has become the aggressor, however, and thus, upon Hamlet's return
to Denmark, the duel with its tragic outcome ensues.

As a king cannot govern his state wisely without the support of
subordinate officers, so the reasonable faculty cannot function rightly without the proper restraint and co-operation of lower faculties.
In Hamlet this relation has been disturbed. Rationality and the
sensitive powers struggle against each other for supremacy, as they
do, for example, in Mark Antony; and in many instances the latter
triumph. Hamlet, like the other tragic heroes, fails to maintain

---

[70] Loc. cit., p. 547.

[71] Act II, sc. ii, ll. 627-632.

[72] Stoll, "Hamlet: an Historical and Comparative Study," loc. cit., pp. 47-49.

[73] Act III, sc. iii, ll. 80-81.

[74] Stoll, "Hamlet: an Historical and Comparative Study," loc. cit., pp. 50-56.

[75] Professor Stoll (ibid., pp. 25, 38-39) directs attention to this resolution and to the actions which follow thereupon. He states further that in the re-mainder of the play Hamlet is himself—"what he has always been." Hamlet does not of course reproach himself again; nor does he show signs of ir-resolution. According to Elizabethan thinking, however, his outburst against Laertes at the grave of Ophelia is probably an indication of weakness.

a proper balance between head and heart, and this lack of modera-
tion is an important motive for the delayed revenge.[76]

If we now consider these tragic heroes as a group, we shall find
that they are not all cast in the same mold. Notably in Hamlet and
in Antony, a warfare of the soul has begun before the opening of
the play; in other cases, it develops during the progress of the
action. Men like Coriolanus have by nature a disposition against
the rule of reason, a disposition which is indeed a tragic *hamartia*.
King Lear has "ever but slenderly known himself;" "the best and
soundest of his time hath been but rash."[77] Flattery has nourished
his weakness.[78] His old age combines the "imperfections of long-
engraffed condition" and the "unruly waywardness that infirm and
choleric years bring with them":[79] Lear becomes a tragic figure.
Hardly may one describe such characters as Brutus and Othello as
men having by nature either too much heart or too much imagination. Although Brutus confesses in Act I that he has been troubled
of late with "passions of some difference," "conceptions only proper to himself,"[80] and eventually does allow his state to suffer "the
nature of an insurrection,"[81] we are to believe that he was a man
in whom the elements were so mixed that nature might stand up
and say to the world, "This was a man!"[82] and as such, generally
a man of unusual self-control. Othello has a heart not easily made
jealous;[83] he has kept himself well in hand, for he is reputed a man
who is "all in all sufficient."[84] Why, then, are Brutus and Othello
tragic characters? We may take the answer from *Timon of Athens*:
"A noble nature May catch a wrench;"[85] "every man has his
fault."[86]

---

[76] Professor Stoll (*ibid.*, pp. 8 ff.) has pointed out that before 1780, critics
did not consider Hamlet a perplexing character. The reason for this fact is
probably that men continued to think as did the dramatist. The passions were
still held to be enemies in the soul, often carrying man beyond the knowledge
of himself. No one who succumbs to passion, as does Hamlet in several instances, was expected to follow a very orderly and successful course of action.

[77] *King Lear*, I, i, 296-298.

[78] *Ibid.*, IV, vi, 97 ff.

[79] *Ibid.*, I, i, 300-303.

[80] *Julius Caesar*, I, ii, 39-42.

[81] *Ibid.*, II, i, 69.

[82] *Ibid.*, V, v, 73-75.

[83] *Othello*, V, ii, 345.

[84] *Ibid.*, IV, i, 275 ff.

[85] Act II, sc. ii, l. 218.

[86] *Ibid.*, III, i, 29.

For who so firm that cannot be seduc'd?[87]

asks Cassius, planning a way to arouse Brutus against Caesar. According to Elizabethan theory, there is no perfect temperament.[88] Brutus and Othello, like Gloucester and Edgar in *King Lear*, possess a noble, free, and unsuspecting nature, which is a tragic *hamartia*.

At the close of Hamlet's "To be, or not to be" soliloquy are the lines,

And thus the native hue of resolution
Is sicklied o'er with the pale cast of thought,
And enterprises of great pith and moment
With this regard their currents turn awry,
And lose the name of action.

The psychology expressed here, that "thinking too precisely on the event" may cause one to forego action, underlies the deeds of more than one tragic hero. Romeo stands upon sudden haste.[89] Macbeth knows that the "flighty purpose" is never overtaken unless the deed goes with it; he makes the principle the basis of his criminality.[90] Richard III is sudden if a thing comes into his head.[91] He has learned that "fearful commenting" is a "leaden servitor to dull delay."[92] These men are afraid of thought. They know that the imagination, which often urges men to desperate action, also "checks and enfeebles Men in their hottest Career; balks their Pleasures, and chills all their Spirits."[93] Upon the basis of this principle King Claudius urges Laertes to seek vengeance against Hamlet immediately:

That we would do,
We should do when we would; for this "would" changes,
And hath abatements and delays as many
As there are tongues, are hands, are accidents.[94]

Troilus goes so far as to discredit reason:

Nay, if we talk of reason,
Let's shut our gates and sleep. Manhood and honour
Should have hare hearts, would they but fat their thoughts
With this cramm'd reason. Reason and respect
Makes livers pale and lustihood deject.[95]

---

[87] *Julius Caesar*, I, ii, 316.
[88] See La Primaudaye, *The French Academie*, p. 535.
[89] *Romeo and Juliet*, II, iii, 93.
[90] *Macbeth*, IV, i, 145-148. Cf. Act III, sc. iv, ll. 139-140.
[91] *3 Henry VI*, V, v, 86. Cf. *King Lear*, V, i, 68-69.
[92] *Richard III*, IV, iii, 51-54.
[93] Charron, *Of Wisdom*, Bk. I, p. 158.
[94] *Hamlet*, IV, vii, 119-122.
[95] *Troilus and Cressida*, II, ii, 46-50.

At times these men who speak against deliberation also express a fear of conscience. Conscience, for Richard III, has "a thousand several tongues," each one condemnatory with several tales.[96] It is

> a word that cowards use,
> Devis'd at first to keep the strong in awe.[97]

Like the "pale cast of thought," conscience makes "cowards of us all."[98]

Desire for hasty action is contrary of course to the Elizabethan ideal for right conduct. In discussing such passions as cowardice and rashness La Primaudaye says: "He that doth anie thing at all aduentures . . . . not considering how well he doth it, ought not to be called vertuous: but onely if he put it in execution, after knowledge, consultation, and election."[99] And in Shakespeare men whose faculties are well balanced rely upon thought and conscience. Oxford, marching against Richard III, finds in conscience a spur to action:

> Every man's conscience is a thousand men,
> To fight against this guilty homicide.[100]

"And modest wisdom plucks me From over-credulous haste,"[101] says Malcolm when he places himself at Macduff's direction.

Enough has been said, I trust, to show that a wrong state of heart is the key to many of Shakespeare's characters. "Affection is my captain," says Tarquin in *The Rape of Lucrece*;[102] his course eventuates in banishment. To Isabella, Angelo says:

---

[96] *Richard III*, V, iii, 193.

[97] *Ibid.*, V, iii, 309-310.

[98] *Hamlet*, III, i, 83. Cf. the words of the Second Murderer in *Richard III*, I, iv, 137 ff.

[99] *Op. cit.*, 1586, p. 286.

[100] *Richard III*, V, ii, 17-18.

[101] *Macbeth*, IV, iii, 119-120. Accepting reason as a guide does not preclude rapid action:

> "True hope is swift, and flies with swallow's wings."
> —*Richard III*, V, ii, 23.

Eager to "advance the war" against Macbeth, Siward says:

> "Thoughts speculative their unsure hopes relate,
> But certain issue strokes must arbitrate."
> —*Macbeth*, V, iv, 19-20.

Such men as Macbeth and Richard III (who desire hasty action) are afraid of "thoughts speculative," which, through relating "unsure hopes," prevent bold undertakings.

[102] L. 271.

I have begun,
And now I give my sensual race the rein;[103]

but through the intervention of the Duke reason is restored and
Angelo saved from the ignominy toward which his heart led him.

From my succession wipe me, father: I
Am heir to my affection,[104]

declares another character, but one who is allowed to prosper because he has chosen more wisely than he knows. The tragic heroes
are less fortunate. The heart over which Cleopatra's charms have
gained full mastery sells an empire without a thought; the heart
fired by anger and jealousy kills the object of its love, and pre-
cipitates destruction upon itself. The supremacy of the imagination, of the affections, or a conjunction of the two—there can hardly
be one without the other—whether it be due to an innate disposition
against the rule of wisdom or to an "uncleanly apprehension"
keeping "leets and law-days" with lawful meditations in a well
regulated bosom and finally insinuating itself into the mind, is
nearly always fatal to an individual; hence this supremacy becomes
a dominant force leading to tragedy.

Shakespeare, as did his contemporaries, thought of action in terms
of the relation maintained among the faculties of the soul. He
not only presents great characters in which the "mental" and the
"active" parts are at war with each other, but he constantly keeps
before us the danger of yielding to the heart. Romeo's "I stand
on sudden haste" brings a warning,

Wisely and slow; they stumble that run fast.[105]

Later Friar Lawrence urges:

These violent delights have violent ends,
And in their triumph die, like fire and powder,
Which as they kiss consume. The sweetest honey
Is loathsome in his own deliciousness
And in the taste confounds the appetite;
Therefore love moderately; long love doth so;
Too swift arrives as tardy as too slow.[106]

Hector opposes Troilus;[107] and Enobarbus, we have found, reminds
us of Antony's folly in swerving from the rule of wisdom. Against

[103] *Measure for Measure,* II, iv, 159-160.
[104] *Winter's Tale,* IV, iv, 490-491.
[105] *Romeo and Juliet,* II, iii, 94.
[106] *Ibid.,* II, vi, 9-15.
[107] *Troilus and Cressida,* II, ii, *passim.*

the protestations of the Player Queen in *Hamlet* the Player King
posits a clear analysis of conduct guided by the heart:

> Purpose is but slave to memory,
> Of violent birth, but poor validity;
> Which now, like fruit unripe, sticks on the tree,
> But fall unshaken when they mellow be. . . . .
> What to ourselves in passion we propose,
> The passion ending, doth the purpose lose.
> The violence of either grief or joy
> Their own enactures with themselves destroy.[108]

In the last play, perhaps, to which Shakespeare gave his hand one
comes upon an extended argument against the violence of passion.
Cardinal Wolsey has just crossed the stage and Buckingham is about
to follow him. Norfolk protests:

> Stay, my lord,
> And let your reason with your choler question
> What 'tis you go about. To climb steep hills
> Requires slow pace at first. Anger is like
> A full hot horse, who being allow'd his way,
> Self-mettle tires him. . . . .

When Buckingham insists again that he must go to the King and
"cry down" the insolence of Cardinal Wolsey, Norfolk continues:

> Be advis'd;
> Heat not a furnace for your foe so hot
> That it do singe yourself. We may outrun,
> By violent swiftness, that which we run at,
> And lose by over-running. Know you not,
> The fire that mounts the liquor till 't run o'er,
> In seeming to augment it wastes it? Be advis'd.
> I say again, there is no English soul
> More stronger to direct you than yourself,
> If with the sap of reason you would quench,
> Or but allay, the fire of passion.[109]

Over against this emphasis upon the treachery of secondary
faculties in Shakespeare's plays and in psychological treatises, is
unlimited praise of the man who knows how to control emotion.

> Give me that man
> That is not passion's slave, and I will wear him
> In my heart's core, ay, in my heart of heart,[110]

says Hamlet to Horatio; and here one may feel reasonably sure
that the dramatist speaks also. A man who governs his passions
is "truely wise";[111] he is a king, although he may be without earth-

[108] *Hamlet*, III, ii, 198 ff.
[109] *Henry VIII*, I, i, 128 ff.
[110] *Hamlet*, III, ii, 76-78.
[111] John Davies of Hereford, "Microcosmos," *loc. cit.*, p. 40.

ly possessions.[112]   The heavens have not seen nor has the earth borne a more glorious person than the man who always obeys reason. Not all the crowns of the world can adorn his head fittingly; only eternity can recompense one of such high virtue.[113]   To have a quiet soul is the only pleasure of the world.[114]

The soul, it will be recalled, depends for its operations upon the body and the spirits.   The microcosm is subject in many ways to influences from the macrocosm.   Unless one indeed has strength of will, any variation in the humors or in temperament produces a corresponding variation in thought and action.   Furthermore, the faculties of the soul are by nature inclined to rebel against each other.   From these principles, fundamental in Elizabethan thinking, arises a conception of life different in an important respect from that to which we have become accustomed, and therefore significant in its bearings upon Shakespeare's method of handling character.

Psychological treatises accord high praise to the man who is at all times master of himself.   They enumerate devices to be used in control of the passions and continually urge us to patience; yet they represent life as a series of conflicting purposes and inexplicable actions.   The Elizabethan did not search for unity in human behavior.   His theory of the soul and of its relation to the macrocosm accounts for inconsistencies.   Our actions, Montaigne tells us, "commonly contradict one another so strangely, as it seemeth impossible they should be parcels of one Warehouse."[115] In the following passage Charron, also, stresses the variability and inconsistency of human conduct:

"Man is a Creature wonderfully Various and Mutable; and the great Difficulty of coming to any Judgment concerning Him, which should be certain, fixt, and universal, proceeds from hence, That our Lives are not all of a Piece, but made up of disagreeing and

---

112 Elyot, *Of the Knowledg which Maketh a Wise Man*, loc. cit., p. 95.

113 Senault, *op. cit.*, p. 98.

114 Burton, *op. cit.*, Vol. II, p. 117.

115 *The Essays of Michael Lord of Montaigne*, done into English by John Florio, 3 vols., London, 1908, Vol. II, p. 1.   Cf. the following: "Our ordinary manner is to follow the inclination of our appetite, this way and that way; on the left, and on the right hand; upward and downe-ward according as the winde of occasions doth transport us: we never thinke on what we would have, but at the instant we would have it: and change as that beast that takes the colour of the place wherein it is laid.   What we even now purposed, we alter by and by, and presently returne to our former biase: all is but changing, motion, and inconstancy.—*Ibid.*, p. 3.

different Parcels. Most Part of our Actions do not arise from steady Thought, but are sudden Starts and Sallies, the Effects of Accident and Impulse, and look like Shreds of several Stuffs patch'd up, and sewed together. . . . . And our Actions, 'tis plain, do so strangely cross and contradict one another, that it is not easie to believe so many Contrarieties should all be deriv'd from the same Original. We change and are not sensible of it: We run eagerly after every Whimsie of our own Appetites, and are born away by the Stream of Accidents and Passions; Tis no more Reason, but Inclination that governs us . . . . Thus our very Minds and Tempers vary too; the Climate, the Weather, and the Motions of Time and Seasons, make considerable Alterations and Differences in us. . . . . Our whole Life is nothing else, but one unequal, irregular, and many-figur'd Motion; nothing strait, nothing steady; We are perpetually moving and turning; and the very change of our Posture is so frequent, as to be an Uneasiness and Trouble to us. *No Man continues to wish and Design the same thing two Days together.* . . . . *Thus we shift our Characters each Moment, and act a Thousand several Parts.* . . . . [Man] is full of Doubles and Trickings; the closest, cunningest, and most Counterfeit part of Creation. He hath a Thousand little Closets and false Doors, where he hides, and comes out again; Sometimes a Man, sometimes a Monster; a Thousand Breathing-holes, at which he blows sometimes Hot, sometimes Cold, and almost blinds you with Cloud and Smoak. Every Agitation is but a fresh Folly; and the Course of his Life One Continu'd Errour. . . . .' "[116]

Modern psychology finds unity in human behavior; hence we have come to demand of our literary artists works that are well-knit in purpose and impeccable in characterization. We have also allowed ourselves to forget that Elizabethan thinking emphasizes variability and even inconsistency in conduct.

> Our wills and fates do so contrary run
> That our devices still are overthrown;
> Our thoughts are ours, their ends none of our own,[117]

says the Player King in *Hamlet.*

Shakespeare, accepting the view held by his contemporaries, could not have been greatly concerned with consistency in characterization. When we look for absolute unity in his characters, we are looking for something the Elizabethan did not recognize except as an ideal rarely attained; and consequently for something Shakespeare could hardly have striven to present in his tragic heroes. Usually, moreover, he was handling old material, sometimes even

---

[116] *Op. cit.*, Bk. I, pp. 328-330.
[117] *Hamlet*, III, ii, 221-223.

old plays. His characters do the things previously set down for them to do, and this fact may account in part for their inconsistencies.[118] Shakespeare was also making use of a theory which teaches that our lives are "not all of a Piece, but made up of disagreeing and different Parcels." Conflicting motives and contradictory actions could not have troubled him as they trouble us today. In the light of Elizabethan thinking, therefore, his characters are more rational beings than we have hitherto supposed. His plays in other respects, also, are richer in meaning.

[118] See Professor Stoll's articles on *Hamlet* and *Othello,* cited above and listed in the bibliography which follows; Professor Schücking, *op. cit.,* pp. 19 ff., 111 ff., etc.

BIBLIOGRAPHY

Abridgment of Sir Walter Raleigh's History of the World, 5 bks., London, 1698.

Aristotle's Psychology (*De Anima* and *Parva Naturalia*), William A. Hammond, translator, Macmillan Company, 1902.

Bacon, Francis, *Works*, new edition, 7 vols., edited by Spedding, Ellis, and Heath, London, 1889.

Barckley, Sir Richard, *The Felicitie of Man, or his Summum Bonum*, London, 1631. The work appeared first in 1598.

Bartholomaeus Anglicus, *De Proprietatibus Rerum*, translated and enlarged by Stephen Batman under title, *Batman vppon Bartholome, his Booke De Proprietatibus Rerum*, London, 1582.

Baskervill, Charles Read, "Bassanio as an Ideal Lover," *The Manly Anniversary Studies in Language and Literature*, University of Chicago Press, 1923, pp. 90-103.

Boaistuau, Pierre, *Theatrum Mundi, the Theatre or Rule of the World*, John Alday, translator, London, 1581. Earlier editions appeared in 1566 (?) and 1574.

Boll, Franz, "Die Lebensalter," *Neue Jahrbücher für das klassische Altertum Geschichte und deutsche Literatur*, Bd. XXXI, 1913.

Boorde, Andrew, *A Compendyous Regyment or a Dyetary of Helth*, 1542 (?). Reprinted in *Early English Text Society* (Ex. Ser.), No. 10.

Bradley, A. C., *Shakespearean Tragedy*, 2d ed., Macmillan Company, 1922.

Bright, Timothy, *A Treatise of Melancholy, Containing the Causes Thereof*, newly corrected and amended, London, 1613. Two editions appeared in 1586.

Bundy, Murray W., "Shakespeare and Elizabethan Psychology," *Journal of English and Germanic Philology*, XXIII (1924), 516-549.

Burton, Robert, *The Anatomy of Melancholy*, 3 vols., A. R. Shilleto, editor, George Bell and Sons, London, 1896.

Castiglione, Baldassare, *The Courtier*, translated into English by Thomas Hoby, 1561. Reprinted in *The Literature of Italy*, 1265-1907, 16 unnumbered vols., edited by Rossiter Johnson and Dora Knowlton Ranous [ed. de luxe], New York, 1907.

Charron, Pierre, *Of Wisdom*, 3 bks., George Stanhope, translator, London, 1697. The original, *De la Sagesse*, was printed at Bordeaux in 1601. There is a translation by Samson Lennard contemporary with Shakespeare.

Coeffeteau, Nicholas, *A Table of Humane Passions*, Edw. Grimeston, translator, London, 1621.

Conrad, Bernard R., "Hamlet's Delay—a Restatement of the Problem," *Publications of the Modern Language Association*, XLI (1926), 580-587.

Craig, Hardin, "The Ethics of *King Lear*," *Philological Quarterly*, IV (1925), 97-109.

————, "Shakespeare's Depiction of Passions," *Philological Quarterly*, IV (1925), 289-301.

Davies, Sir John, "Nosce Teipsum," 1599, *Works in Verse and Prose*, 3 vols., A. B. Grosart, editor, Fuller Worthies' Library, 1869, Vol. I, pp. 39-162.

Davies, John of Hereford, *Complete Works*, 2 vols., A. B. Grosart, editor, Chertsey Worthies' Library, Edinburgh, 1878.

Dialogues of Plato, 4 vols., B. Jowett, translator, Jefferson Press, New York.

Dowden, Edwin, "Elizabethan Psychology," *Essays Modern and Elizabethan*, London, 1910, pp. 308-333.

Elyot, Sir Thomas, *Of the Knowledg which Maketh a Wise Man; a Disputacion Platonike*, London, 1533. Reprinted in *Palaestra*, LXXXIII, 1920.

Essayes of Michael Lord of Montaigne, done into English by John Florio, 3 vols., London, Grant Richards, 1908.

Ferrand, James, 'Εϱωτομανία, *or a Treatise Discoursing of the Essence, Causes, Symptomes, Prognosticks, and Cure of Love or Erotique Melancholy*, 2d ed., Oxford, 1645. The earlier edition appeared in 1640.

Fletcher, Jefferson Butler, *The Religion of Beauty in Woman*, Macmillan Company, 1911.

Fletcher, Phineas, ''The Purple Island, or the Isle of Man,'' 1633, *Poetical Works of Giles and Phineas Fletcher*, 2 vols., Frederick S. Boas, editor, Cambridge University Press, 1909, Vol. II, pp. 1-89.

Greville, Fulke, ''A Treatie of Humane Learning,'' 1633, *The Works in Verse and Prose Complete*, A. B. Grosart, editor, Fuller Worthies' Library, 1870, Vol. III, pp. 5-61.

Hooker, Richard, *Of the Laws of Ecclesiastical Polity*, 2 vols., Ernest Rhys, editor, Everyman's Library, E. P. Dutton & Company, N. Y.

Huarte Navarro, Juan de Dios, *Examen de Ingenios, the Examination of Mens Wits*, translated out of the Spanish tongue by M. Camilli, Inglished out of his Italian, by R. C[arew], London, 1596. The first edition was printed in 1594.

La Primaudaye, Pierre de, *The French Academie; Fully Discoursed and Finished in Foure Bookes*, London, 1618. Book II is a treatise on the soul. It was first printed in English in 1594.

Nemesius, *The Nature of Man*, Geo. Wither, translator, London, 1636.

O'Sullivan, Mary Isabelle, ''Hamlet and Dr. Timothy Bright,'' *Publications of the Modern Language Association*, XLI (1926), 667-679.

Person, David, *Varieties: or a Surveigh of Rare and Excellent Matters*, London, 1635.

Rea, John D., ''Jacques on the Microcosm,'' *Philological Quarterly*, IV (1925), 345-347.

Schücking, Levin L., *Character Problems in Shakespeare's Plays*, Henry Holt and Company, 1922.

Senault, Jean Francois, *De l'Usage des Passions, derniere edition*, Amsterdam, 1668.

Spenser, Edmund, *The Faerie Queene, Complete Works in Verse and Prose*, 10 vols., A. B. Grosart, editor, printed for private circulation, 1882, Vols. V-VIII.

Stoll, Elmer Edgar, ''*Hamlet*: an Historical and Comparative Study,'' *University of Minnesota Studies in Language and Literature*, No. 7, 1919.

————, ''Hamlet and Iago,'' *Anniversary Papers by Colleagues and Pupils of George Lyman Kittredge*, Ginn and Company, 1913, pp. 261-272.

————, ''*Othello*: an Historical and Comparative Study,'' *University of Minnesota Studies in Language and Literature*, No. 2, 1915.

————, ''Shakespeare, Marston, and the Malcontent Type,'' *Modern Philology*, III (1906), 281-303.

Tilley, M. P., ''Good Drink Makes Good Blood,'' *Modern Language Notes*, XXXIX (1924), 153-155.

Vives, Joannes Ludovicus, *Introduction to Wysedome*, bound with Sir Thomas Elyot's *Banket of Sapience* and the *Preceptes of Agapetus*, London, 1550. The treatise was first printed in English in 1540.

Wihan, Dr. Josef, ''Die Hamletfrage, ein Beitrag zur Geschichte der Renaissance in England,'' *Leipziger Beiträge zur englischen Philologie, Heft III*, Leipzig, 1921.

Wits Theater of the Little World, Robert Allot, compiler, printed by J. R[oberts] for N. L[ing], 1599.

Wright, Thomas, *The Passions of the Minde in Generall*; corrected, enlarged, and with sundry new discourses augmented, London, 1630. The first edition is dated 1601.

INDEX

Frequently an entry covers both theory and Shakespeare's use of this theory. The lists of items for Shakespeare are therefore not exhaustive. In the section on his works italicized numbers refer to pages of this volume.